THE
GEOGRAPHY
OF
SOUTH DAKOTA

Third Edition

by
Edward Patrick Hogan
State Geographer
South Dakota State University
and
Erin Hogan Fouberg
Mary Washington College

Cartography by
Orville E. Gab
South Dakota State University

The Center for Western Studies

Published by
The Center for Western Studies
Box 727, Augustana College
Sioux Falls, South Dakota 57197

The Center for Western Studies is an archives, library, museum, publishing house, and educational agency concerned principally with collecting, preserving, and interpreting prehistoric, historic, and contemporary materials that document native and immigrant cultures of the northern prairie plains. The Center promotes understanding of the region through exhibits, publications, art shows, conferences, and academic programs. It is committed, ultimately, to defining the contribution of the region to American civilization.

Library of Congress Cataloging-in-Publication Data:

Hogan, Edward Patrick, 1939- , and Erin Hogan Fouberg, 1970-
    The geography of South Dakota / by Edward Patrick Hogan and Erin Hogan Fouberg.
       p. cm.
    Includes bibliographical references and index.
    Summary: Examines the geography, natural resources, people, history, and culture of South Dakota.
    Revised Edition: ISBN 0-931170-61-3 (hardcover)
    Third Edition: ISBN 0-931170-79-6 (paperback)
    1. South Dakota—Geography—Juvenile literature. [1. South Dakota.] I. Title.
F651.8.H64 1995
917.83—dc20   95-45370
                                                                    CIP
                                                                            AC

Funded by a grant from the Mary Chilton Chapter, Sioux Falls, of the National Society of the Daughters of the American Revolution, and by a gift from the Elmen Family Foundation, Sioux Falls, South Dakota.

Photo credits: Unless otherwise indicated, all photos are courtesy of the South Dakota Governor's Office of Economic Development. Front cover photo courtesy of USGS EROS Data Center. Back cover photo courtesy of South Dakota Art Museum.

Printed in the United States of America

PINE HILL PRESS
4000 West 57th Street
Sioux Falls, S.D. 57106

TO JOAN, WHO MADE
SOUTH DAKOTA HOME.
WE LOVE YOU.

PREFACE

The geography of South Dakota is comprised of the physical and cultural environments of the state. The physical environment includes the phenomena of nature, while the cultural environment encompasses the human-made ways of utilizing the earth and extracting wealth from it. Thus, geography can be defined as the study of the earth as the home of humankind.

Almost two hundred years ago, President Thomas Jefferson selected Meriwether Lewis and William Clark to undertake their now-famous "Journey of Discovery and Exploration" into the American West. At that time, Jefferson was one of the most geographically literate people in the world. Lewis and Clark utilized the vast knowledge of Jefferson and other scholars to prepare for their journey. Yet, as history demonstrates, in reality they were geographically unaware of the physical and cultural environments, and challenges, facing them.

Unfortunately, most Americans are still unaware of what geography really is. This does not surprise the geographer. For years, geographers have been warning the nation that the American people have become geographically ignorant of the world in which they live and compete for survival. In the case of South Dakota, this can be illustrated by the fact that prior to 1995, the last major geography of South Dakota was written in 1918, by Stephen S. Visher.

Fortunately, the Congress of the United States, two presidents, the nation's governors, corporate America, and boards of education have taken or are taking steps to restore geography to its proper place in the nation's schools. In South Dakota, we are especially proud of the fact that the South Dakota Board of Education was the first in the country to restore a geography requirement for high-school graduation. Many other states have since followed its lead.

Geography and geographers are concerned with five essential ingredients or phenomena. The first of these is place, that is, where things are. In the case of this book, South Dakota is the place. The second ingredient is location, or a position relative to other places. For example, South Dakota to Minnesota, or Brookings to Sioux Falls to St. Paul. The third phenomenon is the interaction between humankind and the natural environment. This concern relates to how people use or change the natural environment. The fourth concern is the interaction between and among peoples and places. How is the ranching environment of western South Dakota related to the farming environment and industrial economy of eastern South Dakota? Finally, the fifth phenomenon is region. A region is a homogeneous area having some unity determined by selective criteria. Examples of regions include the Great Plains, the Corn Belt, the Black Hills, the Sioux Empire, and Brown County.

While this work is primarily a topical study of the physical and cultural environments, it also utilizes aspects of the regional approach. This book, then, is an overview of the geographic environment known as South Dakota. It intentionally draws together the diversities of the discipline of geography in order to provide a comprehensive understanding of the state.

CONTENTS

CHAPTER

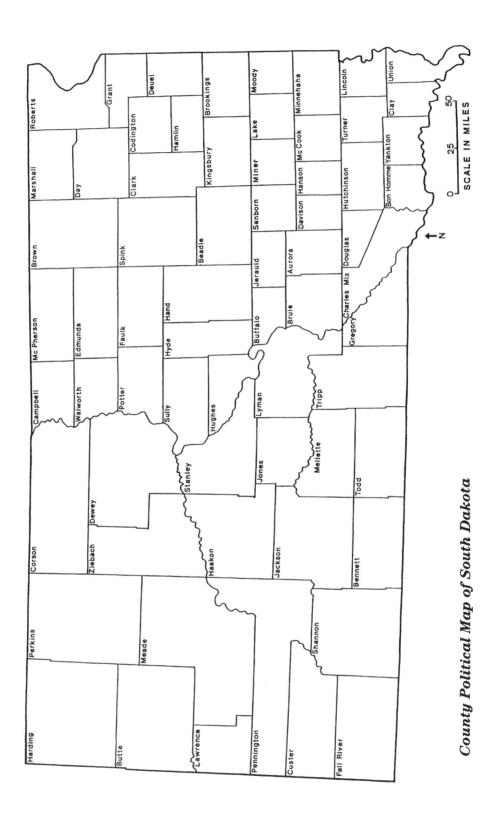

County Political Map of South Dakota

SCALE IN MILES

0   25   50

N

MAPS AND FIGURES

MAPS

FIGURES

Chapter One

THE GEOGRAPHY OF SOUTH DAKOTA

INTRODUCTION

In 1804, after the Louisiana Purchase, President Thomas Jefferson sent Meriwether Lewis and William Clark to explore the new American territory. These two explorers encountered new physical geographic environments and described and collected samples for scientists to study. However, Lewis and Clark also encountered many Indian peoples, whose descendants are living in present-day South Dakota, and wrote in their journals about their interactions with them.

During their exploration, Lewis and Clark journeyed along both sides of the Missouri River. They traveled through present-day South Dakota from August 22 to October 13, 1804, writing about the flora and fauna of the region. They explored physical geographic features such as Spirit Mound, six miles north of Vermillion; Calumet Bluffs near Gavins Point Dam; and found their way across and around the Big Bend on the Missouri River. Lewis and Clark reported violent thunderstorms, fog, vegetation types, pelicans, prairie dogs, which they called "barking squirrels," and noted encounters with vast herds of elk, deer, antelope, and buffalo. In addition to these physical geographic phenomena, Lewis and Clark recorded and reported meetings with the Yankton Sioux near Gavins Point; the Teton Sioux, where the Bad River enters the Missouri; and the Arikara Indians in the area of present-day Gettysburg and Mobridge.

Because of these physical and human encounters, the account of Lewis and Clark's "Journey of Discovery and Exploration" was a geographic study of the Missouri River region in 1804. The first geography text written about all of South Dakota was in 1918 by Steven Sargent Visher. In 1995, Edward Patrick Hogan published the first major geography of the state in over seventy-five years. This text is a revised and updated edition of the 1995 book.

Today, South Dakota is quite different from the land explored by Lewis and Clark. South Dakota is poised to enter a new century as a land of impressive environmental diversity. Physically this is reflected in the diversity of its landscape, climate, soils, flora, and fauna. Culturally, the state varies from agricultural to industrial. Manufacturing, commerce, and service are increasingly important economies. The greatest concentrations of economic growth are centered in the larger communities. Small towns face the continual loss of population and businesses. Their survival continues to depend upon local leadership, hometown loyalties, and time.

A DEFINITION OF GEOGRAPHY

The geography of South Dakota is comprised of the criteria that make up the physical and cultural environments of the state. The geographic environment is the sum total of the surrounding external conditions within which we exist. In other words, it is everything and everyone around us. The environment is comprised of two parts, the physical environment and the cultural environment. The physical environment includes the phenomena of nature, while the cultural environment is comprised of the human-made and developed ways of utilizing the earth and extracting wealth from it. Thus, geography can be defined as the study of the earth as the home of humankind.

AN ANALOGY

In a sense, an analogy can be drawn between geography and a stage play. The physical environment is the stage, with its design, shape, construction, and surface conditions. The cultural environment is the set upon that stage, with its buildings, furnishings, design, construction, costumes, props, and so forth. Human beings in each case, whether it be in the world of theater or of geography, are the actors. The completed play itself is the geography. In both theater and life, humankind's performances can be good or bad, depending upon many factors: the script, how well they know their roles, their ability to take direction, and the ability to improvise when necessary.

Like a good stage play, geography must be evaluated by a critic. Just as the drama critic rates our performances as poor, good, or even outstanding, it is the geographer's role to serve as the critic for the environment. Like a critic, the geographer must describe and evaluate the stage, the sets, the props, and the performances of the actors. Presently, one can rate humankind's treatment of the environment as poor or mediocre, with only a few examples of excellence. For the future, humans must all improve their performances, scripts, sets, props, and stage design, or like a poorly developed play, the environment will continue to suffer.

In rehearsals, the actors learn about the stage, the set, the costumes, props, and how to act out their roles. This learning is essential in order to understand what the actual performance will be like. The purpose of geography is to understand the physical and cultural environments in which we live, as well as what we must do to develop properly the present and future world in which we can successfully live and function.

The authors' concept of the role of geography and the geographer may not be what you expected. Unfortunately, many people have misconceptions about what geography is. Some people still think that geography is the memorization of state capitals, or flowers, or birds. Others expect something similar to the vacation trip across the United States that they read about in grade school, with Dick and Jane, their Mom and Dad, and dog Spot. If you went to a Catholic school, as did one of the authors, you might expect to continue that exciting travel adventure by canoe, with Father Marquette and Father DeSmet.

The fact that most Americans are unaware of what geography really is does not shock the geographer. For years, geographers have been warning the nation that the American people have become geographically ignorant of the world in which they live and compete for survival. Fortunately, the Congress of the United States of America, two presidents, the nation's governors and legislatures, and boards of education have taken or are taking steps to restore geography to its proper place in the nation's schools.

It is commonly known that geography is among the most ancient of the present-day fields of study. Unfortunately, history, geography's ancient sister, is also often overlooked in our education system. Geography finds its roots in the eastern Mediterranean region where the Greeks, Phoenicians, and others developed a science to explain the earth many centuries before the dawn of the Christian era. The meaning of "Geography," as given by the ancient Greeks, is defined within the word itself: Geo = earth, and Graphy = to write about, or to describe.

THE SCIENCE OF THE EARTH'S SURFACE

Most modern-day academic definitions begin by stating that geography is a science. Indeed, it can be both a physical science as is the case with physical geography, or it can be a social science as is cultural geography. Geography and geographers are concerned with five essential ingredients or phenomena. The first of these is **place,** that is, where things are. In the case of this book South Dakota is the place. The second ingredient is **location,** or a position relative to other places. For example, South Dakota to Minnesota, or Brookings to Sioux Falls to Minneapolis. The third phenomenon is the **interaction between humankind and the natural environment.** This concern relates to how people use or change the natural environment. The fourth concern is the **interaction between and among peoples and places.** How is the ranching environment of western South Dakota related to the farming environment and industrial economy of eastern South Dakota? Finally, the fifth phenomenon is **regions.** A region is a homogeneous area having some unity determined by selective criteria. For example the Great Plains, the Corn Belt, the Black Hills, the Sioux Empire, or even Brown County.

From geography's very beginning geographers have attempted to describe the earth and its various natural and human-made features. Today, however, this 2,000-plus-year-old definition of geography must be further clarified. This is because today there are other geo-sciences. The easiest way to distinguish between the geo-sciences is to remember that geography is primarily concerned with the earth as the home of humankind. Therefore, geographers are most interested in the earth's surface, or the human habitat.

The earth's surface, however, must not be taken too literally. It is not limited to the precise point at which the land (lithosphere) and water (hydrosphere) meet the air (atmosphere). Instead, geography views the earth's surface as being a very thin layer of Earth's outer crust extending downward into the earth as far as humans go to extract metals, mineral fuels, or water, and upward to include the lower atmosphere. This very thin layer is the human habitat. It is the life layer upon which humankind must depend for survival. When compared to the huge mass of the planet itself, the human habitat does indeed appear to coincide with the earth's surface.

MODERN GEOGRAPHY AS RELATED TO THIS BOOK

Geography is study of the earth as the home of humankind. While this definition may seem confusing to some people, it actually provides a sound understanding of both modern geography and this book. Modern geography has both a physical and cultural focus. Indeed, most geography students begin their higher education in the discipline with work in both physical geography and cultural geography. Physical geography studies the various aspects and phenomena that comprise the physical environment. Likewise, cultural geography studies the cultural environments that people have developed around this planet. Both are reflected in this book, which emphasizes the physical and cultural environments of South Dakota.

The focus of modern geography also varies in relation to regional geography and systematic geography. Geographers may study the human habitat by investigating it in relation to regions and places through regional geography, or topically, utilizing systematic geography. While this book is primarily a topical study of the physical and cultural environments of South Dakota, it also utilizes aspects of the regional approach. This book, then, is an overview of the geographic environment we know as South Dakota. It intentionally draws together the diversities of the discipline of geography in order to provide a comprehensive understanding of the state.

Physical geography traditionally examines the various aspects of the physical environment, either topically or systematically. In the same manner, cultural geography investigates the cultural environment, that is, the sum total of humankind's ways as inscribed upon the landscape. The physical environment is comprised of the terrain, weather and climate, soils, flora and fauna, water resources, and minerals. The cultural environment consists of the human occupance and the human development. The latter consists of hunting, fishing, and collecting; agriculture; mining; industry and commerce; recreation and tourism; transportation, power, and utilities; population; and potential or the future.

A regional geography will then utilize these topics to develop a geographic understanding of a specific place. It traditionally utilizes the topics to delimit each region. This study, while regional in nature, is actually a systematic geography of the state. That is, the geography of South Dakota is studied topic by topic. Many of the topics are studied in relation to sub-regions or micro regions. Also, the second-to-last chapter is a regional study of South Dakota. The final chapter is an effort to provide you with some food for thought. It is about the future of South Dakota. It is not intended to be a crystal-ball prediction but rather a geographer's view of what lies ahead as a result of characteristics, trends, and traditions.

Today modern geography is also blessed with a variety of extremely valuable techniques that strengthen the discipline and geographic understanding. Among these techniques are cartography, aerial photo interpretation, remote sensing and geographic information systems. While some people tend to confuse them with the discipline, it must be remembered that they are tools and not geography. These tools of the trade are utilized throughout this work in order to provide you with additional understanding of the geography of the state.

A GEOGRAPHIC ADVENTURE

Studying the geography of South Dakota can be thought of as a very special learning adventure. Such a study may be thought of as being a geographic play, or, if you prefer, a geographic tour of South Dakota. Although the play or trip will be by the written word, map and photograph, ideally, your mind's eye will provide you a stage upon which you will view the state's geography.

You will witness the ever-changing human habitat as you view the state's surface. South Dakota is located near the center of the North American Continent (Map 1). This

Map 1. **South Dakota Located Near Geographic Center of North America.**

rectangular-shaped state is situated on the Missouri Plateau. Here, the land that comprises what we call South Dakota for the most part slopes gently in a southeastward direction from the north, northwest and southwest.

The state is located from 43° N latitude to 45° 56' N latitude and from 96° 25' W longitude to 104° 02' W longitude (Map 2). The state's eastern boundary separates it from Iowa on the southeast and Minnesota to the east. The northern boundary separates it from its sister state of North Dakota.

The western border of South Dakota is marked by the historic Black Hills Principal Meridian. The meridian was a measure of distance in degrees of longitude from Washington D.C. This line played a vital role during the statehood period, when it was utilized to separate South Dakota from Montana on the northwest and from Wyoming to the west and southwest. The southern border separates South Dakota and Nebraska.

South Dakota is the sixteenth-largest state in the United States. It extends over an area of 77,047 square miles. Its areal extent is greater than all of the New England states combined. The state extends approximately 370 miles from east to west, and 210 miles from south to north.

The highest point in the state is Harney Peak located in the Black Hills at 7,242 feet above sea level. The lowest point in South Dakota is near the Continental Divide between Big Stone Lake and Lake Traverse in the northeastern corner of the state. At that point the land is only 965 feet above sea level.

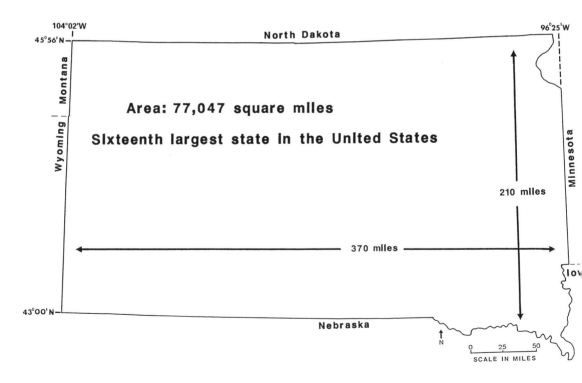

Map 2. Latitude, Longitude, and Areal Extent of South Dakota.

The major topographic features of South Dakota were carved by glaciers in the eastern portion of the state, and by streams and wind in the western portion. The Missouri Plateau upon which South Dakota is situated is divided into three major physiographic provinces, which in turn are further divided into sub-regions. East of the Missouri River most of the land is typical of the Central Lowlands Province. It is a humid environment frequently referred to as "Prairie Country." The Great Plains Province begins along the east side of the Missouri River and extends across the western border to the Rocky Mountains in Wyoming and Montana. This is a land of semiarid climate and of short prairie grasses. At the extreme southwestern edge is the Black Hills, a dome mountain region that leaps skyward from the plains. The Black Hills are a land of abundant forests and minerals and great natural beauty.

The prairies and plains of South Dakota have been occupied by humankind for thousands of years. The paleo-Indians, and Native Americans such as the Arikaras and Sioux, have made this their home. European explorers and Anglo-American settlers came to South Dakota over the last three centuries and also made this their home.

The human habitat of South Dakota has proven to be a zone in which people were able to obtain an abundant food supply either through hunting or agriculture. In recent years the people of South Dakota have increasingly turned to industry, commerce and tourism for all or portions of their livelihoods. The state has developed all the modern facilities and systems needed to enable it to function efficiently in providing the people with transportation, utilities, markets, goods and services. Indeed, it is in a position where, with proper understanding of its human habitat, the people of South Dakota will be able to make the wise decisions necessary for a bountiful future.

By the time you have completed this study, like a geographer you will be in a position to explain the importance of the various aspects of the state's physical and cultural environment. Ideally, this book can lead the 700,000 people who take pride in calling South Dakota home to a better understanding and appreciation of the geographic diversity of this wonderful place.

Chapter Two

THE TERRAIN OF SOUTH DAKOTA

INTRODUCTION

George Catlin, the noted artist, in 1835 painted a verbal picture of the high terrain of a portion of eastern South Dakota, describing it as "undoubtedly the noblest mound of its kind in the world: it gradually and gracefully rises on each side, by swell after swell, without tree or bush . . . and is everywhere covered with green grass, affording the traveller, from its highest elevations, the most unbounded and sublime views of nothing at all, save the blue and boundless ocean of prairies that lie beneath and all around him, vanishing into azure in the distance, without a speck or spot to break their softness." What a beautiful descriptive image of the Coteau des Prairies. It gives you a real sense of the beauty of the landscape we know as South Dakota.

Similar mental landscapes could be painted of the other major physiographic regions of South Dakota. The land surface varies from flat, dry ancient lake beds, to massive erosional plateaus scoured by ice and water, to deeply incised stream valleys bounded by rounded hills, to steplike tablelands rising in elevation like a staircase, to the majestic peaks of the Black Hills. Actually, an artist would discover thousands of opportunities to paint scenic views of the major and minor landforms that comprise the landscape of this "Land of Infinite Variety."

Over 4 billion years ago, earth-building forces began a series of processes that were to result in formation of the present-day landscape of South Dakota. Somewhere between 600 million and 1.6 billion years ago the land surface began to emerge. First the parent materials of the Black Hills and later the eastern portions of the state were born. The granites, schists, and quartzites formed at this time provide the basis upon which the rest of the state's geologic structure was to be laid.

Located in the center of North America is the Missouri Plateau. This vast continental landform slopes gently in a southeastward direction from the north, northwest and west. The Missouri Plateau contains a wide array of surface features (topography) ranging from low river valleys and lake beds carved by ancient streams to flat plains that were once the floors of glacial lakes, to hills formed by wind-blown soils and sands or by water erosion, to castellated badlands, to plateaus dotted with mesas and buttes, to the beautiful Black Hills.

All these landforms are found within the borders of present-day South Dakota. They are among the many natural features that formerly gave South Dakota the name "Land of Infinite Variety." Let's begin our journey across the map of South Dakota and examine the physiographic diversity of the state. In order to assist geographic learning, a general understanding and overview of the state's landforms and terrain is essential.

THE RELIEF OF SOUTH DAKOTA

The relief of South Dakota is the difference in elevation between the lowest point in the state and the highest point. The lowest point in South Dakota is at Big Stone Lake in the northeastern corner of the state. At that point the land is 965 feet above sea level.

Elevation	Area	Percent of Total
Below 1,000 feet	270 square miles	0.3%
1,000-2,000 feet	42,300 square miles	54.5%
2,000-3,000 feet	23,000 square miles	30.0%
3,000-5,000 feet	10,700 square miles	13.5%
5,000-7,000 feet	1,380 square miles	2.8%

Figure 1. **Elevation of South Dakota.**
Source: Visher (1918)

The highest point is Harney Peak in the Black Hills at 7,242 feet above sea level. The difference between the state's highest and lowest elevations is the relief. South Dakota's relief is 6,276 feet. The average elevation of South Dakota is 2,200 feet, which, by the way, is approximately the average elevation of the earth.

Overall, the relief of South Dakota can be said to be gentle to rolling. Thousands of square miles of the state's land fit into these two categories. Indeed, rugged land is limited for the most part to the Black Hills and portions of the Badlands. Less than fifteen percent of the state's land has slopes of over fifteen degrees.

THE SUBSURFACE GEOLOGY OF SOUTH DAKOTA

Eastern South Dakota is built on a deep base of ancient granite and quartzite. These Pre-Cambrian deposits are over 600 million years old and predate the earliest known forms of life on this planet. This area was then inundated by the sea and later occupied by various forms of sea and animal life, including the dinosaurs. During the Cretaceous Period, about 100 million years ago, the dinosaurs became extinct. Marine deposits during this period left a new blanket of bedrock composed of sandstones and shales.

About 1 million years ago, the Pleistocene Epoch introduced the Ice Age to the region. During this Epoch's four major glacial periods, continental ice sheets covered the area, scoured the surface, and retreated, leaving a changed surface with each movement. The glaciers last retreated from eastern South Dakota some 10,000 years ago. They left the surface covered with a blanket of glacial drift or rubble across the region ranging up to 700 feet in thickness, but averaging 40 feet. The glacial drift is comprised primarily of sandstones and shales.

During the most recent Wisconsin Glacial Period some 10,000 to 75,000 years ago, ice moved into the area from the north and northeast. The extreme limit of Wisconsin glaciation is essentially marked by the Missouri River, although the ice did cross much of its present-day course. The visible surface terrain of eastern South Dakota is a result of glaciation. Except for deep river trenches, almost all the surface materials are a direct result of glacial ice sheet covering the land during the Pleistocene glacial epoch.

The ice sheets moved over the land, breaking, scraping, cutting, grinding, polishing, and crushing the weak shale, chalk, sandstone, and limestone rocks in their path. When the ice retreated in numerous stages, eastern South Dakota was covered with glacial drift (rock debris). The heterogeneous (dissimilar) rock mixture termed *till* is predominantly local rocks ranging in size from clay to boulders and deposited directly from ice without water transport. Streams from melting ice carried most of the silts and clays out of the area. Where ice melted and water accumulated in streams and lakes, layers of sorted clays, silts, sands and gravel called *stratified drift* accumulated.

In the time since the glaciers retreated some 10,000 to 15,000 years ago, other forces of nature have shaped eastern South Dakota. Weathering, mass wasting, erosion, transportation, and deposition have all impacted the landscape. Their effect has created a variety of geographic landforms that, combined, give the eastern part of the state its unique physical character.

Western South Dakota is a part of that region of the Missouri Plateau more commonly known as the Great Plains. This region is located primarily west of the Missouri River. The landscape west of the Missouri River was not significantly affected by Wisconsin glaciation. Thus the landscape is quite different from that in the eastern part of the state. The recent geologic history of western South Dakota is a record of erosion and repeated partial deposition by water and wind.

The western portion of the state was built up from the floors of ancient Cambrian geologic seas. Among the oldest materials that form the geologic basis of the region are Mississippian and older limestones, sandstones, and shales deposited over 310 million years ago. Limestones from this zone also form the plateau in the Black Hills. This layer of strata is covered with a blanket of Pennsylvanian-Permian-Triassic-Jurassic rocks which are primarily sandstones and shales. It also includes a purple limestone that today is used for cement. This layer was deposited between 230 million and 310 million years ago.

The next rock layer in western South Dakota is a zone of sedimentary rock comprised of sandstones and shales. This zone includes the Dakota sandstone, the primary artesian aquifer of the region. This stone is covered by a deposit of mixed sedimentary materials, which in turn is blanketed by the Niobrara-Greenhorn zone of limestone, chalk and shale that outcrops in places in western South Dakota.

This zone of sedimentary rock is overlain by the dark-gray-colored Pierre shale, the principal material of the region's surface. Pierre shale was deposited between 63 million and 135 million years ago on the bottom of a vast shallow Cretaceous sea. The Pierre shale is noted as being weak and flaky when dry and thick and sticky when wet.

Post-Cretaceous sedimentary deposits are found covering Pierre shale in the Big Badlands along the White River. These fine sands, clays, and volcanic ash were deposited by streams during the wearing down of the Black Hills and Rocky Mountains.

Much of the terrain of western South Dakota was shaped from water carving weak Pierre shale into river valleys, while older valley floors covered with gravel and sands resisted erosion and became highlands. The terrain was also affected by larger streams capturing smaller, often intermittent, shifting tributaries. The result is a landscape ranging from buttes, to hills, to terraces. Streams flow eastward from the Black Hills and the lands to the northwest, as they have for thousands of years. They have incised laterally and have become entrenched in Pierre shale valleys between gravel-capped hills and buttes.

In extreme southwestern South Dakota, the Black Hills comprise a miniature version of the Rocky Mountains. The Black Hills were upthrust through the Great Plains at the same geologic time as the Rocky Mountains to the west, and by the same forces. These earth-building forces are collectively called tectonics. Together they caused the uplift, faulting, folding, and warping that resulted in a 300-mile-long buckle in the earth that extended three miles up at its highest point. Over time, this great earth block has been carved into the nearly elliptical-shaped Black Hills. The hills are comprised of a crystalline central core, surrounded by a limestone plateau, sandstone valley, and hogbacks.

The geology of the Black Hills is very complex and provides a 1.6-billion-year history of the state's rocks. The oldest rocks in the Black Hills are believed to be ancient slates and quartzites which can be found high in the central crystalline core. High temperatures and pressures resulting from earth building metamorphosed these rocks from weaker older clays and sandstones. Included in these ancient rocks are the gold veins and deposits famous to the Black Hills. Granite rock also intruded into this region and is the principal rock in the central core.

More recently, sandstones, clays, and limestones were deposited in the Black Hills region. These were deposited over a 400-million-year period and included the red sand-stones and the Paha Sapa limestones. Depositions ended with the close of the Cretaceous period. It was at this time, 63 million years ago, that the Rocky Mountains and Black Hills were formed.

THE PHYSIOGRAPHIC PROVINCES OF SOUTH DAKOTA

Today the variation in landscape in that portion of the Missouri Plateau that lies in present-day South Dakota is referred to by physical geographers as the three main physiographic provinces (Map 3). Each province is a subdivision of land based on topography and relief. These three physiographic regions are known as:

1. The Central Lowlands of eastern South Dakota
2. The Great Plains of western South Dakota
3. The Black Hills

Each of these regions extends into other parts of the United States. Each major physiographic region is also divided into several subregions that give us an even greater understanding and appreciation of the state's physical geography.

The geographic journey across South Dakota begins with a closer look at the eastern one-third of South Dakota (Map 3). This region, known as the Central Lowlands, extends eastward through Minnesota, Iowa, and other neighboring states, and provides the physical stage for the American Corn Belt. During the journey across South Dakota it is important to remember that the major topographic features of eastern South Dakota and especially the Central Lowlands are a result of glaciation. Today this region is an area of gentle rolling hills, with water-filled depressions, all resulting from the movement, scraping, scouring, and melting of ice.

Our journey begins in extreme northeastern South Dakota. Situated here in a portion of the Central Lowlands province is a subregion known as the Minnesota River-Red River

Lowlands. While part of this subregion lies in South Dakota, the bulk of it extends into Minnesota and North Dakota.

THE MINNESOTA RIVER-RED RIVER LOWLANDS

The Minnesota River-Red River Lowlands were formed by an ancient, large northward-flowing river. Later the area was attacked by glacial erosion. In South Dakota, this region is dominated by a narrow trench that was a spillway for the ancient glacial Lake Agassiz. Today this trench is occupied by Lake Traverse on the north and Big Stone Lake to the south. Between the two elongated lakes is a continental divide, at about Browns Valley, Minnesota.

Here the divide separates the waters of Lake Traverse, which flows into the Boise de Sioux, then the Red River of the North, and finally into Hudson Bay and the Arctic Ocean from the waters of Big Stone Lake, which flows into the Minnesota River, the Mississippi River, and into the Gulf of Mexico. The continental divide here is so low that minor rises in the water level of one or both lakes can result in the two lakes flowing together into a single water body and actually draining into both the Arctic Ocean and the Gulf of Mexico at the same time.

Big Stone Lake and Lake Traverse form the eastern border of the physiographic region. The central portion of the Minnesota River-Red River Lowlands is comprised of about 1,600 square miles of glaciated basin land. This land is covered with ground moraine and end moraine. The relief here averages less than 20 feet per mile. The western portion of the lowlands is made up of the eastern slopes of the Coteau des Prairies.

The most conspicuous feature in the Minnesota River-Red River Lowlands is located in Grant County and is known as Big Tom Hill. It can be observed from old U.S. Highway 12 between Milbank and Big Stone City. Comprised mainly of medium to coarse gravel, it is an end moraine about 100 feet high and about one-half mile wide at its base. The moraine runs eastward into Minnesota, where it is known locally as the Antelope Hills.

A large portion of the Lowlands is covered by waters from Big Stone Lake and Lake Traverse. Both lakes cover extensive areas, are long and narrow in shape, and are shallow in depth. Big Stone Lake is the larger of the two. It runs from Ortonville, Minnesota, north-west to Browns Valley, Minnesota. It is 25 miles long and about one and one-half miles wide at its widest point, and from 15 feet to 18 feet deep. Lake Traverse runs essentially north-northeast from Browns Valley for about 15 miles. It is about one mile wide at its widest point, and has an average depth of 10 feet.

In order to understand fully the importance of the physical geography of the Minnesota River-Red River Lowlands, one must be aware of the subsurface geology of the region. The principal underlying rock of the region is Pre-Cambrian granite. Just southeast of Milbank, South Dakota, is a small, unique area of extensive granite outcrops. The granite rock in this area is believed to be several thousand feet deep. It is a high-quality granite that is today commercially quarried for monument and building stone.

Throughout the rest of the region the granite bedrock is covered by ascending layers of sandstones, shales, and limestones. Glaciation played a major role in the shaping of the surface of this region. It left some very distinct physiographic features in the Lowlands.

One of these features is a series of very low beach ridges formed by Lake Agassiz. During the Wisconsin Glacial Period, Lake Agassiz was formed by the ice block of northward-flowing rivers. The lake built up behind the blockage and eventually drained to the south

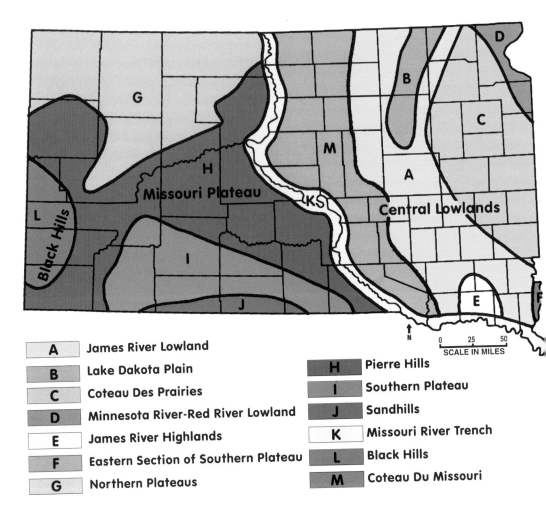

Map 3. The Physiographic Provinces of South Dakota.
Source: Flint (1955)

A James River Lowland
B Lake Dakota Plain
C Coteau Des Prairies
D Minnesota River-Red River Lowland
E James River Highlands
F Eastern Section of Southern Plateau
G Northern Plateaus
H Pierre Hills
I Southern Plateau
J Sandhills
K Missouri River Trench
L Black Hills
M Coteau Du Missouri

through present-day Lake Traverse and Big Stone Lake. During its existence Lake Agassiz developed a series of beach ridges at its southern end. The ridges can be seen in a ten-mile-long band at the South Dakota-North Dakota border area. The old floor of Lake Agassiz to the north is today very flat and partially occupied by Mud Lake. To the south the beach ridges range, for the most part, from the barely noticeable to 100 feet in width.

The other glacial features are two moraines, the Big Stone Moraine and the Gary-Altamont Moraine. The former begins at the south end of Big Stone Lake and extends northwest. The latter parallels the east edge of the Coteau des Prairies.

Travelling westward out of the Minnesota River-Red River Lowlands subregion one can note a highland a short distance to the west, and about 800 feet higher in elevation. This highland subregion is the Coteau des Prairies. The Coteau is the most conspicuous landform in eastern South Dakota.

Sica Hollow State Park. Carved into the Coteau des Prairies is a land of Indian legends and great seasonal variations.

THE COTEAU DES PRAIRIES

The Coteau des Prairies subregion is a flatiron-shaped plateau about 200 miles long and ranging from 1,700 feet to 2,000 feet above sea level. The point of the iron is in Sargent County, North Dakota, about 15 miles north of the border with South Dakota. On the southern end or heel of the iron, the Coteau merges into the general upland areas of Minnesota and Iowa. At its maximum, the Coteau des Prairies is about 70 miles wide.

The Coteau des Prairies reaches its highest elevation in the northeast near Roberts and Grant counties where its elevation surpasses 2,000 feet. The Coteau decreases in elevation as it slopes to the southeast, finally merging into the land near the South Dakota, Minnesota, Iowa border just southeast of Sioux Falls.

The Coteau des Prairies is actually a plateau. It is a part of a much larger plateau that extends through North Dakota into Manitoba and Saskatchewan. The Coteau des Prairies is an erosional remnant reduced in elevation in the geologic past. The northern escarpment of the Coteau is striking on its eastern side. The northern portion of the eastern slope rises over 800 feet above the Minnesota River-Red River Lowlands to the east. It achieves this rise in elevation through an incline that rises some 200 feet a mile from the western edge of the Lowlands to the upper lip of the Coteau.

The western edge of the Coteau des Prairies is less noticeable than the eastern slope. This is due to the fact that the James River Lowland to the west is much higher in elevation than the Minnesota River-Red River Lowland to the east. Also the Coteau des Prairies itself slopes gently to the west, decreasing in elevation from 100 feet to 200 feet at its western edge. The Coteau then gently drops off into the James River Lowland which is 100 feet to 300 feet lower than the edge of the Coteau des Prairies to the east.

Geologic evidence indicates that the bedrock of this sub-region is buried some 100 feet to 400 feet below the surface of the Coteau des Prairies. The bedrock is believed to slope to the south and west, with a relief of 400 feet to 500 feet. The bedrock formation is primarily composed of Pierre shale, which underlies all of the Coteau except for a small area composed of Sioux Quartzite located in Minnehaha County and portions of Moody and Lincoln counties.

Pierre shale is comprised primarily of clay with small amounts of quartz and bentonite. This combination results in a material that is poorly consolidated and highly subject to erosion. If the Pierre shale is dry, it remains very firm and compact. However, when exposed to moisture, the bentonite within the shale absorbs water easily and makes the material highly plastic. The constant swelling and drying decomposes the material and it breaks up into flaky substances that can be easily transported by water, wind, and ice.

It is believed that the Coteau des Prairies exists because of ancient stream valleys that gave it its flatiron shape. During the glacial periods drift was deposited around the edges of the Coteau which was to impede the advances of the most recent ice sheet movements.

The Wisconsin glacial sheet attacked the Coteau des Prairies in stages. Three of its four substages are relevant to the Coteau des Prairies. These are the Mankato, Cary, and Tazewell deposits. The Mankato deposits are youngest of the Wisconsin-stage drift sheets found in South Dakota. They include more stratified drift than the Cary or Tazewell stages. In the Coteau des Prairies, the most conspicuous evidence of the Mankato stage is the Altamont moraine that lies along the northeast side of the Coteau. The Mankato substage also contains outwash along its borders, thin deposits of till, ground moraine, and end moraine.

Beneath the Mankato substage is an interval layer of loessial soil. Below the loess is the Cary substage. It is marked in the Coteau des Prairies by an end moraine called the Bemis moraine. The Cary substage contains a mixture of loess, stratified drift and till. Its topographic expression was a ground moraine made up of swells and swales with a relief of 10 feet or less. The Cary substage is underlaid by another layer of loess and then the Tazewell substage. The Tazewell substage is marked by drift with irregular swells and swales, and discontinuous end moraine.

During the Ice Age, the Coteau was attacked by the glaciers, and when the ice retreated, it was irregularly covered with large deposits of glacial drift varying in thickness from 100 to 400 feet. Both margins of the Coteau contain nearly parallel recessional moraines or ridges of dumped debris left by retreating glaciers.

The Coteau des Prairies is drained by the Big Sioux River, which almost divides the subregion in half. The course of the river appears to be a result of the melting of two ice lobes that flanked the coteau. While both lobes drained into the Big Sioux River, the lobe to the east melted faster than the western lobe. This resulted in the eastern tributaries of the Big Sioux carving stream valleys. The slower melt of the western lobe resulted in glacial drift blocking off former valleys. This resulted in the area west of the Big Sioux River being dotted with perennial and intermittent lakes and sloughs. The largest of these lakes are 5 miles to 10 miles in length.

Traveling to the western edge of the Coteau des Prairies you can see that the land is about to drop some 200 feet to 300 feet in elevation as you move down the escarpment (steep slope) into the next subregion of the Central Lowlands.

THE JAMES RIVER LOWLAND

The James River Lowland subregion is a broad lowland situated between the Coteau des Prairies to the east and the Coteau du Missouri to the west. The James River Lowland is about 50 miles wide and 200 miles long from north to south. The lowland ranges in elevation from about 1,300 feet to 1,400 feet above sea level. The James River Lowland is about 200 feet to 300 feet lower in elevation than the Coteau des Prairies to the east. It is about 300 feet to 800 feet lower in elevation than the Coteau du Missouri to the west.

In the geologic past two ancient streams drained northward through this area, carving broad valleys below the neighboring coteaus. During the Wisconsin Glacial Stage, ice widened and united the two ancient valleys. As the ice retreated deposition occurred.

More erosion occurred in the James River Lowland than in other portions of eastern South Dakota. Because ancient streams had already eroded the land below the adjacent coteaus, there was far less resistance to glaciation. Indeed the glaciers were thickest in this subregion, and as a result far more erosion occurred.

Essentially every visible topographic feature of the James River Lowland is a result of glaciation. Ice widened and filled in valleys, deposited till and drift, and left recessional and end moraines. The surface of the James River Lowlands is smoothly rolling, covered with glacial drift, with some recessional moraines forming low west-to-east ridges. The glacial drift consists of numerous layers of stratified drift, till, and loess and indicates successive glacial retreats and advances. There are also three areas of isolated hills near Mitchell, Redfield, and Doland.

All three of these areas are believed to be shale bedrock divides of ancient streams today covered with glacial drift. The Mitchell Ridge, located five miles south of Mitchell, is a low knobby ridge that rises 80 feet above the surrounding terrain. The Redfield Hills lie south and east of Redfield and rise 80 feet in height. Bald Mountain is located 6 miles southwest of Redfield and reaches 140 feet above the surrounding landscape. The Doland Ridge is a zone of low hills located 10 miles south of the city of Doland. They rise 60 feet to 80 feet above the surrounding land.

The James River Lowland is underlain by Pierre shale that resulted from ancient inland seas that deposited a thick layer of clays on their floors. Glaciers later entered the region from the north and northeast, moving to the west and south. The glaciers created deposits of drift that range from 50 feet to 300 feet thick in places.

Today this region is a gently rolling plain incised by the James River and the other streams located in the subregion. The relief of the Lowland averages 10 feet to 20 feet and in places as much as 30 feet. The highest elevations in the subregion are end moraines, and the lowest elevations are stream valleys.

This subregion is drained by the James River which flows through the central axis of the area. The Jim River, as it is also called, is often referred to as the longest non-navigable stream in the world. It flows some 250 miles through South Dakota, flowing from north to south. The James River has carved a very narrow, steep-sided valley through the subregion. This valley was the main drainage way through which glacial ice melt drained southward to the Gulf of Mexico. The valley is fairly uniform in size, ranging in width from one-half mile in the north to almost a mile in width at the southern end of the Lowland.

The valley is bordered by steep, nearly vertical bluffs that rise from 20 feet to 100 feet from the lowland's surface. The James River's gradient averages only 5 inches a mile. In fact, during its course throughout South Dakota, the James River drops only 129 feet in its 250-mile course. Indeed, because of the flat gradient, stream volume normally takes three weeks to traverse the meandering 250-mile journey through South Dakota. The James River is so flat that at flood stage, its tributaries may cause it to experience reverse flow. The river may also go temporarily dry during drought years.

The James River Lowland is also drained by two other rivers. The Big Sioux River exits the Coteau des Prairies and forms the extreme eastern edge of the subregion south of Sioux Falls. The Vermillion River drains through the southeastern portion of the region. It has a deep-cut trench formed by glacial melt water. Local relief in the Vermillion basins is generally from 20 feet to 50 feet.

Aside from the rivers, local drainage in the region is poorly developed, with interior drainage dominating the surface. The James River Lowland contains numerous lakes, ponds, and marshes which fluctuate greatly depending upon precipitation, snow melt, evaporation, or drought. These features owe their existence to the climatic characteristics of the area and to glacial drift that blocks ancient drainage ways.

THE LAKE DAKOTA PLAIN

As one looks north from the James River Lowland, the land suddenly appears flatter on the horizon. That's because one is approaching the next subregion, the Lake Dakota Plain. This area sits in the middle of the James River Lowland. It is physically distinct from the lowland because it is the floor of an abandoned glacial lake or, as it is also called, a lacustrine plain.

The Lake Dakota Plain extends from south of Redfield northward for over 100 miles. Some 90 percent of it is in South Dakota, the rest in North Dakota. It is about 25 miles wide. More importantly, it is remarkably flat, with a local relief of less than 10 feet. Indeed the elevation of the plain is 1,300 feet above sea level at the North Dakota-South Dakota border and remains at almost 1,300 feet at the southern end of the lake bed.

The Lake Dakota Plain is a flat lacustrine plain comprised of alternating layers of fine and coarser silts, sands, and clays. The finer materials were deposited when the lake was frozen, and the coarser materials during open periods. The movement of water at the bottom of the lake spread out the materials, producing an extremely flat floor. Once the lake drained, the lacustrine plain resulted.

The Lake Dakota Plain is dissected by a steep trench carved by the James River and its tributaries. The trench varies from 30 feet deep at the border area to 100 feet deep at the south end. In the northeastern part of the sub-region are patches of low, rounded hills of wind-blown sand that are termed hummocky.

THE JAMES RIVER HIGHLANDS

Located adjacent to the southern end of the James River Lowland is a subregion known as the James River Highlands. The highlands consist of three ridges of drift-covered chalk or limestone bedrock. They are the result of drainage changes that occurred during the last glacial period.

Turkey Ridge is the largest of the three, rising over 300 feet above the surrounding land. It is about 10 miles wide and 40 miles long. It is comprised of a bedrock of Niobrara chalk overlain with some Pierre shale and a 30-foot- to 200-foot-thick mantle of glacial drift. Turkey Ridge forms a divide between the nearly parallel Vermillion and James rivers. The northeast side of the ridge slopes gently down to the glaciated Vermillion River valley. The steeper southwest side of Turkey Ridge was undercut over time by both the James River and the Missouri River. Turkey Creek, an interlobate stream, divides the ridge flowing almost 20 miles through a 200-foot-deep narrow canyon.

The James Ridge is the smallest of the three ridges. It reaches about 260 feet higher than the surrounding land and is one mile wide and 9 miles long. Like Turkey Ridge, which it parallels, the James Ridge also consists of a thick mantle of glacial drift over bedrock of chalk and shale.

Yankton Ridge is the third highland. It makes up the northern border of the Missouri River Trench. The Yankton Ridge is about 500 feet above the Missouri River and extends from Yankton westward for about 16 miles. It is composed of the same materials as Turkey Ridge and the James Ridge, except along the bluffs of the Missouri River where chalk is continually exposed.

Actually, a fourth and smaller ridge is also located in the area. The town of Lesterville is situated on top of this ridge. All indications are that it is similar in origin to the other three ridges. The land between the four ridges is comprised of portions of the James River Lowland and is, of course, essentially the same as described in the paragraphs about that subregion.

EASTERN SECTION OF THE SOUTHERN PLATEAUS

East of the James River Highlands and Lowlands, and along the South Dakota-Iowa border, is a very small subregion known as the Eastern Section of the Southern Plateaus. It is located in eastern Lincoln and Union counties and is basically a stream-dissected loessial highlands (of wind-blown surface materials deposited over time). The land here varies in elevation from 1,200 feet to 1,500 feet above sea level.

SOUTHERN SECTION OF THE MISSOURI RIVER TRENCH

The extreme southern boundary of South Dakota is made up of the South Section of the Missouri River Trench. This subregion is that portion of the Missouri River that extends southeast and southward from Gavins Point. The river lies about 100 feet below most of the surrounding sections of South Dakota, and 200 feet to 400 feet below the Nebraska and Iowa uplands.

The Trench varies in width from 2 miles to 3 miles between the Niobrara River and the James River, and from the James River to the mouth of the Big Sioux River it ranges from 6 miles to 10 miles in width.

This subregion is non-glaciated and a flat river valley. It contains extensive marsh land, natural levees, and the lower portions of the James, Vermillion, and Big Sioux Rivers. The Missouri River itself carries sand, silt, and other debris. With changes in the flow, it creates various channels, islands, and bars that appear and disappear during the year.

THE GREAT PLAINS PROVINCE

The Great Plains Province is comprised of six subregions: the Coteau du Missouri, the Missouri River Trench, the Northern Plateau, the Pierre Hills, the Southern Plateau, and the Sand Hills. This province encompasses the western two-thirds of South Dakota except for the Black Hills (Map 3).

THE COTEAU DU MISSOURI

The easternmost subregion of the Great Plains is the Coteau du Missouri. This subregion lies east of the Missouri River. The Coteau du Missouri is the western version of the Coteau des Prairies. It is an extensive remnant of a plateau that has been carved by ancient major streams. The bedrock of the Coteau is Pierre shale that has been covered by glacial drift. The bedrock is gently inclined toward the Missouri River.

Indeed, before the glaciers scoured this subregion, the Coteau was a nearly flat bedrock region incised by major streams draining to the east and northeast. The bedrock of the area is Pierre shale. This is a material that is highly subject to erosion because it is firm and compact when dry. When wet, it absorbs water easily and becomes plastic. As a result of its elasticity the rock becomes highly subject to erosion by wind and water.

In portions of the Coteau du Missouri the Pierre shale is overlain by a more resistant sandstone cap rock. Examples of this include an area in eastern McPherson County where the land reaches an elevation of 2,100 feet; the Ree Hills, located southwest of Miller; and the Bijou Hills in the northwest corner of Charles Mix County. The sandstone caps of all three highland areas are covered with glacial drift.

The eastern edge of the Coteau du Missouri is composed of a variety of features. In the northern part of the Coteau, the Altamont moraine forms what are locally known as the Bowdle and Lebanon Hills. They reach an elevation of about 2,000 feet. To the south of these hills there exists a 30-mile gap where the Coteau and James River Lowland gently blend. Then a 75-mile-long escarpment rises 200 feet above the lowland, clearly reflecting the Coteau's eastern edge. The northern edge is the Ree Hills and the southern end is called the Wessington Hills.

The entire course of the western edge of the Coteau is marked by the Missouri River Trench. Here the Coteau simply blends into "the Missouri Breaks." One of the principal effects of glaciation on this area has been to reduce the local relief. Evidence indicates that the bedrock surface of the Coteau is highly irregular. However, the glacial drift that has covered the bedrock has given the surface less relief than the subsurface. This is in spite of some of the hills and moraines. Actually, throughout the Coteau du Missouri, the thickness of the glacial till varies from a trace to several hundred feet.

Another very significant feature of the Coteau du Missouri is landforms known as sags. Lowland areas called sags are former west-to-east-running abandoned ancient stream valleys, now covered with glacial drift. The Great Ree Valley is the most conspicuous sag and has an elevation of about 1,750 feet above sea level. This is some 450 feet lower in elevation than the great mesa known as the Ree Hills that parallels the sag's southern edge. This sag extends through Hughes, Hyde, and Hand counties.

There are four other sags that extend across portions of the Coteau du Missouri. The first of these is situated in southwestern Edmunds and Potter counties and northeastern Faulk County. The second is in the northern portion of Brule and Aurora counties. The third extends eastward across northern Douglas County. The fourth runs northeast across eastern Charles Mix and southeastern Douglas counties. These sags are not as clearly defined as the Great Ree Valley because they have been covered with drift during several periods of glacial action.

Today, no major stream drains the Coteau du Missouri. The eastern edge of the Coteau is marked by short parallel streams that drain into the James River. The western edge is highly irregular and runs into the breaks of the Missouri River. Indeed, the Coteau is dominated by symmetrical interior drainage. The northern portion is marked by many local depressions that are filled by runoff and then dry up.

The historical drainage pattern of the Coteau du Missouri has been very complex. In earlier times glaciation streams drained to the east and north. Today drainage is to the interior or to the west and south.

THE MISSOURI RIVER TRENCH

A second subregion of the Great Plains is the Missouri River Trench. This subregion extends from the North Dakota border to Gavins Point. The Missouri River Trench is a deeply cut landform carved by and containing the Missouri River and its reservoirs. The Trench is a very steep cut into the Missouri Plateau that results in a narrow river valley, forming a barrier to east-west travel.

In its natural state, the floor of the river trench is narrow, normally about one mile wide. In a few places the valley widens as it flows through older valleys. The sides of the trench are very steep, extending 300 feet to 700 feet down from the plateau to the floor.

21

Slim Buttes and the Cave Hills in the northwestern part of the state provide fascinating landscape and beaut⬤ Removed from major tourist routes, they are not seen by most travelers. Courtesy Edward P. Hogan.

Bedrock of Pierre shale is exposed all along the Missouri River Trench. The weak non-resistant material has been dissected into badlands or extensive slumping. The trench also shows evidence of glacial drift to varying degrees.

Over the ages, the Missouri River has been rejuvenated many times. Physiographically, this is a result of land being uplifted by various tectonic forces, often resulting from the removal of the overburden by the erosion of the river. As the region is uplifted, the stream again starts downcutting, seeking to reduce the land surface to sea level. Terraces along the valley walls signify that the Missouri River has been rejuvenated several times, each time resulting in more downward cutting of the valley.

The trench is bordered on both sides by steep-sided ravines extending several miles into the surrounding subregions and locally termed "the Missouri Breaks" or "the Breaks." They are an indication that this portion of the Missouri River is again in the youthful stage since these short tributaries have not had time to develop longer, gentler valleys.

The Missouri River drops in elevation about one foot per mile. At about the time the dams and reservoirs were constructed, between 1946 and 1966, the Missouri River was at equilibrium. That is, the amount of debris entering the stream was equal to its ability to carry it out. The dams changed this, and today silting is a problem.

It should be noted that the present course of the Missouri River is a result of glaciation. The last ice sheet sealed off former streams that flowed across South Dakota from west to northeast. As a result of ice blockage, the Missouri River developed its present-day course.

THE NORTHERN PLATEAUS

West of the Missouri River, the Great Plains Province offers a diverse landscape, comprised of four more subregions. The Northern Plateaus comprise the northwestern portion of the state. The Northern Plateaus increase in elevation in a staircase-like series of terraces from the Missouri River to the state's western border.

Each terrace is a broad, rolling sandstone plain. The steps have experienced various degrees of erosion. In the geologic past this region was at least one thousand feet higher in elevation. Over time, that one thousand feet of rock has been carried off this landscape by water and wind. From the Missouri River west, the steps tend to increase in height as they rise over the valley floors. Looking eastward from each stair, the observer is provided a view of the multi-colored buttes that litter the zone below and the extensive rolling landscape of the lower step.

The edge of each step or terrace is marked by flat-topped or rounding sandstone buttes. The sandstone cap rock is part of a sandy rock blanket deposited by the ancient Cretaceous sea. A butte is an erosional remnant resulting from the wearing away of softer sands and clays below a sandstone caprock. Water attempts to wear away the weaker materials and the cap rock, of course, resists this and prevents downward erosion.

Patches of buttes occur throughout the region where sandstone tops the less resistant Pierre shales. The largest and most famous buttes in the subregion are the Cave Hills in Harding County. They are about 3 miles wide and 12 miles long, capped by a salmon-colored 50-foot-thick sandstone cap. The name, Cave Hills, was given to this area because it contains a large cave in the northern hill.

Slim Buttes and the Short Pine Hills are especially beautiful butte areas with white caprocks accentuated by dark evergreens. They rise about 400 feet above the surrounding landscape. Slim Buttes are one of the best kept beauty secrets in South Dakota. Because the area is remote, most tourists are unaware of this narrow, thirty-mile-long patch of great beauty. Other notable buttes in the sub-region include Fox Hills, Antelope Butte, Two Top Buttes, Castlerock Butte, and the Deer's Ears.

THE PIERRE HILLS

The Pierre Hills subregion occupies the center of western South Dakota. They comprise a mature geologic subregion of smooth, rounded, contoured hills. The area is a result of erosion of dark Pierre shale bedrock, which breaks down into a sticky clay called "gumbo." When wet, the clay resists water absorption and when dry, it tends to cake, flake, and decompose.

The Pierre Hills are a subregion of unique appearance. From season to season they reflect a palette of shades of greens, yellows, browns, and whites. The hills rise and descend in a roller-coaster-like pattern, interrupted here and there by white or gray buttes. The landscape is dotted with blue or green pools of water and gray-white alkali spots. The result is an ever-changing painting of priceless natural beauty.

During wet periods, water that is unable to saturate the "gumbo" rapidly runs off the land, cutting deep into the land. In other places, valley water holes and intermittent standing pools collect the runoff. It then evaporates or very slowly seeps into the land while providing sustenance to wildlife and livestock. Alkali spots contain a salt in the soil, resulting in a surface that is essentially devoid of vegetation.

Streams have cut eastward-flowing trenches some 200 feet to 300 feet below the hills, while several prominent buttes stand above the surrounding landscape. The buttes are capped with white or gray sandstones, and the highest rise some 400 feet above the surrounding lands. Among the more notable buttes are Medicine Butte, White Clay Butte, and Rattlesnake Butte. In the western portion of the Pierre Hills a unique geologic formation called a tepee butte is found. Tepee buttes are symmetrical cones ranging from 3 feet to 30 feet in height. They have developed around vertical cores of limestone rather than under sandstone caps.

The Pierre Hills landscape is one of the most interesting in all of South Dakota. To some it is desolate in appearance, to others it is the most beautiful part of the state, and to many people it is where the West really begins. Unfortunately, most visitors to South Dakota travel the interstate highway, built on more level ground. As a result, tourists seldom get to appreciate the phenomenal beauty of the Pierre Hills. They could enjoy this unique landscape much more if they traveled one of the state highways that cross the region.

THE SOUTHERN PLATEAUS

The Southern Plateaus is another subregion of plateaus or tablelands. This area is comprised of young rock formed by the debris produced by the erosion of the Black Hills and Rocky Mountains and carried eastward by wind and water. Today, this is a region of wide, flat areas of land between streams and contrasting deep, narrow stream valleys and canyons. It is also a region of badlands, buttes, and tables. The Southern Plateaus are dominated by rocks formed from sands and clays, occurring in a variety of colors. Streams have cut deep into the landscape, exposing the sub-surface rocks.

The northern part of the Southern Plateaus is noted for its badlands topography. Of the several badlands areas found here, the largest and most famous is the Big Badlands, which follow the White River for over 100 miles. In 1910, Professor C.C. O'Harra, of the South Dakota School of Mines, described the Big Badlands as "magnificent ruins of a great silent city, painted in delicate shades of cream, pink, buff, and green." Badlands result from a combination of geologic and climatic factors: falling and running water; the sands, clay and volcanic ash that form the soil and rock materials; and elevation that results in rapid downcutting by streams. The name "badlands" is given the region because of the lack of water and vegetation, the rugged landscape, and the hindrances to travel and agriculture.

The bulk of the land in the northern part of this subregion is composed of level plains. The land is today covered with grasses or is farmed. Along the northern side of the White River Valley is an elongated badlands feature known as the Great Wall. It runs some 60 miles and contains numerous valleys, gullies, and passes. Big Foot Pass and Cedar Pass are the most famous passes in the area since the roads now follow these previously formidable barriers to travel. This is the portion of the Badlands most often visited by tourists.

The southern section of the subregion is locally known as the "Tables." It is comprised of large, wide-topped buttes and mesas. Among the more notable tables are Cuny Table, Sheep Mountain Table, and Hart Table. They stand over 400 feet above the surrounding landscape and may be over five miles in both length and width.

THE SANDHILLS

The smallest subregion of the Great Plains Province in South Dakota is the Sandhills. This subregion is actually an extension of the Nebraska Sandhills across the border into South Dakota. Here fixed sand dunes, now covered for the most part with grasses, form a topography of moderate rounded hills, dotted with a few lakes and low swampy areas.

Sand dunes are the principal features of the subregion. The Sandhills are an eolian formation that was worked by wind into a succession of dunes in the Post-Pleistocene Era. Across the region three types of dunes are found. They are First Series (broad-massive-elongated dunes); Second Series (narrow-linear dune ridges); and Third Series (relatively small multi-shaped dunes). The First Series dunes are massive and have great breadth. They vary in height from 75 feet to 200 feet and often extend several miles in length. They result primarily from northwest winds during their formation and are oriented to the southeast. As a result of climatic change, these massive dunes stabilized and soil and vegetation developed.

Dunes of the Second Series developed over the First. They are similar to the First in orientation but are narrower and shorter in length. They range from 30 feet to 60 feet in height and range from one-half to two miles in length. While these dunes grew out of the original dunes, like them they also stabilized during periods of modified climate.

Dunes of the Third Series are smooth and rounded or sharp and abrupt shapes. They are generally less than 10 feet in height. It is believed that they developed during periods of drought where less vegetation allowed increased erosion in the Second Series dunes. Again over time these dunes also became stabilized.

The lands between the Sandhills are essentially flat valleys. They tend to run from northwest to southeast parallel to the First Series dunes. These valleys vary greatly in area, ranging from a few acres to several square miles. They are dotted with intermittent marshes and lakes lacking external drainage.

THE BLACK HILLS

The Black Hills are the third major physiographic province of South Dakota (Map 4). They are a miniature version of the Rocky Mountains and were formed at about the same geologic time and by the same earth-building forces. Diastrophic earth-building forces caused the earth to buckle and thrust a great block upward some three miles in the center of a long fold. The dome-like block extended from present-day northwestern Nebraska to Glendive, Montana.

Time and erosion have worn this great block into today's Black Hills, an elliptical-shaped region about 60 miles wide and 125 miles in length. They rise almost four thousand feet above the Missouri Plateau to the east. Some two-thirds of the Black Hills lies in South Dakota, and the rest in Wyoming. The Black Hills are made up of four subregions, each quite different in appearance and size.

THE GREAT HOGBACKS

The Great Hogbacks form the outer limits of the Hills. The Hogbacks are a residual monoclinal ridge. That is, they result from sandstone bedrock upturned as the Black Hills

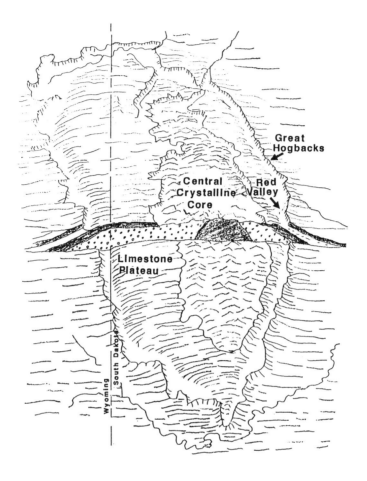

Map 4. The Black Hills Province.

broke through the earth's surface. It is that appearance, resembling the sharp-ridged back of a razorback hog, that gives the region its name.

The hogback ridge of sandstone overlies weaker clays and shale. The hogbacks rise out of the Great Plains at an angle of about 10 degrees and generally stand 300 feet to 600 feet above the surrounding land. The Black Hills side of the hogbacks is much steeper, descending quickly into the Red Valley. At a few points streams have cut water gaps through the hogbacks. These gaps may be as much as a hundred feet deep and are the main passes into the rest of the Black Hills province.

THE RED VALLEY

Inside the hogbacks, appearing like an elliptical course on the map, is the second sub-region of the Black Hills. This impressive subsequent valley is known as the Red Valley. It gets its name from the deep-colored red sandstone of the Spearfish Red Beds that overlies a limestone bedrock.

The Red Valley lies as much as 500 feet below the hogbacks and can be from one-fourth mile to six miles in width, but for the most part is one to two miles in width. The Red Valley is generally devoid of streams. However, the rocks of this region are very weak and offer little resistance to any of the agents of erosion, especially rainfall. The Red Valley nearly encircles the main section of the Black Hills.

THE LIMESTONE PLATEAU

The Limestone Plateau is the third major subregion of the Hills. This area also encircles the central portion of the Black Hills. However, the bulk of the Limestone Plateau lies on the west side of the Central Core with a much narrower limestone formation on the east. As a result, the western portion of the Limestone Plateau is indeed a true plateau

Scenic Spearfish Canyon cuts through the Limestone Plateau of the Black Hills.

area. It reaches 7,100 feet in elevation and is actually higher than all but the highest peak in the Hills. In fact, from the plateau in the west, one can actually look down on the mountains in the core. The eastern limestone area ranges up to 6,000 feet in elevation and appears more as a ridge than a plateau.

The Limestone Plateau subregion is also canyon and cave country. Streams have cut 1,000-feet-deep canyons into the limestone. Spearfish Canyon in the north is the most famous of the canyons. Its lovely valley follows Spearfish Creek for 20 miles in a canyon so narrow that the sun cannot shine on much of the canyon floor. Other canyons include Spring, Hill, and Bush Springs. The scenic canyons contain multi-hued sheer cliffs, sparkling waterfalls, rushing streams, and a colorful variety of plant life. Several caves also dot the Limestone Plateau. Among the more notable are Wind Cave and Jewel Cave. The former is spectacular enough to be named a national park, while the latter was designated a national monument. Other caves are Crystal Cave, Onyx Cave, Sitting Bull Cave, and Jasper Cave.

THE CENTRAL CRYSTALLINE CORE

The fourth subregion of the Black Hills is the Central Crystalline Core. This area is the very heart of the Black Hills. It is an area of mountain peaks and gulches filling the landscape without any semblance of order or reason. The Central Crystalline Core is also referred to as a basin because most of it is lower in elevation than the western portion of

The Needles are erosional spires of granite located in the Central Crystalline Core of the Black Hills.

the Limestone Plateau. In reality, however, this is a true highland area. Many peaks exceed 6,000 feet in elevation, the most notable being Harney Peak at 7,242 feet, Terry Peak at 7,071 feet, and Bald Mountain at 6,613 feet. Harney Peak is the continent's highest landform east of the Rocky Mountains.

This subregion has been carved from a crystalline rock core. The crystalline rocks were formed deep within the earth by volcanic magma. Later the tectonic forces that created the Black Hills crushed and altered the crystalline rock core as the mountains were thrust upward. The result was some exceptionally strong quartzite and granite, and some soft shining mica. The more resistant granite forms the mountain tops while weaker mica and schist are eroded into the valleys.

The Black Hills also contain an area knows as "the Needles," where erosion in vertical cracks has resulted in long spires of granite as much as 60 feet high. The Needles are especially popular today with tourists.

OBSERVATIONS

One can see from the journey across the map of South Dakota that the landscape of the state reflects physiographic diversity, ranging from river valleys to ancient lake beds, from plateaus to badlands to mountains. All these landscapes form the basic stage upon which the people of South Dakota enact their drama of life.

The highways and railroads must seek the best paths across the landscape. Some areas are conducive to large-scale farming, others to ranching, and still others to mining or recreation. All this variety of topography contributes to the diversity of uses to which the people of South Dakota put the land upon which they live.

Chapter Three

THE ATMOSPHERE: WEATHER AND CLIMATE

INTRODUCTION

How many times a day do you say or hear, "Hi, beautiful day, isn't it!" or "Wow, it's really a cold one today!" How many times a day does your favorite radio or TV station present the weather? How often do you get up early on cold, snowy winter days to turn on the radio to listen to school closings? How many times a day do you check that outdoor thermometer? When do you winterize your automobile? What emergency supplies do you take with you when you travel in winter? We could go on infinitum with questions such as these, all related to South Dakota's weather and climate.

Weather and climate in South Dakota, a continual topic of daily life! Perhaps the geographic uniqueness of South Dakota is more obvious in the state's weather and climatic systems than in any other physical characteristics. The geographic importance of weather and climate is more than a topic: it is so great that it extends into almost every aspect of one's daily life.

Weather and climate are of great importance to South Dakotans. Just look around the state. Each spring witnesses the arrival of life-giving, moisture-laden clouds, the warming of daily temperatures, and the greening of the vegetative surroundings. By summer South Dakota is experiencing some very hot days, with temperatures even exceeding 100° F. Summer can also bring drought, a lack of rainfall resulting from a lack of moisture-bearing clouds, and high temperatures, and can end with the parching of our landscape. By fall, the changes in the length of daylight signal the deciduous trees to change color and drop their leaves. Frost returns, along with dampness and cool northerly winds. Soon, winter arrives, with accompanying snowfall, below-zero temperatures and occasional blizzards.

Weather and climate extend into everyone's daily life, affecting the way people feel, the way they dress, and the way they play. Weather and climate influence the growing season, crop types, and crop yields. On occasion, agricultural production is destroyed by flooding, hail, drought, or wind. At other times, atmospheric conditions result in bumper crops.

WEATHER

Weather consists of the atmospheric conditions at any given moment. Climate is simply weather averaged over a long period of time. South Dakotans obtain their weather and climatic data from official weather stations that are distributed across the state and maintained on a continuous basis. Each weather station contains four simple instruments. These four instruments provide information that is continuously incorporated into our daily lives and yearly planning. They collect all the data utilized in weather summaries and forecasts. The four instruments are:

1. **The Rain Gauge.** This instrument provides precipitation data for rainfall, snowfall, sleet and hail, all of which occur in the state. Rainstorms can sweep across the land much of the year. Obviously, during periods of colder temperature, precipitation falls from snowstorms instead. Hail and sleet can and do occur, damaging crops, trees, power lines, and automobiles, and causing other inconveniences as well.

2. **The Thermometer.** This instrument measures the temperature on a continuous basis.

3. **The Barometer.** It measures the barometric pressure. Air pressure is always rising or falling and that fact indicates changes in weather. Generally a falling barometer indicates warmer and more humid weather, while a rising barometer means cooler and drier weather.

4. **The Anemometer.** This instrument measures wind speed, and the wind vane indicates wind direction.

In order to understand the weather and climate of South Dakota, one begins with an examination of the atmospheric conditions that can be measured at any given moment, or "the weather." It is important to understand that no matter what time of year, the four weather instruments are measuring the same characteristics. But to understand weather variation better, geographers look at the weather characteristics by season and event. Let us begin with spring for, as was mentioned at the beginning of this chapter, spring is when one witnesses the arrival of the moisture-laden, life-giving clouds, the warming of temperatures, and the greening of the landscape.

SPRING

In South Dakota, spring is a short transitional season. It has been said, "Don't blink or you will miss spring in South Dakota." Actually, that statement has some truth to it. Throughout the state, spring is the shortest of the four seasons. It is marked by a rapid change in the weather. Cold winter temperatures begin to moderate, first changing to cool temperatures and eventually to warm. By the middle of May, nighttime temperatures have warmed to the point that they could be described as cool. Daytime temperatures in mid-May can even be hot, reaching the mid-eighties and above.

Beginning in May, frost gradually disappears, generally being absent statewide by the end of the month. Many of the state's residents, anxious to plant their crops, gardens, and flowers, challenge the weather by planting them early. However, Mother Nature almost annually rises to the occasion and forces them to cover their starter plants at night or be frozen out.

The most important single weather factor in spring is a very marked increase in precipitation. Spring rains are vital to the success of the state's agricultural economy. They add moisture to the ground and provide lifegiving sustenance to the plants and animals as they begin their seasons of growth. Statewide, over 40 percent of the total yearly precipitation falls from the period of April through June.

SUMMER

Summer in South Dakota is generally the season of growth, the period when the crops and livestock grow fastest, thrive, and mature. It is the season when the state's tourism and recreation sectors reach peak activities. South Dakotans love the summer outdoors, with the late sunsets resulting from Daylight Savings Time.

Summers are generally pleasant, with a maximum of sunshine. In fact, South Dakota receives 70 percent or more of possible summer sunshine. For that reason, it is sometimes referred to as "the Sunshine State." Daytime summer temperatures range from warm to quite hot. Daytime temperatures are generally highest between 2 p.m. and 4 p.m. Nighttime is normally warm to cool with comfortable nights. It should be noted that nighttime temperatures are quite important in that 80 percent of the corn plant's growth occurs on warm nights.

Daily high temperatures will exceed 100° F several times during a normal summer. This is especially true for the central portion of the state, which generally has the summer daily high temperatures. However, even with the high temperatures, summer days can be pleasant as a result of low humidities and brisk winds. It should also be noted that the diurnal (daily) temperature range is great as a result of rapid cooling at night and a lack of cloud cover to hold in the heat at night. So one might observe people running around in a T-shirt during the day and a light jacket at night. The result, then, is that physical discomfort from high summer temperatures is not as great in South Dakota as temperature figures alone may make it appear. Indeed, many homes still are not air conditioned and are quite comfortably cooled with fans and breezes.

FALL

Fall is a most pleasant season. For many South Dakotans it is also their favorite season. It signals football, hunting, more fishing, and the return to school. Autumn is marked by changes that include mild daytime temperatures, cool evenings, ample amounts of sunshine and a decline in the occurrence and amount of precipitation. However, autumn rainfall can be quite forceful, with cold rains and chilling winds that announce the pending arrival of winter.

Normally, the first fall frost occurs about September 15. It is important to note, however, that the first frost can occur as early as late August or as late as October in a given year. By the middle of October, normal nighttime temperatures will be at or near the freezing level. By late October, the temperature at night will reach the 20° F range.

WINTER

Winter season is generally described as cold, dry, and long. Storms of frequent but short duration are normal occurrences in winter. Actually, rapid weather change can and does occur all year long as storms sweep across South Dakota. Occasionally, some winters can be described as open and relatively storm free. In a normal winter one to three heavy snow storms strike, with some years experiencing many more. In fact, the season can range from one with essentially bare ground to winters with three or four feet of snow-cover from December through March.

Winter temperatures by late December can reach well below zero. This condition can last off and on until mid-February. Nighttime winter temperatures can reach -30° F to -40° F or lower. The combination of low temperatures and strong winds produce the wind-chill factor, a measurement of the combined effect of cold and wind on the exposed surface bodies of human beings and livestock. Anyone outdoors in periods of low temperatures and strong winds risks frostbite and even death. A temperature of 0° F with a 15 mph wind is equal to a temperature of -33° F without a wind. This, then, is the wind-chill effect. In recent years, it has become increasingly important on radio and TV weather reports. In addition to providing an excellent warning to dress properly for the weather, it seems to make some people feel that they are tough pioneer-type survivors of bitter weather.

It was during a South Dakota winter when the greatest temperature variation in a limited time period occurred. On January 22, 1943, the temperature at Spearfish at 7:30 a.m. was -4° F. Two minutes later it increased to 45° F, a change of 49°. This freak weather event is known as the Spearfish Chinook.

While the seasons provide a vital understanding of a portion of the total weather picture, events provide the rest of the story. Weather events include thunderstorms, tornadoes, winds, and blizzards and snowfalls.

THUNDERSTORMS

Two very important aspects of spring and summer in South Dakota are thunderstorms and tornadoes. Thunderstorms are frequent in these seasons, with the greatest occurrence from mid-May through July. Thunderstorms are most likely to occur in the late afternoon and evening. If you are observant, you can watch the clouds build up to the west or south all afternoon long. A second daily storm period occurs in the early morning, generally between 2 a.m. and 5 a.m., when thunderstorms and crackling bolts of lightning may suddenly wake you from a deep sleep.

The most severe thunderstorms are generally accompanied by lightning, very strong winds, occasionally hail, or even tornadoes. These storm features occur as cold fronts or squall lines sweep southeast or eastward across South Dakota. Lightning can cause fires, destroy plant and animal life, and frighten humans. At the same time, it can provide the most spectacular fireworks display you will ever see. Hail occurring with a thunderstorm is most likely in late May and June. It should be noted, however, that hail can also occur in late summer and fall. Hail pellets can range in size from pea size to baseball size. Obviously, the larger the pellets and the greater in number, the more destructive the hail is to crops and possessions.

TORNADOES

Tornadoes occur commonly in South Dakota. In fact, anyone who listens to radio and television knows that tornado watches and warnings generally begin in mid-May and can last all summer. The greatest frequency, however, is in June and July. Tornado watches tend to be daily occurrences during summer days. Because of frequent watches, some people discount the potential severity of tornadoes. However, such watches should always be respected, and tornado warnings must be obeyed for one's safety.

A tornado is the smallest yet most intensive type of storm. It is relatively rare outside of the United States and Australia. A tornado is a small, intense cyclone. It appears as a dark grey to black funnel cloud suspended from a cumulo-nimbus cloud. Winds inside a funnel cloud can reach 250 mph. The clouds contain moisture, dirt and dust, and debris. While the path of a tornado is narrow, destruction is often tremendous as a result of wind stress and reduced air pressure.

South Dakota is not part of America's famous "Tornado Alley," which extends through Texas, Oklahoma, Kansas, Nebraska, Missouri, and Illinois. However, because of the intensity of tornadoes, it is not the frequency but rather the event that one must respect. Tornadoes can occur throughout South Dakota and, in actuality, can occur during any month. However, the storms are most likely in summer. When a tornado watch is announced, it means that atmospheric conditions are such that a tornado could occur. A tornado warning means that a tornado has been spotted and one should seek immediate shelter.

South Dakota can experience from a few to dozens of tornadoes during a normal year. While the number of tornadoes seems to be increasing almost yearly, it is not a result of weather changes. The increases are generally a result of improved spotting and detection and greater understanding of these intense storms.

There are numerous examples every summer of farm buildings, house trailers, and other structures being damaged by tornadoes. Some of the destructions are not observed until after the event. The state has been fortunate in that no large city has sustained significant damage from tornadoes. This does not mean that such damage will not occur. However, tornadoes like all forces of nature tend to take the path of least resistance. If one touches down in open country, it is more likely to go around a town than through it. That is why house trailers, which tend to be sited on the outskirts of town and offer weak resistance, are so susceptible to storm damage. The greatest destruction occurs when a tornado touches down in an open area such as a park or school ground in a city. Then the storm must travel through surrounding structures in its path.

WINDS

Fall is a good time to begin talking about the winds. This is so because fall marks the time of year when wind patterns shift. The arrival of fall winds brings piercing chills to people acclimated to warm summer weather. During summer and early fall, prevailing winds are from the south. In the fall, wind direction shifts to the east and then to the north and northwest for the winter.

Winter brings blasts of Arctic and sub-Arctic temperatures and winds to the state, winds that try to blow the freezing outdoor temperatures through the walls and windows of your home. South Dakota has an average wind velocity of 11 to 12 mph. However, it should be understood that winds can hit 70 to 90 mph at any time of the year. Indeed, winds of over 100 mph have been clocked in the state. For example, in 1968 winds of 100 to 150 mph for an extensive period (up to 20 minutes) were clocked in many communities in eastern South Dakota. These powerful winds destroyed many trees and damaged numerous farm and town structures.

BLIZZARDS AND SNOWFALL

Two other winter phenomena common to South Dakota are snowfall and the blizzard. Snowfall can occur anytime from early October until the first part of May. Obviously, those are the two extremes, and snowfall is most likely in the intervening months. Blizzards in the state average three a year. Of course, some years there are none, and in other years there may be four or more.

South Dakota usually experiences three or four severe cold waves a year. During these cold waves, temperatures at night can reach -30° or lower. Snowfall may occur during cold waves. When these low temperatures are accompanied by strong winds and heavy snowfall, a blizzard can develop. Some 8 inches to 12 inches of snowfall can occur within a 24-hour period. In fact, on occasion over 20 inches of snowfall has occurred in South Dakota in a day's time. During storms and blizzards, snowfall is accompanied by drifting. When this occurs, highways and roads can be blocked for up to a day or even longer. People and livestock must obtain shelter or perish.

Before examining blizzards in greater detail, one should learn about snow. In understanding snow, it is important to realize that the moisture content of snow varies greatly.

Geographically, the general rule is that ten inches of snow is equal to one inch of rainfall. During a very wet, slushy type of snowfall, as little as two inches of snow might equal one inch of rainfall. These are the snows that quickly soak through your shoes and socks, chilling your feet. During a dry, drifting snowfall it might take as much as thirty inches of snow to equal one inch of rainfall. Snowfall in a blizzard is often the latter fine and relatively dry type. The dry snow is extremely dangerous during windy periods since it can be blown around, blocking roads, isolating farms, and closing city streets.

Weather conditions favorable to a blizzard will normally result in the issuance of a blizzard or severe blizzard warning. A blizzard warning is issued when winds with speeds of 35 mph or more are accompanied by considerable falling and or blowing snow, when temperatures are 20° F or lower, when visibility is 500 feet or less, and when these conditions are expected to continue for an extended period. A severe blizzard warning is issued when winds reach 45 mph or more, the temperature is 10°F or lower, and visibility is near zero.

It should be noted that blizzards can be statewide or closely localized. They may last from one to three days, occasionally even longer. In some years a series of blizzards and severe storms will sweep across South Dakota in an unexplainable pattern. During the winter of 1968-1969, much of the state experienced an almost-weekly blizzard or heavy snowstorm from each Thursday evening through Saturday. That year many communities received three to four times their normal snowfall. In fact, the snow in some towns was so deep that people put big, red ribbons on their car radio antennas to enable cars approaching from intersecting streets to see them coming.

An examination of South Dakota's historical records reveal that the first blizzard in recent recorded history was also the latest in terms of seasonal date. That storm occurred when John J. Audubon, the famous naturalist, was traveling through present-day South Dakota in May 1843. On May 5, he recorded that a tremendous blizzard hit, resulting in the deaths of thousands of newborn buffalo calves.

The most famous blizzard in South Dakota history was the terrible "School Children's Blizzard." This death-dealing storm roared out of the northwest on January 12, 1888, with little warning. Early morning gave no clue of the pending storm. As the weather began to change, many children in the eastern portion of Dakota Territory were sent home from school, only to be trapped by the storm and die. There were 174 human deaths, virtually all children, that occurred that day as a result of the blizzard. It is also very likely that the Native Americans suffered great loss of life during that storm, but because of isolation and the time, that supposition cannot be documented.

CLIMATE

As a result of the examination of weather conditions and seasonal patterns, one is now in a better position to understand climate. Remember, climate is simply weather over a long period of time. South Dakota's climate is Continental. This name reflects the fact that the state's location is in the heart of the North American continent. The state is about the same distance from the Atlantic and Pacific oceans, and the same distance from the Arctic Ocean and the Gulf of Mexico.

Because of its interior location, South Dakota is also at a crossroads of climatic types. It is important to remember that climate is an average. Therefore, a climatic zone is based on average conditions, and its boundary determined by averages. It must be remembered that each climatic zone is an idealized type that in reality can shift in a given year.

The climate of South Dakota is comprised of four climatic types or zones (Map 5). They are:

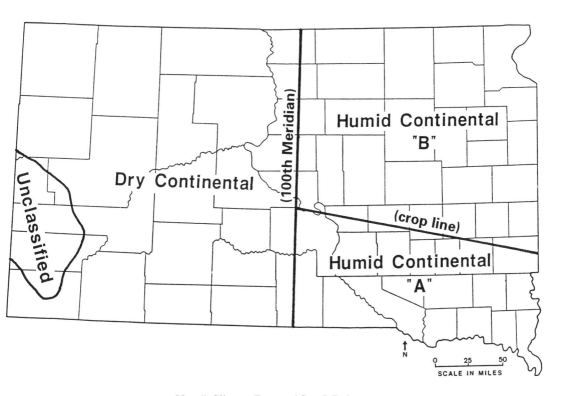

Map 5. Climate Zones of South Dakota.

1. The Humid Continental Type "A"
2. The Humid Continental Type "B"
3. The Dry Continental
4. The Unclassified Continental

In South Dakota, the Humid Continental Type "A" climate runs roughly from the 100th meridian west, northward to about 44° north latitude at Big Bend Dam. From there the line runs east-southeast to just south of Dell Rapids to Luverne, Minnesota. Historically, that line has been known as the crop line. The "A" climate includes everything south of this line. It must be remembered throughout this discussion that these are idealized lines, and in reality the lines are movable from year to year.

The Humid Continental "B" climate is in all of South Dakota north of that line (crop line) and east of the 100th meridian. The Dry Continental zone encompasses everything west of the 100th meridian (roughly from Winner to Blunt to Herreid), with the exception of the Black Hills, which constitute the Unclassified climate. A geographic description of each climate will give you a better understanding of the differences in the four types.

THE HUMID CONTINENTAL "A" CLIMATE

The Humid Continental "A" is the long-summer type. It is characterized by narrower seasonal temperature variations, receives more precipitation, and exhibits a greater evaporation rate than the other types. It is separated from the "B" climate by a "crop line" which is historically based on corn maturity. South of the crop line, summer is long enough for corn to reach full maturity in the field.

In the "A" climate there are four well-defined seasons, with a longer summer and a shorter, milder winter. Rainfall is well distributed. South Dakota's portion of the "A" climate is in the extreme northwestern portion of the belt for the United States and is really a transition zone. Therefore, South Dakota's extremes are greater than other portions of the "A" climate except for the northeastern sections of the U.S.A.

The average temperature for the Humid Continental "A" climatic zone ranges from 45° F in Minnehaha County to near 50° F along the southern border of the state. The winter temperatures range from 18° F average in the north to near 26° F in southern Tripp County, while the average summer mean temperatures range from 71° F in the north to near 75° F in the southern limit of the state.

In the fall the first freeze occurs around September 18 in Minnehaha County and as late as September 29 along the Nebraska border. The reverse is true for the last spring freeze. In this instance, the last freeze in the south is May 6 and in Minnehaha County about May 15. Using these figures, one can see that the annual average growing season for the Humid Continental "A" climate in South Dakota ranges from 130 days in the northern part of the zone to 150 days in southern Bon Homme, southeast Charles Mix, and southwest Yankton counties.

It is during the growing season that this zone receives the best rainfall, with 40 percent to 60 percent of it falling during that time. The May to September rainfall averages from 11 inches in the west to near 18 inches in the southeast portion of the zone. The importance of this can be seen from examining the annual average precipitation. It ranges from 18" near Big Bend Dam to almost 26" in Union County. The annual average rainfall increases from west to east within this zone. The same is true of annual snowfall. Snowfall at Big Bend averages about 26", while in Union County it approaches 40" a year. There is one big exception as regards snowfall. In Todd, Tripp, and Gregory counties snowfall averages 52" or more. Snowfall here is heavier because it is outside the effect of the Black Hills, which pirates moisture from the rest of the state, and because this zone is attacked by many fronts as they move across the continent.

Data from four key weather stations are useful to an understanding of the Humid Continental "A" climate:

Sioux Falls has an all-time high of 110° F and an all-time low of -36° F, with an average 25" of precipitation. Average annual snowfall is 41" and the record is 95".

Vermillion has a high of 114° F and low of -38° F. Precipitation averages 25", and snowfall 30" with a record of 67".

Mitchell has a high of 116° F, low of -39° F with 22" of precipitation. Snowfall averages 32" with a 72" record.

Academy has a high of 116° F, low of -37° F, with 21" of rainfall. Snowfall averages 26" with a 92" record.

THE HUMID CONTINENTAL "B" CLIMATE

The Humid Continental "B" climate also has four seasons. Its summers are warm to hot and medium in length. The winters are long and cold. Precipitation is moderate, and both rainfall and snowfall are well distributed.

The Humid Continental "B" climate covers northeast South Dakota north of the crop line (Map 5). The mean temperature in this zone ranges from 43° F in the north to near 47° F in the south. The winter temperatures range from 13° F in the northeast to 19° F at the crop line. Summer averages range from 68° F in Campbell County to 72° F at the crop line.

In the fall the average date of the first freeze is September 13 in McPherson County and runs as late as September 23 in the south. The last spring freeze in Minnehaha County is May 12 and extends to May 27 in McPherson County. This gives the region a growing season of from 133 days in the southeast to 118 days in the north.

The annual growing-season precipitation from May to September ranges from 11" to 15". The annual average precipitation ranges from 16" in the northwest to 24" in Minnehaha County. Snowfall amounts vary in the region. Average snowfall along the crop line is 38", dropping to 28" in the central area, then increasing to 39" along the northern border. The decrease in the central portion is a rain shadow effect caused by the Black Hills.

Climatic summaries from four stations give a good picture of this zone:

Watertown has an all-time high of 110° F and an all-time low of -40° F with 22" of precipitation. Average snowfall is 30" with a record snowfall of 60".

Aberdeen has a high of 115° F and a low of -46° F with 19" of precipitation. Average snowfall is 36" with a record of 96".

Huron has a high of 112° F and low of -41° F with precipitation of 20". Average snow is 42" and record snowfall is 83".

Highmore has a high of 113° F and low of -45° F with 18" of precipitation. Snowfall averages 28" with an 83" record.

THE DRY CONTINENTAL CLIMATE

The Dry Continental climate is very much like the two Humid Continental types in temperature. Summers are hot. Since the atmosphere is dry and clouds and fog are rare, sunny days prevail. Both the relative humidity and sensible temperature are low. Winters can be bitterly cold. Wind is changeable all year. The diurnal temperatures are great. Annual temperature variations, too, are great and can be as much as 150° F.

The most striking difference between the Humid and Dry Continental climates is precipitation. In the Dry Zone precipitation everywhere is less than 20" a year. In the Humid zone it exceeds 20" almost everywhere.

The lack of heavy precipitation anywhere in South Dakota is a result of its continental location. The state is a great distance from the principal sources of water, namely the oceans. It is also blocked by mountains on the west that take available moisture from clouds as they move over the uplands. About 80 percent of the precipitation falls as thunderstorms and cloudbursts, resulting from the rapid rise of heated air. Hence, rainfall, especially in western South Dakota, is highly localized, erratic, and can be unreliable.

The Dry Continental climate of western South Dakota covers all the state west of the 100th meridian except for the Black Hills. Here the annual average temperature ranges from a low of 42° F near Lemmon to 48° F in Shannon and Bennett counties. The mean daily temperature for winter is 16° F in Campbell County and increases to 26° F in Todd and Bennett counties. The average summer temperature ranges from 65° F in the north to 74° F in the south.

The average date of the first fall freeze is September 17 in the north and September 25 in the south. The last spring freeze occurs May 12 in the south and May 28 in the north. This provides the area with a growing season of 118 days in the north ranging to 140 days in the southeast. Again the Black Hills provide an additional effect by protecting the area around Rapid City from frost and giving that area a 143-day growing season.

During the growing season, precipitation ranges from 10 to 12 inches. The normal yearly precipitation for the region ranges from 13" in the northwest to 20" in Tripp County. Snowfall ranges from 28" in the north to 52" in Tripp County.

Pierre has an all-time high of 115° F and an all-time low of -40° F with 18" of precipitation. Average snowfall is 31", and record snow is 82".

Lemmon has a high of 115° F and low of -45° F, with 18" of precipitation. Snowfall 33", with a 70" record snow.

Rapid City has a high of 110° F and low of -34° F, with 16" of precipitation. Snowfall averages 41" with a 81" record.

Camp Crook has a high of 114° F and low of -57° F, with an average precipitation of 14". Snowfall averages 32" with a 76" record.

It should be noted that the record low temperature for South Dakota occurred in this region when it fell to -58° F at McIntosh on February 17, 1936. The record high temperature was in the "A" zone at Gann Valley, where it reached 120° F, also in 1936.

THE UNCLASSIFIED CLIMATE

The Unclassified Climate is located in the upper elevations of the Black Hills. It is an area with 20 inches to 24 inches of precipitation. Here the normal lapse rate comes into play. Under normal conditions air temperature drops 3½° F for every 1,000 foot increase in elevation. Elevation, temperature, precipitation, and sunlight produce a variety of micro-climates that distinguish the Black Hills from the surrounding Dry Continental zone.

In South Dakota, the Unclassified Continental climate is found only in the Black Hills. Here the annual average temperature ranges from 40° F in the higher elevations to 47° F in the lower. The winter averages range from 22° F to 27° F. As a result of the higher winter temperatures, the people of this region like to boast that they live in the "banana belt." Summer temperatures range from 65° F in the higher areas to 71° F in the lower elevations.

The average date of the first fall freeze is September 13 to 20. The last spring freeze is from May 15 to 24. The annual average growing season runs from 101 days in the higher elevations to 130 in other portions of the Hills. Precipitation is 10" to 12" during the growing season. The annual average precipitation varies from 14" to 24" in the Central Core area. One notable variation in the Hills is snowfall, ranging from 32" in Butte County to over 140" in the mountains proper.

> Lead has an all-time high of 101° F and an all-time low of -40° F with 28" of precipitation. Snowfall averages 164" with a 261" record.
> Hot Springs has a high of 112° F and low of -41° F with 17" of precipitation. Snowfall averages 36" with a record of 68".
> Deerfield, given its elevation, keeps only snowfall information, with an annual record snowfall of 264" in 1977.

From the examination of the weather and climate of South Dakota it is apparent that great variation exists in the state's atmospheric conditions. South Dakota indeed has its beautiful weather. It also has extremely cold days. On occasion, for some people, it is too hot, or too windy, or has too much snow. For others, the snow is an opportunity to enjoy outdoor winter sports; the wind is fine for sailboarding; and the sun and heat perfect for summer relaxation.

Weather and climatic variations have necessitated cultural responses to make residents' lives here better. As a result, people insulate, heat, and air-condition their homes for comfort and survival. Residents learn to dress appropriately whether for summer or winter. People adapt their agricultural practices to hybrids that require shorter growing seasons, and to irrigated fields to increase the crop yields. South Dakota residents practice a diverse recreation pattern that allows and encourages year-long enjoyment of the state. They do this by swimming, boating, and fishing in summer and hunting, cross-country skiing, ice fishing, and snowmobiling in winter.

South Dakota's weather and climate have something for almost everybody. To the state's residents, these physical forces are often the love-it or leave-it factors that encourage people to out-migrate or stay at home. As the lives of Americans become increasingly involved in recreation, the four seasons of the state's climate make South Dakota even more appealing as a place to live.

Chapter Four
PLANT, ANIMAL, AND SOIL GEOGRAPHY

INTRODUCTION

Plant life, animal life, and soil qualities are ever-changing aspects of South Dakota's physical geography. By understanding these changes over time, one can appreciate the impact and unique diversity of nature. Today, as in times past, people have lived close to this land, adapting to the unique natural landscape of South Dakota and depending on its fertile soils and abundant plant and animal resources for their livelihood. The soils provide the nutrients that enable the plants and animal life of the region to form its biosphere.

THE PRE-INDIAN BIOSPHERE

The first residents of this environment, Native American hunters who roamed the region more than 10,000 years ago, found a biotic environment much different from that of the pioneers or that in which people live today. Elephants, musk ox, caribou, primitive horses, saber-toothed tigers, and a number of other ancient fauna (or wildlife) shared this then-wooded land with its earliest human settlers at the close of the Ice Age.

In the Badlands, archaeologists have discovered an arrowhead imbedded in the bones of a huge mammoth. It is from this important discovery that we now know that humans and these huge extinct mammals occupied this land together at the end of the Pleistocene. Bones of mammoths and other ancient fauna are on display at the Hot Springs Mammoth Site in Fall River County and the South Dakota Museum of Geology in Rapid City.

Some scientists believe that the earliest humans reaching the Great Plains found much of the region to be wooded and that humans, perhaps more than even climatic change, were responsible for the gradual change in vegetation cover from forest to grassland. For hundreds of thousands of years, humans around the world have used fire to clear land, hunt game animals, and to create environmental conditions more favorable for domesticated animals and plants from which they obtained food, hide, fiber, and other useful materials.

Many scientists believe that ancient hunters of the Plains also used fire for these purposes. Gradually, over thousands of years, the native woodlands were destroyed and replaced by prairie grasses. As the vegetative habitat, or environment in which certain animals thrive, was changed by fire, woodland-dwelling animals left the region, to be replaced by grazing animals, among them the bison (commonly called the "buffalo"), deer, and antelope.

Perhaps today's residents should be very thankful for this environmental change done unwittingly by native peoples thousands of years ago. Beneath the dense grassland cover and thick mat of sod, some of the world's most richly organic and fertile soils were formed, the Chernozem and Chestnut soils that made it possible for the region to become one of the world's most productive agricultural "bread baskets." Even today, long after much of the native prairie grassland has fallen to the homesteaders' plows, the rich "A horizon," or highly organic top layer of the soil, can be seen in a soil profile. It is from the nutrients in the topsoil that plants, including our agricultural crops, gain most of their nourishment.

THE PLAINS INDIAN

When we think of wildlife typical to the region, certainly the American bison, or buffalo, stands as a shaggy symbol of the region's past. Plains Indians developed a culture that was heavily dependent on the buffalo. For these skilled hunters, the countless millions of bison that roamed the plains amply provided their essential needs. The buffalo was their chief source of food. It was from the buffalo's hide that the women made clothing, blankets, moccasins, and the coverings of their tepees. The bones of animals were fashioned into tools, and from horns they made cups, spoons, ornaments, and other containers. For those Indians living remote from wooded areas, dried bison dung served as fuel.

From wild plants the Indians obtained food and fiber. They found some of these plants to be very useful for curing sickness and healing wounds. The Native Americans possessed an intimate knowledge of their environment. This included not only knowledge of its plant and animal life, which were their major resources, but also those environmental elements upon which they depended for their survival.

ANGLO-AMERICAN SETTLEMENT

When European peoples first settled Dakota during the nineteenth century, the vegetation of the Plains could best be described as a "sea of grass." Trees grew only in those places that were naturally protected from fire, such as river bottomlands, along the shores of lakes, and in areas of broken terrain such as Pine Ridge and the Black Hills. Millions of bison still roamed the plains in numbers much greater than those of today's domesticated livestock, cattle, horses, and sheep.

From the earliest period of settlement, the European pioneer settlers began changing the environment to better suit their needs. In a few short decades, the bison population declined from millions to near extinction. They were replaced on the range by herds of livestock. Native prairie grasslands were plowed under and replaced by varieties of cultivated grasses, such crops as wheat, barley, rye, oats, and corn.

Many early settlers selected homestead sites near wooded areas, such as along lakes or streams. Here, wood was available for building and for fuel. Those not as fortunate often bundled prairie grasses or hay to burn, a practice remembered today in the name of Hayti, a Hamlin County community. On the plains, away from timber, thick prairie sod was used to build dwellings. The result was the famous "soddies" that were home to many early residents who settled in Dakota.

With the discovery of gold during the mid-1870s in the Black Hills and the rush that followed, mines began to dot the landscape and boomtowns seemed to rise overnight. Trees from the Black Hills' dense forests were cut over rapidly to provide mining timbers, logs, and lumber for construction, and fuel. By the turn of the century, much of the original stand of timber in the Hills was gone, leaving a barren landscape.

During the 1870s the railroads pressed ever westward across the territory. The demand for rail ties further reduced the region's woodland. But as natural woodlands disappeared, they gradually began to be replaced by deliberately planted stands of timber. It must be remembered that most early settlers came from areas that were heavily wooded. These settlers felt exposed and vulnerable in an open, treeless landscape.

Trees planted around homesteads and in towns provided a break in the otherwise monotonous and, to some, bleak landscape. The trees provided some shelter from the howling winds that sweep the plains. The tree claim act of the late nineteenth century further encouraged homesteaders to plant saplings. Some of these early woodlands remain today. In fact, a good example of these tree claims still exists today and is visible as Brookings' wooded Hillcrest Park.

During the twentieth century, the coniferous forest of the Black Hills was gradually restored to its present densely wooded condition. In fact, the Black Hills today contain over three times more trees than existed at the time of the Custer Expedition to the region in 1874. On the Plains, following the "Dust Bowl" era of the 1930s, the federal government began planting "shelterbelts," the long, narrow, strips of woodland that are common on farmsteads throughout eastern South Dakota. From 1935 to 1942, more than 40 million trees were planted in more than 3,200 miles of shelterbelt.

Today, as many of the original trees die, unfortunately they are not being replaced. Some shelterbelts are being removed by farmers to clear additional land for the planting of crops. In other cases the shelterbelts are being enhanced because the farmer realizes that commercial trees can be raised in these areas and provide protection at the same time. The replanting and preservation of shelterbelts is a very important step in conserving the environment. Not only do trees reduce wind erosion, but they also provide a sheltered habitat for wildlife.

The natural vegetation, or flora, is changed in many ways. Changes can be brought about by fire, cutting, tilling the soil, planting, and grazing. For thousands of years, fire has been the greatest agent of change. Some fires begin from natural causes, such as a lightning strike. However, most fires are caused by humans. Not only does fire destroy and often change the character of flora, but by altering or destroying wildlife habitat, it affects animal life as well. Unfortunately, when the land and soil are charred and bare of vegetation, precious soil can be lost through the erosional forces of rain and wind.

Early settlers on the Plains lived in constant fear of prairie fires during the dry seasons of the year. Such fires, often sparked by human carelessness or railroad steam engines, frequently burned across hundreds or even thousands of square miles. Traveling at speeds which often exceeded 50 miles an hour, the intense heat of these "fire storms" destroyed everything in their path, including entire communities on some occasions. In April 1889, a prairie fire at Leola burned over 400 square miles of land. Another in 1909 burned a 15-mile by 30-mile area in Edmunds and Faulk counties. In 1947 the largest prairie fire in South Dakota's history burned an area of over 300,000 acres in northern Hyde and four adjoining counties.

In the Black Hills, forest fires can ravage thousands of acres of timberland, leaving once beautifully wooded slopes a desolate landscape of charred waste. In the Hills, burned woodlands are replanted, but decades pass before small seedlings grow to maturity and the forest returns to its former beauty and economic value. The lumber industry in the

Black Hills is able to succeed because as trees are removed they are replaced by seedlings. In this way our forest resources are both used and renewed for future generations.

Agricultural activities, such as tilling the soil for crop farming and the rangeland grazing of livestock, have done more to change South Dakota's flora than any other factors during the period of European settlement in the region. Virgin prairie grass and sod have been tilled for more than a century in most of the state east of the Missouri River. What was once described as being "a sea of grass, . . . an ocean of earth, undulating in heavy, long-drawn waves, on and on into the blue distance," has been transformed by generations of farmers into a landscape dominated by "amber waves of grain" during the harvest season.

West of the Missouri, large herds of livestock have grazed for a hundred years on the open ranges of nutritious prairie (tall grass) and steppe (short grass). In some places, severe overgrazing has destroyed the original grass cover, with less desirable plants and grasses replacing the native buffalo grass, bluegama, bluestem, and wheatgrass. Often, overgrazing has also caused fertile topsoil to be stripped away by water and wind erosion. Today, many farmers and ranchers improve pasturelands by introducing new varieties of grasses and other types of forage.

One can easily observe how humans have used and changed the flora of this state, sometimes accidentally, often deliberately. Some changes have been beneficial, such as those that have turned large areas of South Dakota into an agricultural breadbasket and the source of food for millions of people around the world. Others, however, have been

The American bison or buffalo, once nearly extinct, is today the symbol of South Dakota's fauna.

very damaging to our natural environment and to the ecosystem, that is, to the combined physical elements of the earth upon which we depend for our survival.

Animal life, too, has been changed greatly by human activity. By 1900, the nation's bison population, which earlier had been estimated by some to have numbered as many as 60 million head, had been reduced to near extinction, with only about twenty remaining. Through careful conservation measures, there are more than 60,000 buffalo today in America, more than half of which are in South Dakota.

Careful management of wildlife resources has protected deer, antelope, waterfowl, pheasants, and other animals and birds. The state bird, the pheasant, was introduced into the United States from its native China. Many of the state's most common birds, such as the sparrow, blackbird, and starling, were brought to this country from Europe. New varieties of fish have been introduced to lakes and rivers. Since 1982, for example, nearly one million chinook salmon have been stocked yearly in Lake Oahe. Fish populations are maintained in all of our sport-fishing waters through careful management and stocking. Many other types of animal life are carefully protected, including deer and antelope, migratory waterfowl, and the proud bald eagle, the symbol of our nation, hundreds of which gather in the Missouri River bottomlands.

Humans depend upon nature for their survival. They use nature's resources to fill many of their social, cultural, economic, and physical needs, and as a result they also change the biotic environment in many ways.

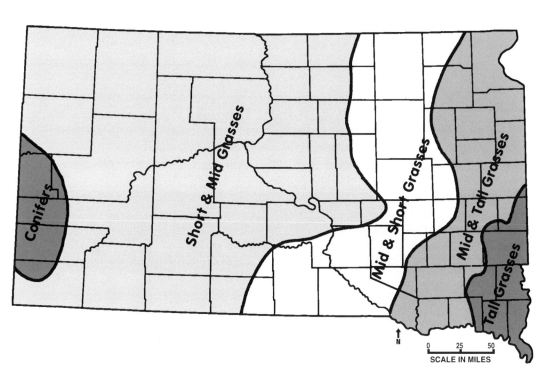

Map 6. **Vegetative Zones of South Dakota.**

The multi-colored Big Badlands resulted from the sand, clay, and volcanic ash that comprise the soil and rock materials.

BIOGEOGRAPHY: THE FLORA AND FAUNA

Although changes in natural plant life may not be obvious to many travelers crossing South Dakota, there are, in fact, five ecosystems, or vegetation regions, that are recognized by geographers and other scientists. From east to west across the state these regions are the Tall Grass Prairie in the southeast corner, the Mid and Tall Grasses Region, and the Mid and Short Grasses Region, all in the eastern third of the state (Map 6). The western two-thirds of South Dakota is comprised of the Short and Mid Grasses or Mixed Prairie Region and the Conifers Region of the Black Hills. A very close relationship exists in these five ecosystems between the flora and fauna as influenced by terrain, climate, and soils.

THE TALL GRASS PRAIRIES

The Tall Grass Prairies in southeastern South Dakota were once comprised of a turf of tall grasses from three to six feet in height. The vegetative surface also contained low shrubs, and herbs. Because of its location, this region has the highest precipitation levels of the state. It also has ground water available at all times and experiences flooding most springs.

The Tall Grass Prairie is an area earlier dominated by big bluestem, little bluestem, sand dropseed, switchgrass, Indian grass, and other tall prairie grass varieties. In the flood plains of the lower Missouri River and the Big Sioux River, grasses such as wild rye, panic-grass, and bluejoint are still found. Shrubs include buck bush and wild roses. These plants furnish the shade that allows the few trees that grow in the region to get seedling starts. Herbs in the region include milkweed, cinquefoil, sunflowers, and goldenrod.

The fauna of the Tall Grass Prairies is dominated by small animals. Among the most common are jackrabbits, cottontail rabbits, and meadow mice. The region that once contained buffalo and antelope today has only one large wild animal, the deer. This area lacks many burrowing animals because the ground water and flood water level would drown them out. Birds include the marsh hawk, bobolink, short-eared owl and short-billed marsh wren.

THE MID AND TALL GRASS REGION

The Mid and Tall Grass Region lies to the southeast of an undulating line running from northeastern Marshall County to southern Charles Mix County. Precipitation in this region averages from 18 inches to 22 inches a year. Plant life ranges from one to three feet in height. The vegetation and animal life of the region reflect the characteristics and types found to both the east and the west.

In this vegetative region, the grass size decreases from east to west. The Mid and Tall Grasses Region gradually merges into a region of Mid and Short grasses. The major grass types are needlegrass and needle-and-thread grass. The eastern portion of the region and the river valleys are similar to the Tall Grass Region, and the western portion of the region and the better drained areas are like the Mid and Short Grass Region.

THE MID AND SHORT GRASS REGION

The Mid and Short Grass Region extends east of a line from central McPherson County in the north to central Todd County in the south. This is a region of reliable and well distributed precipitation. Plant height averages six inches but can easily reach one foot or more. Mid grasses prevail in the lowlands, while short grasses dominate the better-drained areas.

Major grasses are the western wheatgrass, porcupine grass, needlegrass, and prairie June grass. Other medium grasses also can be found in the region. Shrubs include the prairie rose and the lead plant. Herbs and seasonals include the prairie clover and goldenrod among the former, and the pasque flower (the state flower) and pineapple flower among the latter.

Major animal life in this region has changed over time. In the past, bison and antelope dominated the landscape. Now jackrabbit, badger, skunk, weasel, pocket gopher, and deer dominate the land. Reptiles have also changed. The once-numerous prairie rattler has been replaced by the bull snake and the blue racer. Birds include larks, sparrows, owls, hawks, ducks, geese, and pheasants.

THE SHORT AND MID GRASS REGION

Most of the western two-thirds of the state is a region of steppe grasslands. It falls within the Short and Mid Grass Region, or Mixed Grass Prairie Region. This is a region of severe climate: irregular precipitation and often-violent thunderstorms, and hail or blizzards. The region receives thirteen inches to eighteen inches of precipitation a year and is for the most part in the early maturity stage of erosion. The resulting landscape offers little protection for plants, which in turn offer a little shelter for animal life.

Here blue grama, buffalograss, little bluestem, wheatgrass, bunchgrass, and green needleleaf dominate the vegetative landscape. Other common plants include the blazing star, goldenrod, aster, and sunflower. Legumes include prairie clover, buffalo bean, and wild alfalfas. Other plants of note are wild onions, prairie lilies, and evening primroses.

Animal life in the Short and Mid Grass Region is dominated by animals known for their speed. The antelope, which can run up to 32 mph, is the fastest animal in the region. The jackrabbit at 28 mph is generally able to outrun the coyote, who travels at 24 mph. Surprisingly, buffalo can reach almost 25 mph when running at full speed. The kit fox and grey wolf can reach speeds of 20 mph. Speed is important to survival in this region, because the animals must not only be able to outrun or run down other species but also cover a wide expanse of land in order to eat. Other animals include the rattlesnake, the bull snake and the blue racer. Birds include larks, sparrows, blackbirds, owls, hawks, turkey buzzards, falcons, ducks, and geese.

THE CONIFERS

The fifth natural region, the Conifers, is comprised of the Black Hills area, which, because of its higher elevation, stands as an "island" above the surrounding grassy plains and some nearby hills and ridges. It is also affected greatly by the vertical zonation of plant and animal life as a result of weather and climate.

The result is the woodlands of the Black Hills, which are dominated by species of needleleaf, coniferous evergreens. The western yellow pine, or ponderosa pine, is the dominant tree of the area. White pine, lodgepole pine, timber pine, the state tree—Black Hills spruce—and the western red cedar are also important. The yellow pine is the most important lumber tree in the region.

Approximately 4 percent of the state's lands are in forest. This amounts to almost 2,000,000 acres of land, which essentially are limited to the Black Hills. The federal government controls almost two-thirds of the commercial forest land in the state. These National Forest lands are administered from headquarters at Custer. It should be noted that through sustained-yield forestry, the Black Hills today contain over three times more trees than they did when the Custer Expedition first visited them in 1874.

Trees are cut for sawtimber, roundwood and pulpwood. Sawtimber is utilized in the construction and mining industries. Roundwood is utilized both for poles and posts, and also for pulpwood. Sawtimber, poles, and posts are milled in Custer, Hill City, and other Black Hills communities. Large amounts of ponderosa pine, the principal pulpwood, are shipped to pulp mills in other states for processing. Of the natural-resource industries, forest products rank after agriculture and mining in importance.

Other plant life in the Conifers Region includes various species of grasses, shrubs, herbs, and leaves. The major grasses are located primarily in the Red Valley. The blue-joint and bluegrass are the major types of grasses. The major shrubs are wild plum, chokecherry, and Juneberry. Herbs include horse mint, thistles, and violets. The Conifers Region also contains three notable vines, the woodbine, the bittersweet, and the wild grape. The wild grape is world famous in that it serves as the pattern for most Black Hills Gold jewelry.

Animal life in the Black Hills has also changed greatly over time. Once the white-tailed deer, puma, black bear, and grizzly bear were dominant there. Today, they have been forced out of the Conifers Region as a result of development. Cottontail and wood rabbits are common in the region, as are squirrel, raccoon, chipmunk, and porcupine. Mountain goat, mountain sheep, buffalo, elk, wild burro, and bobcat are also found in the region. Some of these survive primarily through efforts of habitat enhancement and species protection. Birds are varied and include the woodpecker, wren, bobwhite, jay, sparrow, and robin.

DECIDUOUS ZONES

Although not a part of the natural vegetation, the Deciduous Zones are distinct patterns that must be noted. These zones are a result of human occupancy. They are found scattered across the state, in shelter belts, tree farms, parks, towns, and river valleys. The major species in these zones vary greatly from one to another. Western cottonwood and green ash are found along the flood plains of many streams. The ash is also found on forested buttes. The Burr oak is limited primarily to portions of Tripp and Gregory coun-

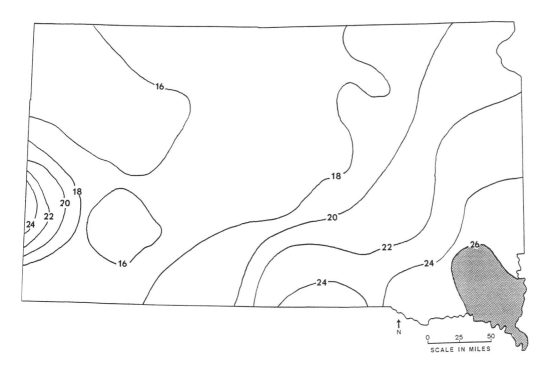

Map 7. **Annual Average Precipitation in South Dakota, in Inches.**

ties. Elm, ash, linden, boxelder, poplar, oak, cottonwood, and other deciduous species are found in our cities and towns.

These deciduous trees, which lose their leaves during the winter season, are supplemented by a wide variety of conifers, including the Black Hills spruce, Colorado blue spruce, pine, and juniper. The coniferous western red cedar is found on the tops and sides of buttes and mesas in western South Dakota and along the bluffs of the Missouri River. Numerous species of shrubs, herbs, and flowers have been introduced into parks and residential areas. Some exist very well on their own in this natural environment, while others require watering and tending.

OBSERVATIONS AND CHANGES

By comparing the map of vegetation regions with that of precipitation, one can see clearly that moisture is the primary factor in determining the state's patterns of natural vegetation (Maps 6 & 7). Taller grasses dominate the more humid eastern portion of the state. The farther west one travels, the drier the conditions become, and the grasses become increasingly shorter and less dense in surface cover. This pattern is broken only in those places such as the Black Hills and other upland areas which receive more moisture or in river bottomlands where available soil moisture supports thick stands of cottonwood, willow, and other broadleaf deciduous trees.

Each of these regions has been greatly changed by human activities. Within each region, however, there remain stands of vegetation relatively unchanged from the time of earliest European settlement. Also, terrain and available moisture vary locally within each region. In Lincoln County south of Sioux Falls, for example, the Newton Hills support a dense woodland, even though the area falls within the Tall Grass Prairie region. West of the Missouri River, the Pine Ridge is but one of several areas of higher elevation where trees are protected from prairie fires and grazing animals and where woodlands provide a break from the rolling grasslands. Near lake shores and in river bottomlands, where adequate moisture is constantly available, woodlands often flourish.

As you have learned, South Dakota is blessed with a considerable variety and abundance of animal life. Deer are common to all areas of the state. Herds of bison and antelope still roam large areas of the west. These are herbivores, or grazing animals. Smaller animals, such as jackrabbits and cottontails, squirrels, and prairie dogs also abound. These smaller herbivores are preyed upon by carnivores, or meat-eating animals, such as the coyote and fox. Wolves and bears, however, are no longer common in the state. Today, the hunting of game animals brings considerable revenue to the state.

Pheasants, ducks and geese, and doves are among the common game birds in South Dakota. In the spring and fall, the Missouri flyway and the state's lakes and prairie potholes and wetlands serve as temporary refuges for hundreds of thousands of ducks and geese during their seasonal migrations.

The state's lakes and streams teem with fish of many types. Anglers from throughout the nation are attracted to our waters in the hope of taking their limit of the state fish, the walleye. Walleye, salmon, trout, pike, and other game fish are regularly stocked in our recreational bodies of water.

Some types of animal life create problems. Insects such as flies and mosquitoes are a nuisance, but others, such as the grasshopper, are pests that can cause millions of dollars

Mule deer are increasingly visible to travelers in western South Dakota.

in crop damage. An adult hopper eats many times its own body weight each day, and swarms numbering millions of insects can strip a field bare in a matter of hours, then move on to inflict their damage elsewhere.

The natural vegetation and animal life of South Dakota, the flora and fauna of the biosphere, are everyone's to enjoy, to use, and to share with others who are drawn to the subtle beauty of the prairie and to the forest-clad Black Hills, to the lakes and streams teeming with game fish, and to the varied wildlife. The fertile soils have long been one of South Dakota's most important economic resources, supporting both crop farming and livestock farming.

SOIL GEOGRAPHY

South Dakota's ecological and economic vitality is influenced by the three principal soil types that dominate the surface zone. Soil formation in the state was influenced by six factors: parent materials, terrain, time, vegetation, biological activity, and climate. The state is part of a vast grassland zone that once extended from the Appalachian Mountains west to the Rocky Mountains. This grassland covered all of the land within the present-day borders of South Dakota except for the Black Hills. Parent materials provided the source from which the soils were to develop. Terrain and time acted as agents that inhibited or facilitated the processes. Vegetation, biological activities, and climate exerted the most significant influences on the development of the soils.

The formation of soils begins with the parent materials from which the soils develop. In the case of South Dakota, the parent materials vary geographically from place to place. In the Black Hills, parent materials include crystalline rocks, and sedimentary rocks including limestone, sandstone, and shale. Sedimentary rocks developed from sands, clay, and silts that were deposited on the floors of ancient inland seas. Parent materials also include the Pierre shale, Cretaceous and Tertiary sandstone, and siltstones that comprise most of the Missouri Plateau. The soils of Eastern South Dakota are more recent and resulted from glaciation. During the Pleistocene, ice sheets scoured the land, topping hills and filling valleys.

Glacial activity left deposits of till, outwash, lacustrine materials, and stratified drift. Till is the most common deposit. It is simply a mixture of various-sized rock particles deposited under the ice. Outwash is primarily sand and gravel deposited by melting waters. Lacustrine deposits are parallel bands of silt and clay on the bottom of ancient lakes and ponds. Finally, drift accumulated against melting ice. The result was numerous small hills that dot the Central Lowlands.

Other parent materials include loess and related wind-blown materials. These materials are blown in primarily from the west, and deposited in veneers of various depths. These silts, sands, and clays are most often deposited along the east side of streams. Alluvium, or stream-laid mixed materials of gravel, sand, silt and clay, is found along stream beds.

Terrain and time are also essential to soil formation. Terrain is the relief of the land. As the previous chapter on the terrain indicated, it varies greatly across the state. It may be

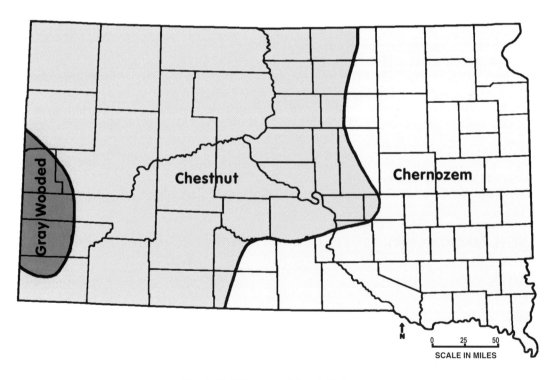

Map 8. **Soil Regions of South Dakota.**
Source: Westin (1967).

flat, rolling, mountainous, glaciated or unglaciated. Indeed, terrain varies greatly even in the local relief. That is, it can vary greatly from acre to acre, or from one's front yard to back yard. Time, of course, is extremely important in that it allows the biological and chemical activities that are necessary to bring about the changes that result in soil variations from type to type and place to place.

Vegetation, biological activity, and climate, interacting with the parent materials, terrain, and time, have resulted in the formation of three soil regions within South Dakota. These three regions from east to west are the Chernozem Region, the Chestnut Region, and the Gray Wooded Region (Map 8).

THE CHERNOZEM REGION

The Chernozem Region is made up of a soil group with a dark color. The name Chernozem in Russian means "black earth." The surface horizon of Chernozem soils is very dark brown or black in color. It is a soil that is very rich in decayed organic matter, having developed in mid-tall and tall prairie grass regions with a cool Humid Continental climate.

The Chernozem Region in South Dakota is located east of a line that extends from McPherson County on the north, southward to Jerauld County, then west to central Mellette and south through Todd County to the Nebraska border. There is some variation within the Chernozem soils from place to place. These variations are primarily a result of temperature averages and organic matter in the soil. Chernozem soils developed in temperature averages of 43° F to 48° F, with 18 inches to 26 inches of precipitation. The upper horizon of the Chernozem zone ranges from 5 inches to 8 inches in thickness. This of course gives plants a deep rich zone from which to extract minerals and moisture.

THE CHESTNUT SOILS REGION

This region includes all of South Dakota west of the Chernozem Region, except for the Gray Wooded Region of the Black Hills. Chestnut soils have developed in a drier climate. In this zone, precipitation ranges from 13 inches to 18 inches a year. Temperatures are also cooler, ranging from 40° F to 48° F over the years. They are similar to Chernozem soils but contain less humus (decayed vegetative matter).

Chestnut soils have developed in areas of short grasses or steppe vegetation. Cooler soil temperatures and lower evaporation rates in the northern portion of the zone supported more luxuriant grasses. This in turn left more organic materials to decay in the soil, resulting in a darker surface color. Southern Chestnut soils are browner in color. The upper horizon of Chestnut soils is thin, generally two inches to four inches in depth. Soils are fertile when there is sufficient precipitation or irrigation. However, they are located in a marginal area for crop production and must be closely monitored, utilizing special cultivation and conservation measures to protect the delicate balance of nature.

GRAY WOODED SOILS

Gray Wooded soils developed in a more humid climate than the semi-arid Chestnut soils. The Gray Wooded soils in South Dakota are principally located in the Black Hills. Here the climate is modified by altitudinal zoning and increased precipitation. The annual average temperature for the region is from 40° F to 47° F. Precipitation ranges from 18 inches to 25 inches a year.

These soils have developed in a region with a native vegetation of coniferous evergreens. Parent materials are essentially a core of igneous and metamorphic rocks, surrounded by sedimentary limestones and sandstone and alluvium. The soil horizon is very thin, ranging from none, to one-half inch, to two inches thick. Like most forest region soils, the Gray Wooded soils tend to be acidic. As a result, they are not important for crop production.

OBSERVATIONS

These precious soil resources cannot be taken for granted. Everyone must work to ensure that the land and abundant floral, faunal, and soil resources are used wisely and protected. This is the practice of conservation. Through the study of ecology, one learns more about the relationships that exist between plants and animals, and the habitats that they occupy. From geography, one knows the patterns of plant and animal distributions now and in the past, and how humans have used and benefitted from these important resources. Geography also enables one to learn those ways in which humans have changed the floral and faunal landscape through time. As living things, plants and animals are renewable resources; so too are the soils. If properly cared for, they will be everyone's to use and enjoy forever.

Chapter Five

WATER RESOURCES OF SOUTH DAKOTA

INTRODUCTION

Life-giving water is the planet's most precious renewable resource and comprises the earth's hydrosphere. Water, the source of life, is essential to the survival and success of South Dakota's agriculture, industry, recreation, and the lives of its people. It has been said that "Water, or the lack of it, has always been South Dakota's currency."

Historically, when water has been plentiful, the state's economy has generally been very prosperous. Likewise, when water supplies have been depleted, as occurred during the Dust Bowl, when drought diminished surface- and ground-water supplies, the economy and the population declined. Much of South Dakota's past, present, and future is directly related to the availability and use of the state's water resources.

South Dakota receives its water supply from two principal sources, surface water and ground water. They provide the state and its residents with water for irrigation, municipal

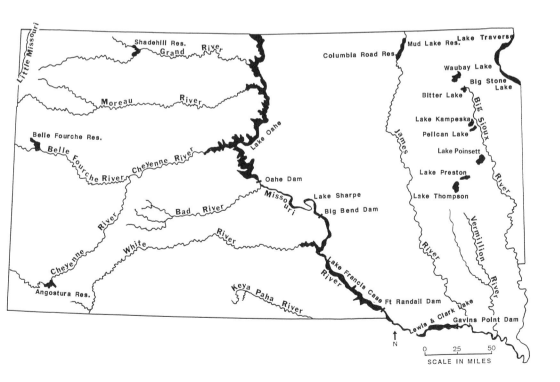

Map 9. Major Rivers and Lakes of South Dakota.

and industrial uses, and for farm and domestic needs. Surface water and ground water, when combined, provide South Dakota with among the most extensive water supplies of any state.

The Missouri River divides South Dakota almost in half. Its present course has resulted from the glaciation of eastern South Dakota in the geologic past and the paths the stream has followed in more recent history. Today all the surface streams in the state drain into the Missouri River except for a very small area in the Minnesota River-Red River Lowland in the northeast corner of the state (Map 9). The portion of that area that drains into Lake Traverse drains into the Boise de Sioux River and then enters Hudson Bay via the Red River of the North.

Today, four huge dams and storage reservoirs on the Missouri River give South Dakota extensive fresh water resources. Total storage capacity of the four Missouri River reservoirs within South Dakota is about 32 million acre feet. That adds up to over 10 trillion gallons of water, or enough water to fill a canal 1,000 feet wide and 100 feet deep reaching from New York City to San Francisco! Or another way to imagine the scale of this much water is that the reservoirs contain enough water to cover 32 million acres of land with one foot of water. In fact, that is enough water to cover the entire state of South Dakota with over one half foot of water.

Ground water is found beneath the surface of South Dakota. Here, contained in water-holding strata called aquifers, there is storage capacity for over ten times the amount of water that exists in all of South Dakota's lakes, reservoirs, and streams. The ground water supply is pumped from its reserve to the surface by wells or arrives by free artesian flow. Ground water provides nearly all of the state's urban and domestic water supply, as well as much of the water used in irrigation. If South Dakota's ground water is used wisely, this great renewable resource will last indefinitely and provide the state with the water necessary for economic enrichment.

Geographically, in order to understand the importance and situation of South Dakota's water resources, three questions must be examined. First, where does South Dakota's water come from? Second, where is it distributed within the state? Third, how has it affected the state's settlement and land-use patterns? In examining these three geographic questions, one also learns of the many ways in which this vital resource is used, and of the major problems associated with South Dakota's water resources.

THE HYDROLOGIC CYCLE

The understanding of South Dakota and indeed the earth's fresh water supply begins with the Hydrologic Cycle. It is an endless cycle in which water from the sea evaporates, is carried over land as water vapor, is precipitated on the land in fresh water form, and eventually returns to the sea by runoff from the land surface (Figure 2).

Over ninety-seven percent of this planet's water is contained within the vast global sea that covers about seventy percent of the earth's surface. This ocean water is of course salty and in that form is of little use to humans. Through evaporation, however, water from the saline sea is changed into salt-free water vapor, or moisture in an atmospheric gaseous state. This change in form from liquid to vapor constitutes the first of four stages of the Hydrologic Cycle. In the second stage, moisture-bearing air is carried by wind to and over the land. Precipitation constitutes the third stage of the cycle. In this stage, moisture is

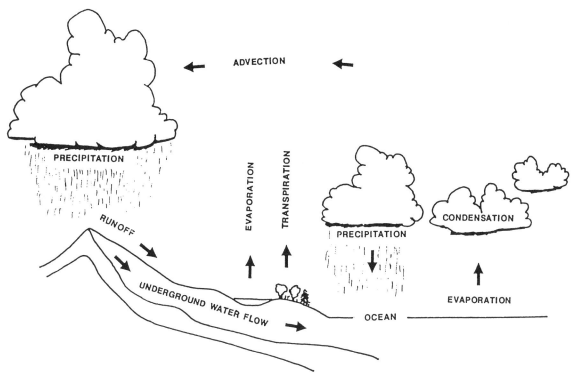

Figure 2. **The Hydrologic Cycle.**

changed from the gaseous to liquid or frozen state, falling in the form of rain, snow, hail, or sleet. Finally, during the fourth, or runoff, stage of the cycle, fresh water on and beneath the earth's surface is available for human use.

At any given moment about three percent of the earth's total water supply is on the land in non-saline form. Of this small amount, nearly three-fourths is in the form of glacial ice in Antarctica and Greenland. Another twenty-four percent lies beneath the earth's surface in the form of ground water. This means that only a small fraction of one percent of the earth's total water is in fresh liquid form, and accessible for use, on the surface as rivers, lakes, or reservoirs. In order to understand better South Dakota's surface and ground water resources, one must further examine the runoff stage of the Hydrologic Cycle as it applies to the state.

Actual surface runoff, that is, water carried by streams and eventually returned to the sea, averages about three million acre feet per year in South Dakota. Much of this water is only "passing through" the state from the upper Missouri River drainage system en route to the Gulf of Mexico via the Mississippi River system. This water is contained for a short period of time in the four large reservoirs built along the Missouri and in thousands of smaller dams that dot the state's landscape.

Some of the surface moisture seeps into the earth and becomes ground water. This water may be stored beneath the surface for tens of thousands of years in aquifers or water-holding beds of gravel, sand, and porous rock. It is estimated that of South Dakota's huge ground-water storage capacity, only about seventy-two million acre feet, or less than one fifth of the total, can be easily recovered using standard pumping methods. However, even this relatively small amount of ground water is enough to cover the entire state to a depth of about one and one-half feet.

Some water, of course, returns to the atmosphere through evaporation from surface waters and the land itself. This can be observed as the roads dry after a rain or lawns begin to yellow without watering.

The portion of the runoff stage that is of greatest importance to humans is the actual availability of water from rivers, lakes, and reservoirs, or from ground water. It is from these sources that water for human needs is easily obtained and used in an endless variety of ways.

The water resources of South Dakota are not evenly distributed across the state, neither as surface or ground water. A "bird's eye" view of eastern South Dakota shows ample vegetation, a dense pattern of farmland uses, and a physical landscape dotted with lakes, wetlands, and winding stream courses. The farther westward one travels across the state, excluding the more moist Black Hills region, the drier the landscape becomes. Indeed, parts of western South Dakota have little if any surface water, scant vegetation, and too little moisture to raise crops without irrigation.

Agricultural land use and the distribution of South Dakota's settlements and population clearly reflect the importance and distribution of adequate moisture. These spatial patterns can be seen quite vividly when one travels from east to west across the state and observes the state's precipitation, land use, and population.

First, from observing South Dakota's precipitation patterns, one can note that the southeastern part of the state receives the greatest amount of moisture and that conditions become drier from east to west across the state and moister again only upon reaching the higher Black Hills.

Next, by examining the agricultural production of the state and comparing it with the changes in precipitation, one can observe that nearly all of the state's corn is grown in areas receiving 20 or more inches of precipitation, or in pockets of irrigation. Wheat, sorghum, and other small grains can be raised most years in areas averaging as little as 18 inches of precipitation. In those parts of the state receiving less than 18 inches of moisture, very little land is used for raising crops of any kind. There a lack of precipitation results in a grassland environment which is used primarily for livestock grazing.

Finally, in traveling from east to west across South Dakota one can see that population density clearly indicates that most of the state's people are clustered in the more humid areas of the east, and that indeed the population declines sharply with decreasing amounts of available moisture until reaching the Black Hills.

Surface waters also are concentrated in the eastern part of South Dakota. As a result of glaciation in the geologic past, the land area east of the Missouri River contains nearly all of the state's natural lakes, ponds, and wetland marshes. The Big Sioux and James rivers and the southern portion of the Missouri River are major streams draining eastern South Dakota. As one might expect, it is in the eastern part of the state where ground water resources are the greatest, having been fed for thousands of years by the higher amounts of precipitation and the many lakes and streams of the region.

In central and western South Dakota, outside the Black Hills, there are very few lakes, streams are small and less reliable in their flow, and ground water is not as abundant. In the Black Hills themselves, there are no natural lakes that feed ground water. All the lakes in the Black Hills are human-made reservoirs.

WATER AND SETTLEMENT

Since people first walked this land, water has played a vital role in the human occupance of this region that is now South Dakota. Native American Arikaras, Sioux, and other peoples established their settlements near lakes or streams in order to have a reliable source of water. The presence of surface water was perhaps even more important to the first European and American settlers, who established their communities along the banks of the Big Sioux and Missouri rivers.

Sioux Falls, Flandreau, and the short-lived Medary were established along the Big Sioux River in 1857. Within only a few years, Bon Homme (which was later abandoned), Yankton, and Vermillion were settled along the Missouri River. Other communities sprang up along these and other streams during the next several decades. Not only did the streams provide a reliable source of water for domestic use, but they were important routes of transportation, with river boats linking communities to larger cities, markets, and sources of manufactured goods located downstream on the Missouri and Mississippi rivers.

Gradually, homesteaders began to settle lands away from major rivers. Lakeside locations afforded both a reliable supply of water and wood for fuel and construction. Elsewhere ground water was pumped by hand from shallow wells. In other cases, windmills made it possible for settlers to move away from sources of surface water and begin to utilize ground water to truly develop the region's agricultural potential.

Many South Dakota communities have names that suggest the importance of water to early settlers. Sioux Falls was built at a site on the Big Sioux River where waterfalls provided power for a mill. The Sioux Falls site provided water power for a milling operation that was once the largest in South Dakota. In the west, Rapid City gained its name from rapids along Rapid Creek. Watertown, named after a city in New York state, occupies a location that is nearly surrounded by lakes. Hot Springs and Wessington Springs were founded because of the water features that gave their names to the communities. The community of Artesian is named for its artesian springs that bring water to the surface under natural flow. All told, some thirty South Dakota communities, or nearly eight percent of the state's towns and cities, have names that reflect the importance of water. Water resources have left their mark not only on the state's patterns of settlement and land use but on many of its place names as well.

THE GEOGRAPHIC ASPECTS OF WATER FEATURES

Geographic aspects of South Dakota's water features are reflected in its streams, lakes, wetlands, and ground-water resources. By understanding these features, one is in a better position to appreciate the importance of water to the people and how better to utilize it for the needs of present and future generations of residents.

Earlier examination of the physiographic provinces of the state showed that South Dakota lies within two continental drainage basins. The Missouri River receives runoff from nearly all of the state and then drains into the Mississippi River and ultimately the

Gulf of Mexico. A very small area in northeastern South Dakota drains into Lake Traverse, the Boise de Sioux, and Red River, eventually reaching Hudson Bay and the Arctic Ocean.

During an average year, water runoff from South Dakota amounts to some 2.6 billion gallons each day, or about 3 million acre feet each year. The actual amount, of course, varies from year to year, depending upon rainfall amounts and on a seasonal basis as well. The greatest amount of runoff occurs from March through July, normally as a result of spring snow melt and early summer rains. During wet years, many rivers and creeks spill beyond their banks and flood surrounding lowlands. Such flooding, which was common during the mid-1980s, can cause considerable property loss to dwellings, public works such as roads and bridges, and the erosion of precious topsoil from flooded fields. During dry years and seasonal decreases in moisture, many streams dry up or flow as mere trickles of water.

South Dakota's river and drainage-basin pattern resembles a tree, with the Missouri River forming the trunk and with essentially all the tree branches connecting to the Missouri trunk. The exception is again the Lake Traverse-Big Stone drainage areas. The land east of the Missouri River generally decreases in elevation from north to the south. Essentially all the land is inclined gently toward the southeastern corner of the state near Sioux City, Iowa. Three streams—the Big Sioux, the Vermillion, and the James—follow the gradient flowing into the Missouri in the southeastern corner of the state. The general relief of western South Dakota drops from west to east, from the Black Hills and other upland features of this region toward the Missouri River Trench. Here the rivers flow in a generally eastward direction to join the Missouri (Map 9).

MISSOURI RIVER

The Missouri River is the "King of Rivers" in South Dakota. The "Mighty Mo," as it is sometimes called, begins in the northern Rocky Mountains and flows through South Dakota en route to its juncture with the Mississippi River just above St. Louis, Missouri. The Missouri River is the greatest source of surface water in South Dakota. Historically, it is the only river in the state with a large sustained flow. It drains through the state, gently dropping in elevation about one foot per mile along its course.

In 1942, as plans to develop the four reservoirs on the river were being developed, it is said that the Missouri had reached equilibrium. That is, the amount of debris and materials being carried into the river from its tributaries was equal to the amount it was able to carry away.

During the mid-1900s, a series of four large dams were constructed along the Missouri River in South Dakota under the Federal Pick-Sloan Plan. The dams are the Oahe, Big Bend, Fort Randall, and Gavins Point. Behind these dams four huge reservoirs were formed. They are Lake Oahe, Lake Sharpe, Lake Francis Case, and Lewis and Clark Lake. The dams and reservoirs now control the flow of the Missouri River. They have essentially turned the river into a chain of four giant lakes except for the southern portion of the river below Gavins Point Dam. The dams and reservoirs also provide flood control for South Dakota and downstream states, power generation, and recreation, and water for agricultural, municipal, and industrial uses.

Oahe Dam with Lake Oahe is the largest water development in the state. The dam itself is 3,500 feet wide at its base and rises to a height of 245 feet above the river bed. The normal operating pool stores some 22,500,000-plus acre feet of water. Lake Oahe at maximum pool level covers over 375,000 acres of land. The dam itself generates almost 600,000 kilowatts of electrical power.

Big Bend Dam and its reservoir Lake Sharpe are second in the chain from north to south. Big Bend Dam rises 95 feet above the river bottom and is 1,200 feet wide across its base. Gross storage in Lake Sharpe is 1,900,000 acre feet. At its maximum it would cover 60,000 acres of land. Big Bend Dam is the second largest of the four in electrical-power generation, with a capacity of 468,000 kilowatts.

Fort Randall Dam and Lake Francis Case are the third link in the lake chain. Fort Randall Dam is the second largest of the four rolled-earth dams. It reaches 165 feet above the valley floor and is 4,300 feet wide at its base. Lake Francis Case is the second largest of the four reservoirs, with a gross storage capacity of 6,100,000 acre feet. At its maximum it covers over 100,000 acres of land. Fort Randall Dam generates 320,000 kilowatts at its peak.

Gavins Point Dam and Lewis and Clark Lake complete the chain. They are the smallest of the four dams and the smallest reservoir. Gavins Point Dam reaches a height of 85 feet above the river bed. It is 850 feet wide at its base. Lewis and Clark Lake has a gross storage of only 540,000 acre feet or about one fiftieth that of Lake Oahe. At its greatest extent it covers only 33,000 acres of land. Gavins Point Dam power-generation capacity is 100,000 kilowatts.

Because of its origin, source areas, and sustained flow, the Missouri River generally contains good-quality water. Communities along its course that utilize the river for municipal supply normally find it to their advantage to do some softening for domestic and industrial uses.

The Missouri River does have some serious potential problems resulting from the construction of the dams. The river was at equilibrium before the dams were built. Over time much of the debris that would have been carried away naturally by the river builds up, silting in the reservoirs and interfering with the dams. This is a problem that will need continual attention in the future.

EAST RIVER STREAMS

BIG SIOUX RIVER

The Big Sioux River begins north of Watertown and drains much of the Coteau des Prairies, essentially flowing down its middle. South of Sioux Falls, the Big Sioux River forms the boundary between South Dakota and Iowa. It has a drainage basin of over 9,500 square miles, of which 70 percent is in South Dakota. The rest is in Minnesota and Iowa. Because the Big Sioux flows through the eastern portion of the state where precipitation is generally the greatest and most dependable, the fresh water is normally of good quality.

The stream does not flow all year along its entire course. From its origin to Watertown, the Big Sioux River generally does not flow for periods in fall and winter. On rare occasions it will cease flowing as far south as Brookings. The lower basin of the Big Sioux River flows all year. Too much flow is another problem of the river, the result being extensive flooding and accompanying damage. Indeed, recent history has shown residents that the Big Sioux can range from a dry stream bed you can walk across to a raging river so wide that its flood waters extend the four miles from Brookings to Volga.

VERMILLION RIVER

To the west, between the Big Sioux and James rivers, is the smaller Vermillion River. It begins in the north as two separate forks, the East and the West Forks. The forks join together near Parker. The Vermillion River drains 2,180 square miles of the southwestern margin of the Coteau des Prairies and flows into the Missouri River east of the James River Highlands near the city of Vermillion, which bears its name. The river will experience periods of no flow about once in every three-and-a-half years. The water quality of this stream is erratic and depends greatly on volume and source.

JAMES RIVER

Originally named the Jacques, the James River is now commonly called the "Jim River." It is the only stream other than the Missouri to flow all the way across the state. It begins in North Dakota, enters the state approximately 35 miles northeast of Aberdeen and flows south to the Missouri just east of Yankton. The James River drains an area of 22,100 square miles, some 70 percent of which is located in South Dakota.

The gradient along the Jim is extremely low as it flows slowly across its floodplain in the James River Lowland. The river drops about five inches per mile as it flows through the state. The result is that at times of high inflow from its tributaries, the river actually flows upstream for a few miles above the mouth of joining streams. This rare natural event is called reverse flow and occurs most frequently just north of Huron.

During a normal year, the James River and the tributary streams will stop flowing for periods of time. Because the banks of the river are so low, a moderate flood will cover much of the flood plain. Floods are the result of heavy rainfall or snow melt. The quality of water in the James River is affected by its flow.

WEST RIVER STREAMS

Six major rivers in western South Dakota flow in a generally west to east direction before joining the Missouri. A seventh river, the Little Missouri River, just passes through the northwestern corner of the state before entering North Dakota and flowing into the Missouri.

GRAND RIVER

The Grand River is the northernmost of the major rivers of western South Dakota. The North and South forks of the Grand join just south of the city of Lemmon at Shadehill Reservoir. Shadehill has a storage capacity of about 400,000 acre feet. The Grand River drains an area of approximately 5,200 square miles in the Northern Plateaus. Its principal source of water is from runoff from snow melt. Unfortunately, the Grand River is high in sodium content and as a result it is not as valuable for irrigation as farmers would like.

MOREAU RIVER

Originating in Butte and Harding counties, the Moreau River begins as the North and South Forks and as Sand Creek. It runs from west to east, nearly paralleling the Grand River about forty miles to the north. The Moreau River drains an area of about 5,400 square miles in the Northern Plateaus and Pierre Hills. Numerous creeks such as Antelope, Deep, Thunder Butte, Red Earth, and the Little Moreau River are tributaries. The Moreau River, which was formerly called the Owl River, and its tributaries have a very erratic stream flow. They are dry much of the time since they depend on runoff from snowfall and thunderstorms. The water quality of this river is generally poor because of high mineral content.

CHEYENNE RIVER

The largest of the western tributaries of the Missouri River is the Cheyenne River, which has part of its headwater drainage in Wyoming. The Cheyenne River drains an area of over 25,500 square miles. About 40 percent of that area is in Wyoming and the other 60 percent in South Dakota. The Cheyenne begins in South Dakota near the Black Hills and flows primarily through the Pierre Hills region. Its largest tributary, the Belle Fourche River, enters South Dakota from Wyoming.

Several very significant tributaries flow into the Cheyenne River or the Belle Fourche; among them are Owl Creek, Rapid Creek, Sulphur Creek, Cherry Creek, and Plum Creek. The Belle Fourche River provides water for the state's largest irrigation project, the Belle Fourche District, located on Owl Creek north of the Black Hills near the town of Belle Fourche. The Belle Fourche Project irrigates over 57,000 acres of land in western South Dakota. Other reservoirs include Deerfield Creek Reservoir and Pactola Reservoir situated along Rapid Creek, west of Rapid City, and the Angostura Reservoir on the Cheyenne and located near Hot Springs.

Waters from a large region including snow melt from the Black Hills are the principal source for the Cheyenne River. Despite the fact that the waters come from such a large area, the river's quality is poor. The stream is higher in dissolved mineral content than any other major river in the state. In the past, mining in the Black Hills deposited significant amounts of cyanide, arsenic, and zinc. Today, water quality regulations have essentially eliminated this source of pollution. Runoff from precipitation below the Black Hills tends to help improve water quality, but it is still poor.

BAD RIVER

South of the Cheyenne, the Bad River drains a small area of about 3,000 square miles in the Pierre Hills and Southern Plateaus physiographic regions. Historically, this stream has been known as the Teton River. It is located between the Cheyenne River to the north and the White River to the south. The flow in this small stream can change from none to flood stage in a single day when heavy rains fall within its drainage basin. During flood stage, the Bad River carries large amounts of silt into the Missouri at its juncture near Fort Pierre. Water quality is hard and poor.

WHITE RIVER

The Southern Plateaus, including the Badlands, and southern Pierre Hills are drained by the White River. It originates in Nebraska and drains about 1,500 square miles of that state and over 8,500 square miles of South Dakota. It flows into the Missouri west of Chamberlain. Since it drains through a dry climatic zone, it is subject to periods of no flow in its Badlands and prairie portions. Likewise intense thunderstorms can cause it to become a torrential destructive stream. The White River has sufficient flow near Chamberlain to run all year downstream. Because of the landscape through which it flows, the White River has essentially good quality water.

KEYA PAHA RIVER

Finally, the small Keya Paha River drains a small portion of south central South Dakota. It begins near Mission and flows in a southeastward direction into Nebraska, where it joins the Niobrara River. The Niobrara, in turn, joins the Missouri near Springfield, west of Yankton. The Keya Paha, though small in volume, generally flows all year except for periods of winter freeze. It is noted for having a quality of water that is generally better than that of any other river in South Dakota.

LAKES AND OTHER SURFACE WATERS

Within South Dakota are nearly 250 publicly owned lakes, which cover nearly 225 square miles of surface. About 90 percent of all the world's natural lakes are located in areas that have been glaciated. The same holds true in South Dakota, where our lakes are tightly clustered in the extensively glaciated Coteau des Prairies physiographic region.

The quality of the state's lakes varies greatly. Some lakes are deep and clear, providing excellent sport fishing and numerous other recreational uses. Others are shallow, lined with reeds and marsh grasses, and having water of quite poor quality. Summer algae blooms infest many such water bodies and make them almost useless for recreational activities. Still other lakes have shriveled in areal extent and depth to the point that they really no longer warrant the name "lake." These former lakes which have nearly dried up are called "wetlands" or "sloughs," and they are extremely important for many reasons.

The landscape of Northeastern South Dakota is dotted with numerous lakes and sloughs resulting from the glaciated terrain.

They help prevent stream flooding by holding water during periods of heavy runoff from snow melt or rain. And they provide an excellent habitat for wildlife, including millions of migratory waterfowl.

The decade from mid-1970 to mid-1980 was the wettest in more than a century. During the latter part of the 1980s, many lakes rose above and well beyond their historic banks. The resulting flooding caused severe economic losses, as lakeside dwellings became partially submerged and thousands of acres of crop and grazing land were covered with flood water. In the spring of 1986 water rose to window level in many homes along the shores of South Dakota's largest natural lake, Lake Poinsett, located between Brookings and Watertown. To the southwest of Lake Poinsett, near the community of Lake Preston, the water of once nearly dry Lake Thompson rose to its highest level in more than a century. Thousands of acres of farmland now lie at the bottom of a water body that in 1986 grew larger than Poinsett to become the state's largest natural lake.

In addition to the natural water bodies and reservoirs, South Dakota has thousands of stock dams and man-made watering ponds. Many of these are not shown on maps, and most people are not aware of their importance and existence. They do pose some potential problems since many of their dams or retaining walls are over half a century old.

GROUND WATER

More than twice as much useful water lies beneath the surface as groundwater as is contained in the state's streams, reservoirs, and lakes. Most of this ground water is in the

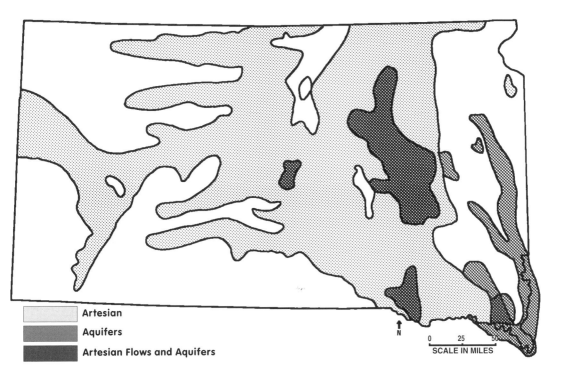

Legend:
- Artesian
- Aquifers
- Artesian Flows and Aquifers

N

0   25   50
SCALE IN MILES

Map 10. **Areal Extent of Ground Water in South Dakota.**

more humid eastern South Dakota (Map 10). It is estimated that the state's ground water supply contains 70 to 80 million acre feet of water that easily can be reclaimed by normal pumping methods. Of the some 350 towns in the state with municipal water systems, over 95 percent obtain most if not all of their supply from ground water.

In general, the chemical quality of the state's ground water is rather poor. A high content of dissolved minerals makes the water hard and in some locations causes it to taste and smell bad as well. Its chemical content is affected by high amounts of sulfate, calcium, or sodium. Iron and manganese are also present in the water supply of many communities. Ground water is the chief source of supply for nearly all the state's farmsteads, and it is the primary source of water used in overhead irrigation.

WATER CONSUMPTION

The average South Dakotan uses about 160 gallons of water daily. Of this amount, nineteen of every twenty gallons comes from ground water supplies, and the other gallon comes from surface water. As regards total water consumption, the greatest user of water is irrigation. It utilizes two-thirds of the water consumed each year in South Dakota. Another quarter of the water consumed is for industry and urban and rural domestic supplies. The remainder is required for livestock needs.

MAJOR USES AND NEEDS

Of the state's several irrigation projects, by far the largest is the Belle Fourche Project, which has more than 57,000 acres of irrigated land. Water used in this project is taken from the Belle Fourche River. Farmers in many parts of the state, however, including the more humid eastern portion, are turning to overhead irrigation to protect their crops from periods of inadequate rainfall during the growing season.

Water is essential to the state's livestock industry, which far surpasses crop production as the chief contributor to South Dakota's economy. Many industries use huge amounts of water. Mining, meat packing, and lumbering operations require millions of gallons of water for various stages of production. Municipalities use water in many ways, including fire protection, waste treatment, and watering parks and other public facilities.

Surprisingly, perhaps, the smallest user of water is people themselves, for domestic use. Household consumption amounts to but a small fraction of the total water used. Yet think for a moment of the countless ways in which we use water. Also realize how much we depend on an abundant supply of clean, fresh water. It should also be noted how often people take this precious resource for granted.

In recent years, the development of rural water systems has not only changed the cultural landscape of farm and ranch country, but also the source of most residents' water supplies. The substantial cost of well drilling, access to better quality waters, and competitive pricing have brought rural water systems to South Dakota. The presence of these systems is reflected in the appearance of the water tower or storage tank on the rural landscape. It no longer stands above the land as an indicator of urban settlement only.

Water is important in many other ways as well. Much of the state's electrical energy is produced by power plants located at dams along the Missouri River. Because hydro-electrical energy is produced by a renewable resource, flowing water, South Dakotans enjoy abundant energy, which ranks among the least expensive in the entire nation.

Water makes people's lives more enjoyable through its recreational uses, such as swimming, boating, and fishing. Even during the winter season, people use water in many ways, such as ice fishing, ice skating, skiing, and snowmobiling. Water also holds aesthetic value, for it provides a pleasing contrast to other landscape features and offers its own beauty within the environment.

Life-giving water is a very precious natural resource. At any moment, only a small fraction of the earth's water, less than one percent of the total, is available to us in fresh liquid form. Yet people depend on water in countless ways. Although water is a renewable resource, we cannot take its availability for granted. South Dakota must continue to develop its water resources. The state must utilize its water wisely and ensure that it remains pollution free. If it does so, residents and visitors will be assured an unlimited supply of clean, fresh water for future use.

Chapter Six
NATIVE AMERICAN CULTURES IN SOUTH DAKOTA

INTRODUCTION

Anthropologists, geographers, archaeologists, and other scientists do not believe that humankind originated in the New World. Indeed, scientific evidence indicates that the first humans reached the New World between 40,000 and 50,000 years ago. Evidence also indicates a second migration period between 10,000 and 28,000 years ago.

Geological and archeological data suggests that during the former period of 40,000 to 50,000 years ago a land bridge existed between present-day Siberia and Alaska. The land bridge was a result of the lowering of the sea level because of an increase in the amount of water frozen in the ice cap. During the period it is believed that the sea level was over 120 feet lower than today, creating a wide land bridge. At the same time, there is evidence that the climate of that area was milder and more conducive to human travel and survival than today.

The second land bridge, which occurred during the last half of the Wisconsin Glacial Period, indicates a much more extensive dry-land route than the former. Scientists believe sea level dropped 300 feet to 400 feet during the Wisconsin stage. The result was a land bridge between Asia and North America some 1,000 to 1,300 miles wide.

Other theories speculate that humankind came to the New World from the South Pacific. There are some interesting artifacts to support these speculations. They are, however, not generally accepted by scientists as major theories of occupance.

Since scientists, then, generally believe that humans lived in the New World about 40,000-plus years ago, they have speculated on where the first arrivals went. Earliest evidence indicates that these first arrivals moved through Alaska into and across the Canadian Shield and then southward east of both the Rocky Mountains and Appalachian Mountains. Their descendants and later arrivals are referred to as Paleo-Indians (Paleo meaning old). By 10,000 years ago, they had reached all of North and South America, including Tierra del Fuego.

PALEO-INDIANS

The Paleo-Indians of the western Great Plains existed as big-game hunters and gatherers. They hunted wooly mammoths and mastodons. With the extinction of these large animals, the Paleo-Indians fed on the gigantic Folsom bison, elk, giant beaver, smaller American bison, antelope, and other smaller game. The hunters ate vegetation as well.

Paleo-Indian hunters utilized deadfalls to down their quarry. Animals were driven over cliffs and other deadfalls by hunters on foot. Often they utilized fire to stampede herds over the deadfalls. Weapons and tools included spears, spear throwers, hand axes, and other Old Stone Age tools such as stone scrapers, projectile points, and knives.

During the construction of Angostura Dam in Fall River County in 1946, a Paleo-Indian campsite was discovered. Archeological remains indicate the campsite as dating to about 5,000 BC. In 1981, the site of a mammoth butchering was located about twelve miles north of Oglala. Carbon dating and the presence of a number of Clovis points place the date of the site around 9,000 BC. Thousands of campsites of more recent origin have been located in South Dakota.

Over time, new groupings of Indians occurred. At about AD 1,000 a number of nomadic peoples occupied the Black Hills. They existed by hunting and by collecting the plants and fruits that thrived in the Hills.

THE MOUND BUILDERS

East of the Missouri River, especially along the Big Sioux River and also near Big Stone Lake, from AD 500 to AD 1,000 or later, the land was occupied by a group of Indians known collectively as the Mound Builders. These people occupied vast sections of the interior of present-day North America. They ranged from near New Orleans to the Upper Mississippi Basin and eastward into Indiana and Ohio.

The American Indian peoples of South Dakota and the surrounding region retain numerous traditions, including the Wacipi or powwow.

The Mound Builders combined hunting and agriculture. They raised corn, squash, and beans and stored food in their storage pits. They lived in earth lodges in villages of 8 to 10 lodges. Their tools consisted of implements made from bison, deer, and antelope bones, and of stone hammers and axe heads. Their weaponry included the bow and arrow, and their artifacts included pottery.

The Mound Builders were named for the burial mounds they left behind. Typically, these mounds are about 100 feet in diameter and may reach heights of 5 to 15 feet. The largest of these mounds is in Cahokia, Illinois, and is about the same mass as the largest pyramid in Egypt.

It is believed that severe climatic conditions resulting in severe drought, dust storms, and devastating winds swept the plains and prairies of the region in the AD 1400s and AD 1500s. These natural disasters would then have pushed the surviving Mound Builders to areas where they could find food and water.

THE PRE-ARIKARAS

From about AD 1250 to AD 1500 an agricultural Indian people migrated into present-day South Dakota from southern Minnesota. These people are believed to be the parental stock of the Mandan, a Siouan-speaking tribe. The Mandan were to become a very powerful and strategically situated tribe who dominated the Upper Missouri River in North Dakota for several centuries.

Several village sites of these Pre-Arikara people have been discovered. Among the more notable are the Arzberger Site, located eight miles east of Pierre and built before the arrival of Columbus in the New World. This site covered over 50 acres and contained a defense system of a moat, bastions, and palisade. Fort Sully Village, which was located 30 miles north of Pierre, contained 200 to 300 earth lodges. Located just below the later Fort Sully military post, it contained an estimated 5,000-plus people. Obviously, such a village would require a great deal of organization and administration and would foster an advanced civilization.

Infra-red imagery of a village site twenty-two miles south of Pierre on the Missouri River shows evidence of bastions that resemble a European fortress. It was built in AD 1362 and allows for considerable speculation about the people who constructed it. We may never know for sure if it was constructed entirely by Pre-Arikara Indians or if some Norsemen, as has been speculated, did indeed reach central North America and interact with the Indians.

THE ARIKARAS

The Arikara (or Ree) Indians are a northern tribe of the Caddoan-speaking peoples. They were related to the Pawnees to the west and south and the Wichitas to the south. It is believed that because of drought, the Arikaras migrated from Texas and Kansas to Nebraska and reached central South Dakota in the sixteenth century.

They were agricultural and hunting people. The Arikaras lived in villages built on the "breaks" along the Missouri River. These spectacular terrace sites provided partial fortification, supplemented by moats and stockades. Inside the fort-like villages were 50 to 200 earth lodges. Tepees were also used by some villages.

Evidence indicates that over time the Arikaras, like many earth-lodge peoples, progressed from the use of a square-shaped lodge to a rounded lodge. This evolution is believed to be the result of a need for a better heating plan utilizing a central fire pit. The earth lodge interior environment was similar to a cave or sod house. The earthen walls helped make the lodge cooler in summer and warmer in winter. As with other tribes, the Arikaras that lived in earth lodges were relatively successful farmers and merchants. They occupied basically permanent homes.

Agriculture's importance in the Arikaras' life is symbolized by their name in sign language, "corn eater." The Arikaras farmed land surrounding their villages. Women were the principal agriculturalists. They worked the fields with hoes made from the shoulder blades of bison. Families also worked small gardens of one to one and one-half acres in size and separate from the tribal fields. Their principal crops were corn, beans, squashes, pumpkins, tobacco, and gourds. The men hunted buffalo, antelope, and a variety of smaller game. They also traded with tribes from other areas and later with Europeans and Americans.

The Arikaras were a very efficient people. They utilized their physical and cultural environments to supply their material needs. They made tools and implements from rocks, wood and bone. They wove baskets from vegetation and made pottery from river-bottom clays. They traded corn, tobacco, and vegetables for meat and skins and buffalo hides. They then processed and decorated the skins and hides. At trading fairs they dealt with the Cheyennes, Arapahoes, Comanches, and Kiowas, as well as with the Sioux. Through this trade, Arikaras became middle men in the traffic of horses, which became accessible to all northern Great Plains tribes by the second quarter of the eighteenth century and thus revolutionized Indian culture.

The coming of the "white men" was most instrumental in the decline in the number of Arikaras. The most serious blow to the Ree people came from diseases introduced by the "white man." They fell victim in the late 1700s because they did not possess any natural immunity to the smallpox epidemics that decimated their population.

Significant historic events of the Arikaras included a meeting with Meriwether Lewis and William Clark in 1804. The American explorers spent five days in three Arikara villages in central South Dakota, where they gained valuable knowledge of what lay ahead.

In 1823 conflict developed between the Arikaras and a combined army of U.S. soldiers, trappers, traders, and Sioux tribal soldiers under General Henry Atkinson. Grey Eyes, an Arikara chief, was killed. The village surrendered. A superior force fled north to settle beside the Mandans. The last left in 1833.

The final chapter of the Arikaras consisted of moving south to live with the Skidi Pawnees in Nebraska. They soon threatened to take over the Rocky Mountain fur trade and were forced by local Indians and non-Indians to return north to the Mandan villages, where they lived in peace.

THE SIOUX

In 1640, Jesuits first encountered and recognized members of a "Nadouessioux" federation, from which the term "Sioux" was derived to identify thirteen tribes (plus Assiniboine) in the present-day United States. The term *Sioux* derived from a derogatory word

used by Ojibwas to identify their neighbors. It has been in common use through the recorded history of the federation. Unfortunately, there exists no euphemism for "Sioux."

The fourteen tribes of the Sioux Federation are linguistic members of the Macro-
Siouan family, as are the Crow, Hidatsa, Winnebago, Mandan, Iowa, Oto, Omaha, Osage,
Ponca, Quapaw, and Kansa. Three dialects of the Siouan language were identified among
the Sioux tribes, and the Assiniboines have a similar language. The dialects are "Dakota,"
spoken by the eastern Sioux; "Nakota," by the middle; and "Lakota," by the western Sioux;
and Assiniboine by the separate group that originated in the Yanktonai tribe.

One of the greatest misconceptions that people make about the Sioux is an assump-
tion that their tribal organization and government was similar to American democracy or
to the government of the "civilized tribes" like the Cherokees. In reality, they lived in related groups called *tiyospayes*, each of which was in effect an extended family. A number of
tiyospayes formed a band. In turn, groupings of bands formed tribes, of which there were
fourteen (see below). Together, they comprised the linguistic cultural federation of Sioux.
All leadership originated at the band level. Non-Indian spokesmen dealt with diplomats,
whom they recognized as tribal or band chiefs of varying rank.

The main divisions of the federation in the United States are the Lakota, Nakota, and
Dakota:

SIOUX FEDERATION

Lakota	Nakota	Dakota	
Two Kettles, Minniconjou	Yankton	Mdewakantowan	} Santee
Black Foot Sioux, Sans Arc	Yanktonai	Wahpekute	
Oglala, Hunkpapa	Hunkpatina	Sisseton	
Brulé	Assiniboine	Wahpeton	

Figure 3. The Sioux Federation.
Source: Herbert T. Hoover

Until about midway through the eighteen century, Sioux people (except Assiniboines)
claimed a common residence along the prairie-woodland border near Mille Lacs, and twice
each year ranged out to hunt and gather food across a vast province comprising at least
100,000,000 acres, which extended nearly to the foothills of the Rocky Mountains.

After mid-century, they scattered to settle across the vast province they previously
used for hunting and gathering. Lakotas traveled across the Missouri River and occupied
the Black Hills area. In the trans-Missouri, Black Hills region, Oglalas and Brulés settled to
the south, the other Lakotas to the north. Dakotas occupied southern Minnesota, a strip
along northern Iowa and western Wisconsin, and some land in northeastern South Dakota
and eastern North Dakota. From this area, Yanktonais ranged south of the Canadian border to eastern Montana. Yanktons owned land eastward from the Missouri to the Des
Moines River. Assiniboines lived mainly in Canada, where they were known also as Hohes
or Stoneys.

By the close of the 1700s, the Dakota peoples occupied large portions of southern Minnesota and extended westward to the Minnesota River-Red River Lowland at Big Stone
Lake and Lake Traverse. The Yanktons occupied eastern South Dakota between the Big

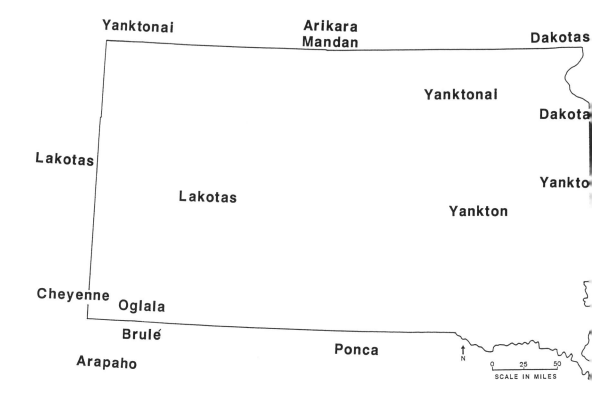

Map 11. **Spatial Distribution of Tribes and Bands About AD 1800.**
Source: Herbert T. Hoover

Sioux River and the Missouri River and as far as eastern Montana. The Yanktonais lived along the middle and upper James River drainage basin and as far as eastern Montana. Lakotas claimed western South Dakota and portions of the surrounding states of Nebraska, Wyoming, Montana, and North Dakota (Map 11).

The Santees (Mdewakantowans and Wahpekutes) practiced "slash-and-burn" agriculture, supplemented with fishing and hunting. As gardeners, the women and teenagers provided labor. Men concentrated on hunting, trapping, and fishing. Women were responsible for tilling the soil, hoeing, and harvesting the crops of corn, squash, beans, and pumpkins, and for preserving food and other supplies. Villages consisted of gabled-roofed lodges of wood and bark.

Lakotas, Nakotas, and many Sissetons and Wahpetons developed very different ways of life after migration from the Mille Lacs area to central and western South Dakota and the surrounding provinces. They changed from agriculturalist-hunters to more dedicated hunters, moving on horseback with travois, tepees, and weapons in search of the buffalo and smaller game. Such game provided them with meat, hides, robes and a variety of other household needs, including buffalo-hide containers and dishes. The horse gave Lakotas, Nakotas, and some Dakotas mobility to follow and hunt the buffalo and to protect their lands and people.

Sissetons, Wahpetons, Yanktons, and Yanktonais established a major trading fair along the James River at Armadale (Grove of Oaks in present-day Spink County near Mellette). There each spring these and sometimes Lakotas would bring goods to trade with British-Canadians representing the North West Company of Montreal. They traded horses, buffalo robes, antelope-skin pants and shirts, bows, pipestone pipes, and the skins of many small animal species for European goods like guns, kettles, axes, and so on. The trading fairs attracted thousands of people to the Grove each spring.

All Sioux in aggregate numbered some 32,000 (in 14 tribes) and belonged to a Great Plain population estimated between 250,000 and 400,000 (in 37 tribes).

In addition to hunting and gathering, warfare became a basic part of Lakota life, carried on to protect tribal hunting grounds, sometimes to earn personal prestige, and to obtain horses or food. A young man became a warrior by raiding enemy camps, counting coup, or taking horses. The Lakotas gained recognition as the best of the Plains Indians warriors, and, along with the Cheyennes, as the bravest and most capable in battle.

When Nakotas and Lakotas moved from the woodland-prairie border, they abandoned their old way of life and learned to live, use, and nurture the environment of the Great Plains. For the most part, they subordinated gardening and fishing to hunting activities and continued to gather food. They gave up the bark lodges, the canoes, and the security of one central permanent village site. It was replaced by scattered villages and a more nomadic life style. They became land travelers, using the horse and the travois to move their goods and people as they followed their food supply.

The lodge was replaced by a tepee constructed from wood poles and buffalo skins. The travois, drawn by a horse, enabled the tepee to be carried from place to place. The buffalo provided the Lakotas and Nakotas the meat that formed the bulk of their diet, which was supplemented by plants gathered as they migrated. Obviously, acquisition of the horse and gun was essential to the successful cultural transition of the western Sioux. They were successful at adapting to environmental changes and challenges without a loss of population. Sioux people belonged to a minority of Great Plains peoples who never have suffered a decline in numbers and since 1870 have more than tripled their aggregate population.

Significant historic events for the Sioux through the last half of the nineteenth century are numerous for they were to center around significant battles and wars against non-Indians. Because of this, down to the present, the "Sioux" have become the prototype of all American Indians in the minds of Americans and foreign people alike. This perception is reinforced by movies and television programs which often seem to use the Sioux to represent the Indian in the story. Unlike reality, in the movies and on TV one might see the Sioux in battle against settlers in Arizona or the U.S. Army in California.

In 1804, Nakotas and Lakotas encountered Lewis and Clark as they journeyed up the Missouri River on the way to the Pacific. It was not a friendly contact, which might have been an omen of things to come, for subsequently, they were frequently in contact with non-Indians in sometimes non-peaceable relationships. In the 1840s, overlanders discovered that the best route to the Far West ran through the lands of the Brulé and Oglala tribes. In 1851, in an effort to secure travel through Indian lands, federal officials called a treaty meeting at Fort Laramie. As a result, the Lakotas and Nakotas were to receive annuity goods for fifteen years.

In 1854, came what American historians remember as the first armed confrontation between Sioux and non-Indians near Fort Laramie. The Gratten Affair was a skirmish near

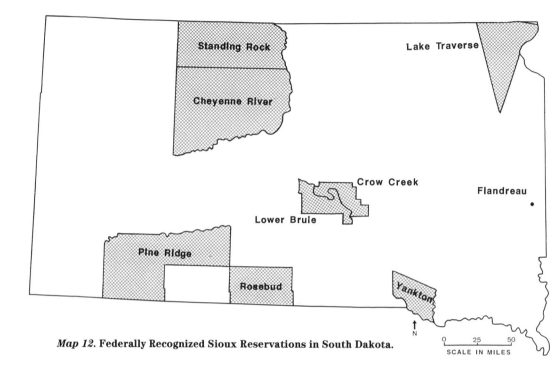

Map 12. **Federally Recognized Sioux Reservations in South Dakota.**

Fort Laramie, during which an entire U.S. Army unit was destroyed. In response General William S. Harney led an army of approximately 1,000 men to punish the Brulés in June 1855. The conflict was settled by March 1856, when Harney advanced to Fort Pierre. There he negotiated a treaty which, although never ratified, led to a few years of peace. Harney then moved down to found Fort Randall in 1856.

The Yankton Treaty of 1858 was the first in which Sioux people ceded large areas of land and agreed to the formation of a permanent Sioux Reservation. In 1862, the Dakota Sioux War disrupted peace in Minnesota and ended in the deaths of some 600 people, and also in the expulsion of all Dakotas from Minnesota. In 1864, gold attracted a horde in Montana. In 1866 a new Peace Council convened at Fort Laramie. The central issue was the opening of a wagon trail from Omaha to Bozeman, Montana. The Indian reaction was Red Cloud's War, including the Fetterman Massacre, the Wagon Box Fight, and the Hayfield Fight. In the spring of 1868 Red Cloud's War ended with federal capitulation. U.S. officials agreed by the Fort Laramie Treaty of 1868 to tear down all forts along the Bozeman Trail, to support Indian agriculture, and most of all, not to allow non-Indian entry into the Great Sioux Reservation without the permission of three-fourths of adult males in every signatory tribe.

In 1874 the Custer Expedition discovered gold in the Black Hills. Soon gold miners entered the Great Sioux Reservation without invitation. Hostilities broke out. In the summer of 1876 the army sent three columns of troops against the Sioux. Lt. Colonel George A. Custer's column was wiped out at the Battle of the Little Big Horn. By the fall of 1876, one-third of the U.S. Army was fighting the Lakota Sioux. By 1878, reservation agencies were in place at Standing Rock, Cheyenne River, Lower Brulé, Crow Creek, Pine Ridge, and the Rosebud. Hostilities wound down and Indians were forced into a new lifestyle, life on the reservation (Map 12). In 1889, the Great Sioux Reservation was further divided into the six reservations.

By 1890, news of Wovoka, the Piaute Messiah in Nevada who preached the Ghost Dance, reached the Sioux reservations. It caused fear among many whites. The final result of this movement was the death of Sitting Bull at Standing Rock on December 15 and the infamous Massacre at Wounded Knee. The latter occurred on December 29, 1890, and resulted in the deaths of 300 Indian men, women, and children. This was the end of the Sioux reign over the region.

Since that time, Sioux people have been forced into accepting reservation life, or moving into urban life in South Dakota, or moving to communities in other states. The nomadic culture was gone, and numerous efforts have been made, in effect, to acculturate Indians. The result has been a series of social, economic, and cultural problems, successes, and tragedies for individuals, families, and the Sioux people as a whole. The late Governor George S. Mickelson's "Year of Reconciliation" was useful in promoting discussions between the Indian and non-Indian peoples of the state, and efforts are still underway to improve understanding.

Chapter Seven

EXPLORATION AND SETTLEMENT: THE HUMAN OCCUPANCE OF SOUTH DAKOTA

INTRODUCTION

Human occupance provides the geographer with both an historical understanding of exploration and settlement and with a series of mental maps that enable one to understand a people's contact with and development of the local environment.

Exploration and settlement of South Dakota by Euro-Americans began with Europeans entering a landscape occupied by American Indians. In the European exploration of North America, present-day South Dakota began as a portion of the French Colonial Empire. Indeed, France's rule over this land lasted until 1763, when as a part of the Treaty of Paris, ending the French and Indian War, the land was ceded to Spain. The Spanish oversaw the land until it was returned to France in 1800.

EXPLORATION

Early exploration of present-day South Dakota by the Euro-Americans is believed to have begun in 1679, when Daniel G. Duluth sent a party from Lake Mille Lacs westward. It is believed that they reached Big Stone Lake and the Coteau des Prairies. In the latter part of that century, reports indicate that Pierre Le Sueur's trading parties entered the Big Sioux River valley several times. These reports are further supported by a 1701 map by William De L'Isle that shows a trail from the Mississippi River to below the falls of the Big Sioux River. In 1839 cartographer Joseph N. Nicollet mapped much of the Coteau des Prairies for the Corps of Topographical Engineers.

French interest in North America was diverted to Canada for the first half of the eighteenth century. The only significant European activity was the LaVerendrye Expedition during which Francois and Louis Joseph LaVerendrye saw the Black Hills and reached the area of present-day Fort Pierre in 1743. Secondly, the British showed some interest in the area by establishing Hudson Bay Company trading posts near present-day Elk Point in 1755 and Flandreau in 1763.

France's Louisiana was ceded to Spain in 1763. Spain developed the southern portion of Louisiana first. New Orleans was the center for expansion for the southern portion of Louisiana Territory. The city of St. Louis was established in 1764 at the junction of the Missouri and Mississippi Rivers. Over time, the British began to show an increasing presence in the northern part of Spanish Louisiana. Spain decided to send fur traders into this area to strengthen their control.

THE FUR TRADE

In 1789, Juan Munier traveled from St. Louis up the Missouri to the mouth of the Nio-brara River and a Ponca village. In 1790, Jacques D'Eglise reached the Mandan villages. There he learned of the British activities in the area from a French trapper. In 1793, the Missouri Company was formed. It sent Jean Baptiste Truteau and later James Mackay on three expeditions into the northern areas. In 1801, Registre Loisel of St. Louis built Fort aux Cedars on Cedar Island some thirty-five miles below present-day Fort Pierre on the Missouri River. It was the major trading post in the region until it burned in 1810.

In 1800, Spain agreed to return Louisiana to France in the secret Treaty of San Ildefon-so. In 1803, Napoleon Bonaparte agreed to sell the land to the United States. Thus, President Thomas Jefferson, because of his interest in geography, secured the land west of the Mississippi River and hoped to expand America's lands to the Pacific Ocean.

THE LEWIS AND CLARK EXPEDITION

On January 18, 1803, President Jefferson asked Congress for funds to send an expedition led by Meriwether Lewis and William Clark to the Pacific Ocean. On May 14, 1804, the Corps of Discovery and Exploration entered the Missouri River. By August 20 they reached present-day Sioux City, where Sgt. Charles Floyd died. On August 22 they camped near present-day Elk Point, and from then until October 13, 1804, they were in present-day South Dakota or Nebraska.

Lewis and Clark came into contact with the Pawnees, the Yankton Sioux and the Teton Sioux, and the Arikaras. On October 13, 1804, they entered the Mandan villages in North Dakota where they met the Indian woman Sacajawea, who would serve as their guide. From there they continued their journey westward, seeing the Pacific Ocean on November 15, 1805. Lewis and Clark returned to the Mandan villages in August of 1806 and to St. Louis on September 20, 1806.

By means of their journey, Lewis and Clark explored the newly acquired lands of the Northwest and Upper Missouri, learned of the Indian tribes, and gained mapping and scientific data. Perhaps most significantly, the reports and writings of Lewis and Clark created the image of "the Great American Desert." As a result of the expedition, the government became more aware of activities of British fur traders in the region. In 1805, in order to reduce that influence, the United States prohibited other countries from trading in the Louisiana Territory.

THE FUR TRADE INDUSTRY

The first half of the nineteenth century in present-day South Dakota was economically dominated for the Euro-Americans by the fur trade. Over 100 fur-trading posts were located in South Dakota during that time. The main post was almost always at the site of Fort Pierre. During this time, many famous and colorful fur traders and trappers roamed the land. Among them were Manuel Lisa of the St. Louis Fur Company; Joshua Pilcher, who succeeded Lisa; General William Ashley and Andrew Henry of the Rocky Mountain Fur Company; and Jedediah Smith of the same company.

However, the most famous and most important fur trader was Pierre Chouteau, Jr. In 1834 the Western Department of John Jacob Astor's American Fur Company was sold to

Pratte, Chouteau and Company. In 1838 it became Pierre Chouteau, Jr., & Company, and it operated in the region for another twenty years. Pierre Chouteau, Sr., had been one of the founders of St. Louis. The greatest impact of Pierre, Jr., on the area was bringing the steamboat *Yellowstone* up the Missouri River in 1831. The steamboat reached Ft. Tecumseh and returned to St. Louis with a wealth of buffalo robes and tongue. In 1832, Ft. Tecumseh was replaced by a new fort at the same location, which was named Fort Pierre Chouteau, Jr., which today we call Ft. Pierre.

Dominance of the region by the fur trade began to decline in the 1850s. The European fur market was replaced by the dominance of silk in fashion. The beaver had disappeared

he first Anglo-American
ettlers in South Dakota
ere native born white
mericans from the
ast and West.

83

as a major fur source, buffalo were declining in number and popularity, and deer also were less important. The decline of the fur trade not only had an impact on the trapper and trader but also the Indian hunters, trappers, and traders. A declining fur trade meant economic decline for the region.

SETTLEMENT

As the fur trade declined, settlement began. In 1856, a company from Dubuque, Iowa, established a town site at the falls of the Big Sioux River. The settlement was short lived since the Indians chased the early residents out. In May 1857, the company returned and successfully occupied the town site, calling it Sioux Falls. In June 1857, the Dakota Land Company of St. Paul, Minnesota, occupied 320 acres adjoining Sioux Falls and named it Sioux Falls City. The Dakota Land Company also established the towns of Medary and Flandreau in June 1857. By 1860, there were about 5,000 settlers in the area, with additional town sites along the eastern edge of the area and along the Missouri River. Among these towns were Yankton, Vermillion, Elk Point, and Bon Homme.

On July 10, 1859, Dakota Territory was opened to settlement. In 1862, Yankton was selected as the capital of Dakota Territory. The Dakota Sioux War that year resulted in the abandonment of all town sites except Yankton. It was not until 1866 that settlers reoccupied most early town sites. By 1870, there were about 10,000 settlers in present-day South Dakota. The Homestead Act was passed in 1862, but it did not have a significant effect on this area until the latter part of the decade.

SETTLERS

Many people believe that the first Euro-Americans to come to the Dakotas were foreign-born immigrants. However, the actual initial settlement of the area was by native-born Americans. These people came to the Dakotas in search of a new life, wealth, and opportunity. They were native-born Americans from the east and south, and they were followed by Yankees and Old American Southerners who established farms and ranches.

Native-born white Americans dominated South Dakota's population until 1890. They came from every state. Some were even third-generation Americans. They brought with them the American culture of the day and the American ways of life in architecture, law, finance, farming, and education.

Foreign-born whites had their greatest impact beginning about 1880, and children of foreign-born whites began arriving in large numbers after 1890. The mixing of the American and the various ethnic groups led to the "Melting Pot" concept in America. In South Dakota, it is more like a pot of stew. The settlers of the state did not melt as much as they mixed. The ethnic groups brought with them their own attitudes, ideas and ideals, inventions, skills, and technologies. They mixed their ways with those of the American and the Indian.

The impact of each ethnic group and its contributions to South Dakota can still be observed in our daily life. A brief overview of their impacts will allow us to recognize this even in our own communities.

The English, Irish, Scottish, and Welsh settlers gave us a great deal. American law and language are derived from English law and language. They came here directly from the

British Isles, Canada, or the Eastern states. They had great mobility and could mix easily in any community. Their presence is reflected in our towns today by Presbyterian, Episcopal, Methodist, and Roman Catholic churches. Their descendants are found across South Dakota.

The Germans are the largest ethnic group in South Dakota. They are made up of Germans from Germany, Wisconsin, Russia, and Hungary. They arrived speaking German, and many settled in ethnic communities while others mixed with their neighbors. They brought with them a love for agriculture, a strong belief in education, and a political conservatism.

Norwegians comprise the second largest ethnic group in South Dakota. Germans are the largest.

Their religions are Lutheran, Reformed Church, Baptist, Methodist, and Catholic. Their influences were significant as regards food, beer, agriculture, and education.

The first Norwegians came to Clay County in 1859. Norwegian immigrants settled in the east first and later the west and north. They came here to farm. Most were Lutherans, proud of their heritage, language, and schools. Swedish settlement differed from Norwegian occupance. The Swedes scattered across the state, quickly integrating with other groups.

Dutch settlers came from New York and Wisconsin. They settled in northwest Iowa, then Milbank, and later throughout the state. They were agricultural people, and their presence is today disclosed by a community having a Reformed Church of America or a Christian Reformed Church.

The French were not especially numerous in recent settlement of South Dakota, although they were here early as explorers and fur trappers. Their presence is seen in place names like Saint Onge, Dupree, the Moreau River, Ft. Pierre, and Belle Fourche. They were men who came without wives. Many came to the New World seeking a fortune so they could return to France wealthy. Most of those who found wealth returned to France to spend it.

Bohemians came to South Dakota from the gold fields in California, or from cities in the east. Czech settlers came to the Yankton and Tabor areas in 1869. Others came to the Rosebud area in 1904. Ethnic ties were and are strong and most are Roman Catholic.

Danes settled mostly in eastern South Dakota. They mixed in the towns and were Baptists, Adventists, and Lutheran. Today many Danish descendants are Mormons. Finnish people settled in four areas: Hamlin County, Buffalo County, Brown County, and Lawrence and Butte counties. They came from New York and Boston. They farmed and ranched, and in the Black Hills they mined. Their impact is seen today in the presence of cooperatives in our communities. On some farms it is also reflected in the presence of saunas.

Other major ethnic groups include the Poles, who settled mainly in the eastern areas; some Russians and Hungarians; and, after 1900, Greek, Portuguese, and Italian immigrants.

These people came to America and to South Dakota for numerous reasons. Among them are social mobility, employment, wealth, escaping persecution, land, marriage, self-esteem, and climate. Over time these immigrants and the Americans, and to some extent the Indians, mixed, intermarried, and became the South Dakotans of today.

DEVELOPMENT AND CHANGE

Other important activities and events in the settlement and occupance of South Dakota include the arrival of the railroad and its development and subsequent decline in importance. Railroad building began in the state in 1873 with the Dakota Southern, which came into Elk Point, Vermillion, and Yankton. Building continued until 1890, when most of the track had been laid. In recent years railroads have experienced great changes. The passenger train is gone. Over the years, miles and miles of railroad tracks have been abandoned. In recent years the railroads have further changed as a result of mergers, new lines, and the emergence of the state-owned railroad.

The Black Hills Gold Rush began with the discovery of gold on French Creek in 1874. By 1876 there were 20,000 miners in the Deadwood area. Millions of dollars in gold were taken out of the Black Hills. Mining in the Hills continues today as a vital part of the state's economy. The Homestake Mine is one of the country's largest gold producers. Presently, several companies are attempting to establish large-scale open-pit mines in the Black Hills to extract gold.

From 1878 to 1887 South Dakota experienced a land rush. This period is often referred to as the Great Dakota Boom. During that decade, claims were filed for over 24,000,000 acres of land. Railroad land and town sites were opened. Population grew from 98,268 in 1880 to 281,000 in 1890. Pioneer settlers occupied the land, broke the prairie, and eked an existence from this harsh environment. They survived blizzards, a lack of water, and prairie fires. They established our farms, ranches, and towns. They built businesses, churches, schools, and courthouses. These people established the communities and economies that are the homes and livelihoods for the state's people today. They provided the basis from which the South Dakota of today grew.

South Dakota communities developed in a very interesting manner. The first settlements were along the lower portions of the Missouri and Big Sioux Rivers in the 1850s and 1860s. Then with the discovery of gold in 1874, settlement jumped across Dakota Territory to the Black Hills with the establishment of mining camps. Much of the land between the eastern and western portions of present-day South Dakota was identified as Indian land or reservations. In 1889 the Great Sioux Reservation was reduced to about the present reservation and the rest of the land opened to non-Indian settlement. This resulted in the establishment of communities such as Mobridge in 1906 and Winner as late as 1909.

In terms of the occupance of South Dakota, several other factors must also be noted. From 1903 to 1924, the Progressive Era dominated the state. Powerful progressive governors and legislatures established far-reaching policies. These included rural credit for farmers, hail insurance, a state-owned coal mine, state-owned elevators, water-power proposals for the Missouri River, and an industrial-development commission. During this period, South Dakota passed and established some of the most interesting social and economic reforms in American history. Some of the results are still present today in such ventures as municipally owned and operated electric, telephone, and liquor entities.

The 1920s was a period of economic crisis. Bank failures began in South Dakota in 1923. The rural-credit system was in trouble. The Great Depression began in 1929, and the state went further in the hole. Many farmers, ranchers, and business men and women lost everything. Depression and the drought of the Dust Bowl put more South Dakotans on relief than in any other state. Economic conditions forced thousands of residents of South Dakota and other Great Plains states to seek better lives elsewhere. Many of those people migrated to California and other western states during the 1930s.

The New Deal and World War II helped to reestablish the economy, but also diminished the population of the state. Hundreds of thousands of South Dakotans left the state to contribute to the Allied victory over the Axis. By 1945, the state's population had decreased to slightly more than one-half million people, a twentieth-century low total.

Following World War II, the state experienced relative prosperity. Many residents who left to fight in the war or work in supporting industries returned home to South Dakota. Farm income increased significantly. Debts of the state and of individuals were paid off. The development of water-power sites and reservoirs on the Missouri River took place. Republican politics tended to dominate the scene, with short periods of Democratic control.

The Federal Interstate Highway System brought two major new roads to South Dakota, I-90 and I-29. These highways, along with improved state and county roads, allowed farmers, ranchers, and small-town residents greater access to the larger communities. At the same time, railroads began reducing passenger service and abandoning track for freight service. The result was increased auto and truck traffic to larger urban communities. Another effect was the loss of retail businesses and professional and financial services to larger communities. Many small towns started to stagnate or die as a result. This was also reflected in declining small town and rural populations as increasing numbers of youth began to seek wealth in larger communities and outside the state.

In recent years, in order to provide increased opportunities for its people, South Dakota has made major efforts to diversify its economy. New industry, financial institutions, and businesses have been lured to or developed in the state in order to provide a greater economic base. Unfortunately, most of the economic expansion has supported continued migration of the population to the state's larger communities. However, state government continues to make a major effort to increase employment opportunities in smaller communities. It will take time to determine if these efforts will be successful for our smaller settlements. Tourism has expanded and yet still has far to go. Farm and ranch sizes have increased greatly, while the number of farmers has declined. South Dakota has changed and will continue to do so. Its future will be diverse. It will indeed be a land of opportunity for its occupants.

Chapter Eight
AGRICULTURE

INTRODUCTION

Agriculture is the single most important segment of South Dakota's economy, with a total economic impact of over $15.1 billion a year. Agricultural output is responsible for 42% of South Dakota's Gross State Product. This $15.1 Billion impact includes livestock and crop production, trade and services, processing, and employment in agricultural industries. In a normal year, 40% of agriculture's economic impact is from livestock, 37% from crops, and 23% from a combination of services, chemicals, farm equipment, processing, and government payments.

Farm income can fluctuate significantly from year to year depending upon crop and livestock production, agricultural prices, and environmental impacts. Crop yields are dependent upon several factors. The amount of land in crops, the yields per acre, and the amount of land harvested are major factors influencing crop production. Crop prices also have significant impact on production and especially on farm income. Livestock production is affected by the number of livestock born each year and the total number on farms. These numbers provide the basis from which livestock marketing occurs. Crop and animal prices are influenced by the amount available at a given time or place and by the demand by consumers.

Environmental factors have tremendous impact on agriculture. Unfortunately, farmers and ranchers have little control over these factors, although irrigation, fertilization, and good agricultural practices help offset detrimental impacts. Historically, the most significant environmental factors impacting South Dakota agriculture are weather related. The agricultural community is constantly worrying whether there will be enough precipitation or not and its timing. It is not too often that farmers worry about too much moisture, although there are rare years when they must. Drought, flooding, hail, and winds are also serious concerns for one or all can occur in a given season, destroying production and the economy. In addition to weather and climatic concerns, farmers and ranchers must deal with threats from insects, a variety of plant and animal diseases, and numerous other minor factors which could destroy their livelihood.

The importance of agriculture to South Dakota and its people is enormous. It is also ever present. On virtually any given day, a trip to the countryside will show the farmer preparing or working the fields. In spring and summer, farmers are busy planting crops, applying pesticides or herbicides, and baling hay. In late summer and fall they are seen harvesting fields, plowing stubble, and driving grain to the elevator. In the fall the roads and railroads are busy as a result of elevators shipping grain and other crops to market. On any given day, one will also see livestock grazing in ranch country or feed yards and feed lots in farm regions. Dairy herds and dairy barns are more common sights in the eastern portion of the state. Hogs are trucked to market from across the state, although they are most numerous in the southeast corner. Livestock auctions are daily or weekly occurrences statewide in the larger communities. The livestock industry reaches its greatest industrial impact on the state's economy at packing houses, where cattle, hogs, sheep, and poultry are processed and sent to consumers around the world.

In town the presence of agriculture is seen in farmers talking to bankers. Farmers and ranchers are seen conducting business with implement dealers, feed and seed dealers, veterinarians, and retailers. Today's farm wife is often working the farm, mowing, shopping, or running farm-related errands, or may be working in business or industry to provide a second income so vital in today's society. Children are seen on the school bus that brings them to school in town, at city recreation activities, and with the family going to church.

South Dakota agriculture is directly related to the physical and cultural environment of the state. By understanding the geographic conditions that exist in South Dakota, farmers and ranchers are able to better utilize the natural resources of the state in agricultural production. Especially important is an intimate understanding of the relationship among weather and climate, soils, and natural vegetation. Likewise, it is important to understand the cultural heritage of agriculturalists and the technological changes that assist and enrich them. The latter are reflected in the rapid adoption of global positioning, using geographic satellite technologies to better manage crop production and land stewardship.

As you will recall, South Dakota is located near the geographic center of the North American continent. Because of its continental location, South Dakota is a transition zone for four climatic types. It is actually at an extreme end for each type. As a result, it is more subject to seasonal variations in weather and climate than the central portions of such climatic zones. In addition to climatic variation, South Dakota can experience abnormal to severe weather phenomena. In a normal year, you will hear about constant fear of drought. Remember the devastating impact of the "Dust Bowl" of the 1930s on the economy and people of South Dakota? At another time in the same or another year, one will hear concern about too much precipitation or snow melt. The fields will be too wet to plant or harvest, or crops will drown and the economy will suffer. In still another year, abundant precipitation will arrive at the proper times and exceptionally high production will occur, to the delight of everyone.

South Dakota's conditions of weather and climate that are of particular importance to agriculture are extensive. The length of the growing season is vital to enable crops to reach full maturity in the field. The growing season is essentially the time between the last frost of spring and the first frost of fall. The timing and the amount of precipitation during the growing season are perhaps the most important weather conditions impacting production. However, hail and wind damages, growing season temperatures, and natural disasters such as drought or flooding can quickly devastate a crop or destroy animal life.

The soils of South Dakota are conducive to the types of agriculture practiced in the state. Rich Chernozem soils occur in the eastern farming section. Chestnut soils of the central and western regions dominate ranch lands and are indicative of declining amounts of precipitation. Gray Wooded soils of the Black Hills, in turn, reflect and affect the vegetation of the state, ranging from tall prairie grasses in the east, to steppe vegetation suitable for livestock grazing in the west, to the coniferous forests of the Black Hills.

Culturally, most of the farmers and ranchers in South Dakota are of European-American descent. European-Americans essentially ignore the agricultural heritage of the American Indian. Unfortunately, instead of utilizing and adapting the positive aspects of Native

Harvest is an especially significant time in South Dakota since it marks the completion of the state's major season of economic growth.

American agriculture, they imposed their European or American agricultural practices on the land. This influenced the types of crops they adopted, the farming practices they employed, farm size, and general farm economy. The Industrial Revolution formed the basis for the Agricultural Revolution with new crops and hybrids, new equipment, and new farming methods and technologies.

CROP AND LIVESTOCK PRODUCTION

Agriculture is the single most important element in the economy of South Dakota. Agricultural records are maintained by the South Dakota Agricultural Statistics Service, located in Sioux Falls. Each spring the service publishes an account of crop and livestock production for the previous year. This material is available to the general public. It is essentially divided into two phases: crop production and livestock production.

For statistical purposes, the South Dakota Agricultural Statistics Service breaks the state down into nine production districts (Map 13). Each year that agency produces a statistical report on each agricultural product produced in South Dakota. The data are reported by county, by production area, and by state totals.

The nine production areas are the Northwest, North Central, Northeast, West Central, Central, East Central, Southwest, South Central, and Southeast. In the examination of South Dakota's crop and livestock production, these production districts will be referred to in order to provide greater geographic understanding.

91

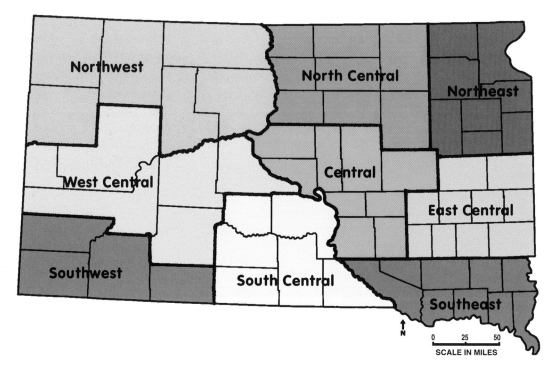

Map 13. **Major Agricultural Production Districts in South Dakota.**
Source: SD Agriculture, 1989-1995.

CROP PRODUCTION

Approximately one-third or more of South Dakota's agricultural economy is from crop production. The state plays a very notable role among the fifty states relative to crop production. South Dakota usually leads the nation in production of two crops, ranking first most years in both oats and rye. It generally ranks second in the nation in production of sunflower seeds and flax seed. The state normally ranks in the top five in other spring wheat and durum wheat. It generally ranks in the top ten states in alfalfa seed, all wheat, corn, barley, soybeans, and alfalfa hay. While not usually in the top ten producing states, South Dakota is also important in other crops, ranking high in sorghum, all hay, winter wheat, and other hays. South Dakota ranks in the top twenty states in potato production.

The major crops can vary each year in production, value, importance, ranking, and other categories as a result of amount planted, yields, disasters, and so on. In a normal year the major crop will be either corn, wheat, or hay. In recent years, soybeans have become an increasingly important crop. Thus, as one examines the variety of crops grown in South Dakota, please keep in mind that in any given year the acreage, yield, production, and dollar value could vary significantly. For this reason, crops are examined geographically rather than statistically.

CORN

When European settlers first arrived in the New World, they found the Indians raising corn. Indeed this crop was grown throughout the New World from low, tropical wetlands to the high mountain regions of the Andes. It had been raised by Indians and their ancestors for thousands of years. It was already available in five major varieties with many sub-varieties.

Today, as a result of Indian corn-growing practices, and tremendous contributions of modern plant breeders, corn can be grown under a wide range of environmental conditions. Plants can range from 2 feet to 20 feet in height; maturity can range from 60 days to 11 months; and corn can be grown from 40° S latitude to 58° N latitude.

In understanding corn production centers in South Dakota, it is important to realize the environmental needs of this plant. Corn is a warm weather plant. It needs high daytime and night-time temperatures during the growing season. Indeed, some 80 percent of corn's growth is during the warm nights. To achieve this, the growing area must have a summer temperature average of 70° to 80° or more. Nighttime temperatures should exceed 58° during much of the growing season. Throughout, a frost free growing season of over 140 days is needed for good corn yields. Rainfall should average 3 inches to 6 inches during each of the summer months. Indeed rainfall should be well distributed during the entire growing season. Corn also thrives on fertile prairie soils that have been enhanced by tall prairie grasses.

These are the environmental conditions that are found in the southeastern portion of South Dakota, and gradate off as one moves west and north. Southeastern South Dakota is the north-western corner of the American Corn Belt and meets the conditions just discussed.

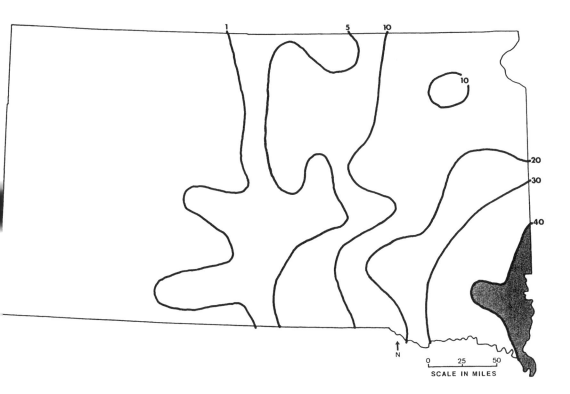

Map 14. **Percent of Harvested Cropland in Corn.**
Source: SD Agriculture, 1995-1999.

93

Geographically, perhaps the easiest way to understand the importance of any crop to the agricultural economy of South Dakota is to understand where it is grown and to what extent. A map of total harvested cropland in corn provides such an understanding (Map 14). From the map it is easy to see that southeastern and east central South Dakota constitute the dominant corn-producing region in the state. In that region over twenty percent of the harvested crop land is in corn. Portions of Turner, Lake, and Moody counties and all of Minnehaha, Lincoln, Clay, and Union counties have over forty percent of their harvested crop land in corn production.

Note how the importance of corn changes as one moves westward or northward. With two occasional exceptions, as far west as the James River Lowlands, corn is down to fifteen percent of the harvested cropland. Those exceptions are in Sully and Hughes counties in the central portion of the state, and in far western Butte County where in any given year corn may be grown by irrigation methods.

About eighty percent of the corn that is grown in this country is fed to animals. Much of the corn is fed to animals on the farms and ranches where it is raised. Corn is also condensed in form and sold as feed for cattle, hogs, sheep, and poultry. In addition to livestock feed, corn is grown for seed, alcohol, breakfast cereal, corn meal, ethanol, starch, syrup, and corn oil. South Dakota corn could end up virtually anywhere in the world; however, most of it is utilized in the state or nearby agricultural regions.

The massive Wheat Growers elevators in Aberdeen reflect the
importance of that commodity to the state's economy.

WHEAT

Wheat, along with corn and rice, is one of the big three world crops. In South Dakota, wheat joins corn and hay as the big three. Like corn, it has a wide area of growth. World wheat production can be found from 40° S latitude to 60° N latitude.

When the wheat plant begins growing, it resembles any other grass at the same stage. As it grows it sends up stalks that carry heads of grain. The amount of wheat grown and the yield from the heads is influenced by seasonal weather conditions. Cool moist seasons following planting generally result in good yields. Warm, dryer seasonal stresses result in lower yields.

In response to the effects of weather on wheat production, different types of wheat are raised. The predominate types are winter wheat and spring wheat. Winter wheat is grown in the warmer regions. It is sown in the fall and harvested the following summer. Spring wheat is raised in colder areas. It is sown in the spring and harvested in late summer.

Wheat tends to do best in environments where it receives from 10 inches to 30 inches of precipitation a year. Less than 10 inches is too little, while too much precipitation is fatal causing the production of straw rather than grain and encouraging rust and fungus diseases.

Wheat farming is a hazardous occupation. It has two main occupational problems: getting a crop and selling the crop. Wheat farming faces the physical hazards of heat, aridity, thunderstorms, hailstorms, freezing, thawing, Hessian Flies, grasshoppers, smut, and rust.

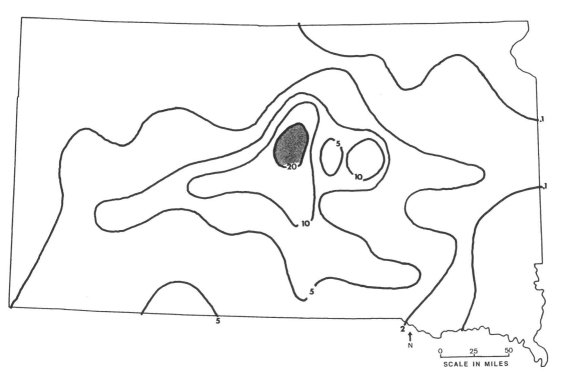

Map 15. **Percent of Harvested Cropland in Winter Wheat.**
Source: SD Agriculture, 1995-1999.

95

It faces the cultural economic hazards of overproduction, market glut, and increasing costs of doing business. At the same time, there is strong evidence to indicate that consolidation of farmland results in significant production increases as a result of more specialization on the part of the wheat growers.

South Dakota plants almost 4,000,000 acres of wheat a year, with historically about equal amounts of land in winter wheat and spring wheat. The yield from spring wheat will normally be higher than from winter wheat.

WINTER WHEAT—Remember, winter wheat is grown in warmer areas where it can be sown in the fall and harvested the following summer. Winter wheat production in South Dakota centers in the west central, central, and south central parts of the state. The most important winter wheat production center is in Hughes and Sully counties, where large portions of that area exceed fifteen percent of the total harvested cropland being in wheat. Essentially all three subregions in the central portion of the state have the greatest percentage of harvested cropland in winter wheat (Map 15).

SPRING WHEAT—Spring wheat is raised in the cooler portions of South Dakota. It is sown in the spring and harvested in late summer. Most of the spring wheat lands lie east of the Missouri River. There are three main areas of production centering in the north central, northeast, and central production regions. The north central and northeast are by far the most important areas. In all three, however, portions of the areas exceed over fifteen percent of the harvested crop lands being in wheat. The area centering on Sully and Hughes counties again utilizes irrigation for production (Map 16). Generally, while the acreages

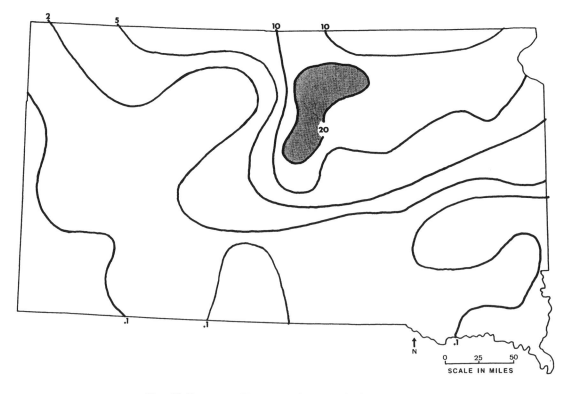

Map 16. Percent of Harvested Cropland in Spring Wheat.
Source: SD Agriculture, 1995-1999.

96

planted for winter wheat and spring wheat are often about equal, about 60 percent of the yield usually comes from spring wheat.

Wheat is the most important commodity on world trade. Both wheat and wheat flour enter the world commodity market. Wheat produced in South Dakota can be shipped to Minneapolis; Duluth to Buffalo, New York, to overseas; to Kansas City for milling; to New Orleans; or to the west coast for export to Asia.

SOYBEANS

Challenging hay for status as the third major crop in South Dakota is soybeans. Soybean production has increased dramatically in South Dakota in recent years and can now equal or exceed the value of corn and wheat. Soybeans are the most important legume crop in the world. Geographically, the plant can be grown over large areas of the earth, since there are hundreds of varieties and since it is a rather drought-resistant summer crop. The soybean has been important in the USA since about 1930, and has been established as a Corn Belt crop. Soybeans are an effective crop to grow in rotation with corn. Its importance in South Dakota is recent, and its future looks good.

Soybean production in the state is closely related to the tall and mid-prairie grass areas. Production is greatest in the southeast and east central areas of the state. The greatest concentrations of soybean production are Union, Lincoln, and Clay counties and portions of Minnehaha, Moody, Turner, and Yankton counties, where over thirty percent of the harvested cropland is in soybeans (Map 17).

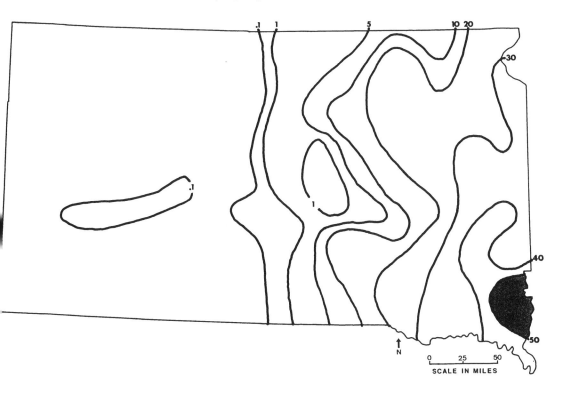

Map 17. Percent of Harvested Cropland in Soybeans.
Source: SD Agriculture, 1995-1999.

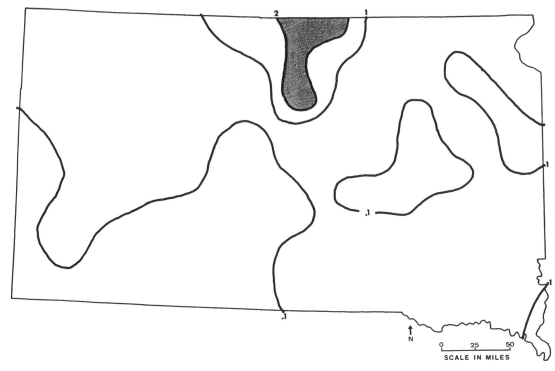

Map 18. **Percent of Harvested Cropland in Oats.**
Source: SD Agriculture, 1995-1999.

Soybeans have a variety of uses for both humans and animals. They are marketed as feed to livestock and poultry. Humans consume soybeans as soybean oil, high protein breakfast foods, vegetable oils, and shortening. Soybeans are also used in the production of soap, plastics, ink, paint, and a variety of industrial products.

OATS

Oats continue to decline in importance in South Dakota, as recent years have demonstrated a significant increase in the importance of soybeans and sunflower. The climatic needs of the plant are similar to wheat, especially spring wheat. Oats are planted in the spring and require more moisture than wheat during the growing season. Oats are primarily grown for horse feed, for breakfast cereal, or are generally fed on the farm where grown. In recent years, however, South Dakota oats have found markets at horse racetracks across the nation.

Oat production centers in five areas of the state: the northeast, north central, central, southeast, and east central. It is most concentrated in Potter, Dewey, McPherson, Campbell, and Corson counties (Map 18).

HAY

Although the amount of land harvested in hay may exceed corn, soybeans, or wheat in a given year, it should be noted that hay is grown throughout South Dakota. Alfalfa hay is the dominant type accounting for over fifty percent of the total production. Hay does very well in this state since the environmental conditions of weather, climate, soil, and vegetation resulted in a natural grassland environment. Hay tends to be drought resistant. The plants develop extensive root systems that grow deep in the soil seeking moisture. Yields are generally good and hay can be cut several times a year in South Dakota. Most of the hay is consumed near its production area. It is primarily utilized as a livestock feed.

BARLEY

Barley production in South Dakota has fluctuated greatly over the years. Since 1948, barley production has declined in importance, although it has shown signs of coming back strongly in recent years. In fact, 1985 was the first year to exceed 1948 production figures.

Barley's greatest attribute is its ability to mature in a short 90- to 100-day growing season. Thus, it enables farmers to respond to colder seasonal temperatures, drought, heat, or wet fields that prevent earlier planting of other crops. Its major production area in the United States corresponds to the Spring Wheat Belt.

Barley production in South Dakota is concentrated in the north central, northeast, and sometimes the central regions. Campbell County produces the most barley. However, the greatest concentration of harvested cropland in barley is in Roberts, Brown, Day, Edmunds, and Perkins counties where over ten percent of the land is in that crop (Map 19). Barley can be used as a livestock feed, in the production of malt, and for seed.

Map 19. **Percent of Harvested Cropland in Barley.**
Source: SD Agriculture, 1995-1999.

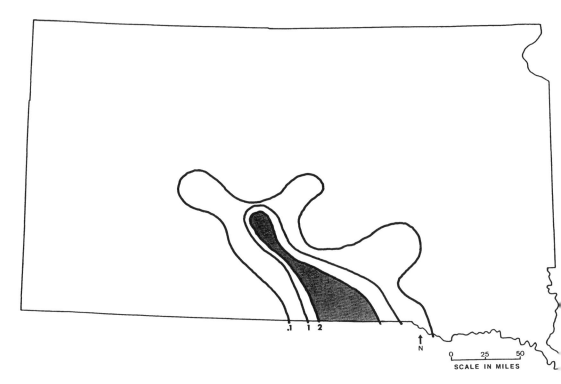

Map 20. Percent of Harvested Cropland in Sorghum.
Source: SD Agriculture, 1995-1999.

SORGHUM

Sorghum is an ancient cereal. It is noted for being the most drought-resistant cereal grain. Sorghum does well in hot temperatures, poor soil, and low rainfall.

The major areas for sorghum production are the south central and the southeast. Over four percent of the harvested cropland in Lyman and Tripp counties is in sorghum. Another small center is found in portions of Charles Mix, Douglas, and Gregory counties (Map 20). Sorghum is very much like millet in appearance and is often confused in the field. Millet has an even shorter growing season than sorghum. Sorghum is grown for grain, fodder, and silage.

SUNFLOWERS

Sunflowers are presently produced commercially in seven states. Almost forty-five percent of the sunflower crop comes from neighboring North Dakota. South Dakota ranks second in sunflower production with about thirty percent of the crop. This crop has become increasingly important in the state. The leading areas of production are the north central, central, and northeast. Sully County has the greatest concentration of cropland in sunflowers with over 20 percent of the land in the central part of that county in sunflowers (Map 21). Virtually all the sunflowers grown in South Dakota are raised for sunflower oil. Less than one percent are grown for seed. Sunflower oil is an important vegetable oil in Europe and is increasing in importance in the United States.

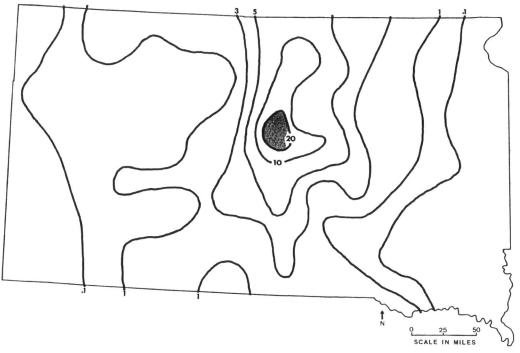

Map 21. Percent of Harvested Cropland in Sunflowers.
Source: SD Agriculture, 1995-1999.

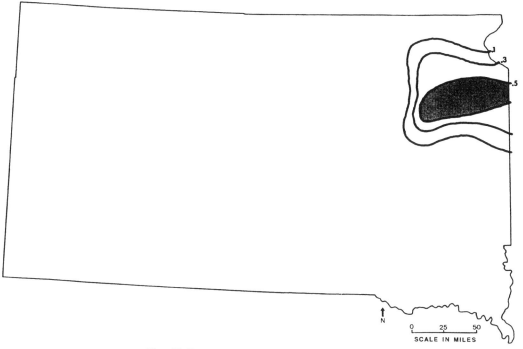

Map 22. Percent of Harvested Cropland in Rye.
Source: SD Agriculture, 1995-1999.

RYE

Rye is the second most important grain in the world's bread production. It can be sown in the fall like winter wheat but actually grows north of the Winter Wheat Belt. Rye can stand temperatures to -40° F which would destroy winter wheat.

Rye production in South Dakota centers in two areas, the north central and the northeast (Map 22). The leading counties for production are Codington, Clark, Grant, Day, Corson, Spink, and Faulk. Rye is used mainly for bread but can also be plowed under as a green manure, thus enriching the soil.

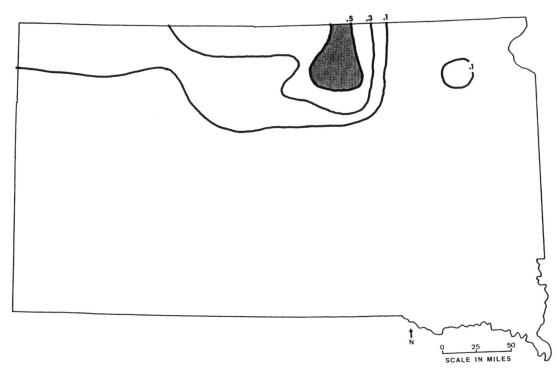

Map 23. Percent of Harvested Cropland in Flax.
Source: SD Agriculture, 1995-1999.

FLAX

Flax is a grain, a fiber, and an oil. In Europe flax is grown for fiber. In South Dakota the crop is raised for flaxseed. The seed can be crushed to make linseed oil for paint and varnish. The oilseed cake or by-product can be used for livestock feed. South Dakota normally ranks first in flax production. Flaxseed production in South Dakota is concentrated in the north central and northeast. The greatest production is in portions of McPherson, Day, Faulk, and Edmunds counties (Map 23).

POTATOES

Fall potatoes are a specialty crop in South Dakota. The state ranks among the top twenty in the nation in potato production. This crop is centered in the northeast, more specifically in Clark County, where now only about 5,000 acres of potatoes are planted yearly. The crop is utilized locally for french fries and potato chips, which are finding an expanding market in both the region and nationwide.

LIVESTOCK PRODUCTION

While crops generally account for 33 to 40 percent of South Dakota's agricultural economy, the livestock industry accounts for the other 60 to 67 percent of the total. Livestock is by far the most important part of the agricultural economy. In South Dakota, the livestock industry is comprised of beef and dairy cattle, hogs, sheep, and lambs, and to a lesser extent poultry and bees.

South Dakota normally ranks in the top ten in the United States for livestock production. It generally ranks seventh in the number of cattle and calves. The state usually ranks fifth in the number of beef cows that have calved and eighth in the number of cattle on feed. South Dakota's calf crop is normally the sixth largest in the nation. The state normally ranks in the top ten states in the number of hogs and pigs and fifth in sheep and lambs.

With the demise of the American buffalo and the opening of the Dakotas to homesteading, farmers and ranchers established an extensive livestock industry in South Dakota. The cattle industry in South Dakota is especially interesting in that it reflects both the

Roundups and cattle drives are still very much a part of the state's livestock industry.

ranching industry of the American West and the farming industry of the American Corn Belt.

CATTLE AND CALVES

Cattle raised in western South Dakota are range cattle. They graze unsheltered throughout much of the year. Ranchers provide them hay and other feeds when snow cover or blizzards prevent grazing. In the fall many cattle are shipped east to Corn Belt farms to be fattened on corn before marketing in the stockyards and the packing-house yards. Cattle also are raised from calf to market on eastern farms.

In South Dakota, the number of cattle on hand can range from about 3,500,000 to 4,500,000 head. The heaviest concentration of cattle and calves is in the southeast and east central areas. In fact a belt of land from Tripp County to Campbell County contains over

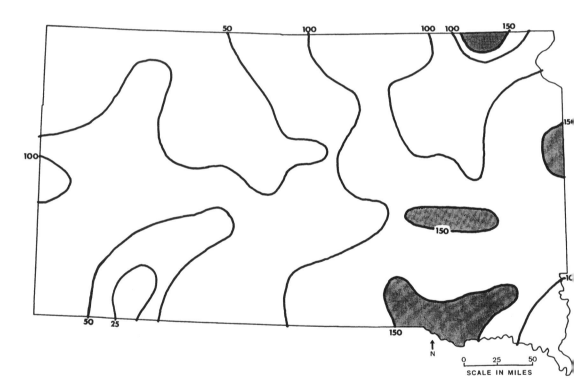

Map 24. **Number of Cattle and Calves per One Thousand Acres.**
Source: SD Agriculture, 1997.

100 head of cattle and calves for every 1,000 acres of land (Map 24). The heaviest cattle density in the state is in the southeast. This is also the portion of South Dakota that is located in the Corn Belt region and where the meat packing and stockyard industries are concentrated. On the other hand the northwest area with the dry steppe vegetation and ranching industry contains fewer than 50 head per 1,000 acres because the carrying capacity is lower.

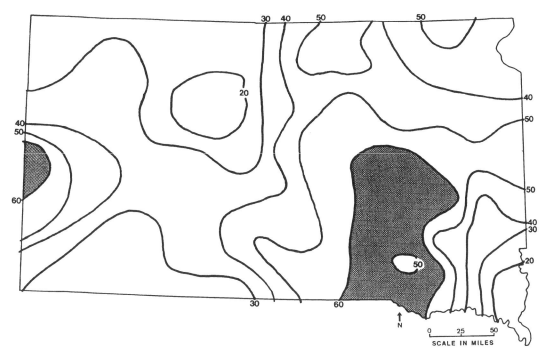

Map 25. **Number of Beef Cows per One Thousand Acres.**
Source: SD Agriculture, 1997.

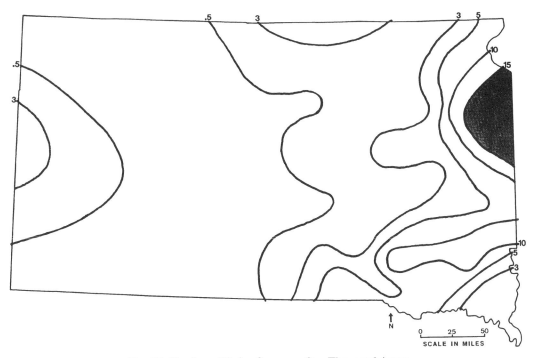

Map 26. **Number of Dairy Cows per One Thousand Acres.**
Source: SD Agriculture, 1997.

For beef cows some variation occurs. The greatest concentration of beef cows is in the east central, central, southeast, and south central areas. Here, there are over fifty head of beef cows per 1,000 acres (Map 25).

Dairy cows on the other hand are concentrated in the northeast, southeast, and east central areas. The greatest concentrations are in Deuel and Codington counties where there are over 20 head of dairy cows per 1,000 acres (Map 26). Milk cow numbers in eastern South Dakota closely parallel the dairy region economy of adjacent western Minnesota.

HOGS AND PIGS

Hog and pig production is a basic part of the farm economy of the American Corn Belt. Hogs have been raised in this portion of the United States since farmers first crossed into Ohio, planted corn, and fed it to hogs. Farmers even had hog drives from Ohio to the East Coast cities. It was so important that Cincinnati, Ohio, was originally named Porkopolis.

Southeastern South Dakota is where the Corn Belt is most visible in the state. It is also where the greatest number of hogs and pigs are found in the state. Statewide, the number of hogs and pigs on farms at a given time can range from about 1,300,000 to over 2,200,000. Several pig crops will be born in the state each year adding several million to the total yearly hog population. Numbers will fluctuate up or down depending upon demand and other economic factors. During the normal year, over 3,000,000 hogs are sent to market. The greatest concentrations of hogs and pigs are in Hutchinson, Minnehaha and Union where

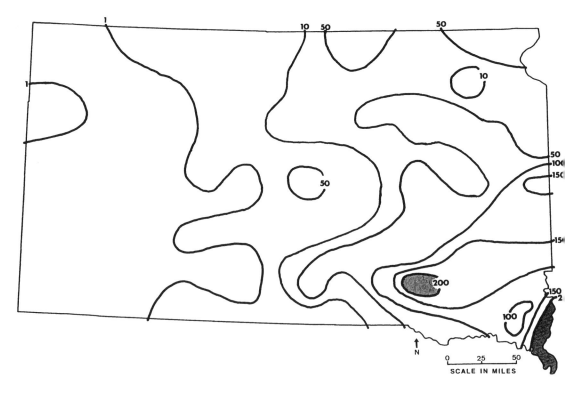

Map 27. **Number of Hogs per One Thousand Acres.**
Source: SD Agriculture, 1997.

over 200 hogs per 1,000 acres are found (Map 27). In fact, most of the portion of South Dakota found in the Humid Continental "A" type climate will average over fifty hogs per 1,000 acres.

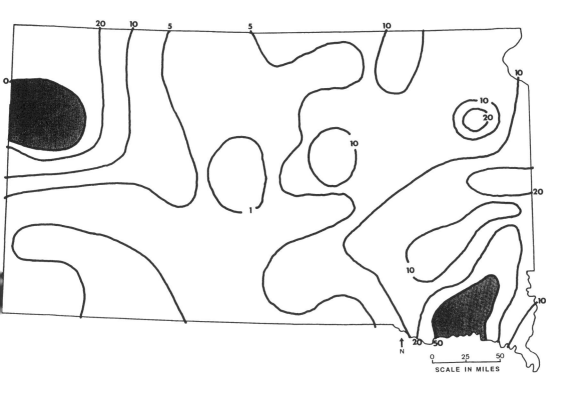

Map 28. Number of Sheep and Lambs per One Thousand Acres.
Source: SD Agriculture, 1997.

In ranching country, to the west, the number of hogs and pigs per 1,000 acres drops off drastically. In Harding County there is fewer than one hog per 1,000 acres. The pigs are concentrated where there is the feed and the need.

SHEEP AND LAMBS

Sheep and lambs are important to South Dakota, although most people do not realize it. Presently the sheep industry is at a record low throughout the nation and in the state. During World War II, over 2,500,000 sheep and lambs a year were raised in South Dakota. In recent years this number has declined to about 400,000 a year. The sheep industry has several centers of production. The major center is in the northwest where in Butte County the number of sheep and lambs reaches over fifty per 1,000 acres (Map 28). The second major area is in the southeast and east central where portions of Yankton County have over fifty head per 1,000 acres. Other centers are in Harding, Perkins, Meade and Turner counties.

Sheep and lambs are raised for wool and for meat. It is interesting to note that a large number of South Dakotans have never eaten mutton. With the decline in sheep and lambs nationally, the same appears to be true for Americans in general.

MILK

Milk production in South Dakota is fairly stable but fluctuates up or down with consumer demand. Production averages about 1.7 billion pounds a year. Approximately 3,000 dairy farm operations serve the state. The production is utilized for fresh milk, powdered milk, cheese, and other dairy products.

POULTRY

The poultry industry of South Dakota is showing mixed signals. At one time, eastern South Dakota had the highest per capita ratio of chickens per person in the country. As recently as 1980 there were 2,400,000 head of chickens in the state. By the late 1980s, that figure dropped to less than 2,000,000 head. Since that time, the number of chickens on farms increased to about 2,500,000. Egg production has also increased. With an increase in chicken population comes a corresponding increase in egg production. It should be noted that chicken production can respond to increased or decreased consumer demands faster than any other meat product.

While chicken numbers were declining, turkey production increased over fifty percent in recent years. In fact, the number of turkeys and chickens on farms is almost equal each year. Pheasants, geese, and ducks are also raised commercially in South Dakota. To date, marketing efforts have concentrated on local sales rather than the national market, which would require a more substantial investment and inspection program.

BEES

One final area of South Dakota's livestock industry is bee keeping. South Dakota has over 250,000 bee colonies working within its borders. Bees are raised for honey and wax. They also provide insect pollination for crops such as alfalfa, sweet clover, cucumbers, and tree fruits. Many of the hives are placed in windbreaks on farms. South Dakota honey production is rated by many experts as among the best in the country.

SUMMARY

The importance of agriculture to the economy of South Dakota is tremendous. More than fifteen billion dollars a year is generated by agriculture for the state's economy. Over time, animals such as buffalo, llama, and ostrich may also become important to the state's agricultural economy. The relationship and dependence upon agriculture by the population and all other segments of the economy is something that must always be considered and understood in order to know truly the geography of South Dakota.

Chapter Nine

MINERALS OF SOUTH DAKOTA

INTRODUCTION

Minerals are one of the most fascinating aspects of geography, for they may be studied as either a part of the physical environment or as a part of the cultural environment. The physical geographer may be concerned about minerals in the same manner as a geologist with the additional concern of spatial distribution. The cultural geographer is concerned not only with location but also with quantity, quality, economic feasibility, marketing, and so forth. It is important to remember that a mineral by itself is essentially of no value. It is only when humankind enters the picture that minerals are of value and demand.

South Dakota contains a large assortment of minerals. This is a result of various factors that resulted in formation of the land. Some are a result of direct deposition, some were exposed by erosion, and still others result from the earth-building forces. With the arrival of humans and their subsequent discovery of the presence of various minerals, some came to possess great economic value. Still other minerals are of little economic value. A few others could be of some worth if necessity or demand for them grows in the future.

Since the discovery of gold in the Black Hills in 1874, mining has been central to South Dakota's economy. Many early European settlers in western South Dakota came for the gold mining. The Homestake Gold Mine was established in 1877 and has been the oldest continuously operating gold mine in the United States. Mining gold in the Hills has become a much more expensive operation, as the cost of mining has increased and the price of gold has decreased. As a result, Homestake closed its doors in 2001, leaving behind 1.5 million ounces of gold that are just too costly to mine.

The economic ramifications of Homestake's closing are not yet known. But, it is known that the jobs at Homestake had high wages and great benefits. The economic loss to the families employed at Homestake will be great. The ramifications will extend beyond Homestake's employees, as the mine's taxes accounted for 9% of the revenue base for Lawrence County and over 20% of the Lead-Deadwood School District's budget. Additionally, the industries and businesses that provided goods and services to the nearly 400 Homestake employees in Lead will be affected.

While South Dakota will still be known for its Black Hills gold, only the gold mine operated by Wharf Resources will continue operating once Homestake closes. As the economic importance of gold mining declines in South Dakota, some of the state's less-tapped resources will increase in importance.

MINERALS BY CLASS

Minerals are normally broken down into three classifications. They are: metallic minerals, non-metallic minerals, and mineral fuels. The first two classes are non-fuel minerals. The latter is of course mineral fuels. Historically, South Dakota's mineral industry has been dominated in terms of production and value by metallic minerals. Some 68% of the value of all the minerals mined in South Dakota has been from gold. Other metallic minerals have accounted for 1% of the mineral value. Non-metallic minerals have comprised the bulk of the rest, about 30% of the total production. Mineral Fuels have accounted for less than 1% of the mineral production in South Dakota (Map 29).

METALLIC MINERALS

GOLD AND SILVER

Gold has, by far, been the most important mineral in the state. Since it was first discovered along French Creek in the Black Hills by members of the Custer Expedition of 1874, it has dominated the state's mineral economy.

Gold is concentrated in the central Black Hills. It is what is commonly known as a mutually occurring mineral. This means that where you find gold, you will also likely find one or more of the following: silver, lead, zinc, copper, and mercury. In the case of the

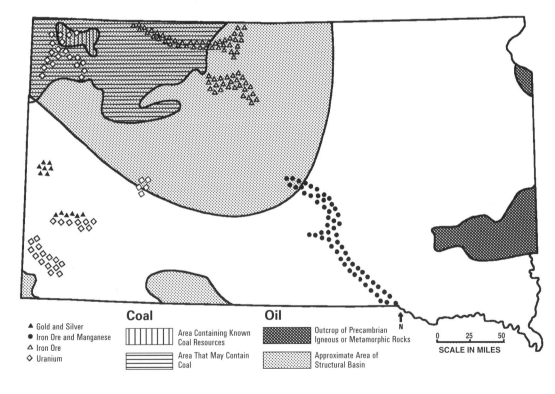

Legend:
- ▲ Gold and Silver
- ● Iron Ore and Manganese
- △ Iron Ore
- ◇ Uranium

Coal
- Area Containing Known Coal Resources
- Area That May Contain Coal

Oil
- Outcrop of Precambrian Igneous or Metamorphic Rocks
- Approximate Area of Structural Basin

0   25   50
SCALE IN MILES

Map 29. **Major Minerals of South Dakota.**

The Homestake Mine in Lead closed in 2001 after 124 years of continuous operation.

Black Hills, the most commonly occurring mineral with gold is silver. However, gold is taken out at a production rate of over five ounces to one ounce of silver.

The precious metal is found in the Black Hills in three major types of deposits. The most important type is known as a replacement deposit. In this type, the presence of gold and silver ore bodies is a result of the replacement of weaker rock with metallic minerals derived from volcanic solutions. The Homestake Mine, which has historically accounted for almost three-fourths of the gold taken out of the Hills, operated in a replacement deposit. Other replacement deposits were mined at the Garden District, Squaw Creek on Bald Mountain, and Keystone.

The other two principal types are the vein and shear zone deposit and the placer deposit. Vein and shear zone deposits are formed when cracks or openings in country rock are filled with mineral bearing volcanic solutions. Placer deposits are generally the first clues to the presence of gold in a region. They are mechanical concentrations of gold found in stream beds. Over the years, as erosion wears away at the land, minerals become increasingly concentrated in ancient and modern stream beds. By mining these beds, minerals are extracted.

Historically, mines such as the Cloverleaf Mine near Lead, the Holy Terror Mine near Keystone, and the Standby Mine at Rochford were important vein and shear zone deposits. Other districts with these deposits were Deadwood, Ragged Top Mountain, Bald Mountain, and Hill City. Placer deposits were "poor man's mines." They consisted of a portion of a stream bed that the miner worked until it played out or the miner started searching elsewhere.

The cost of gold and silver mining in South Dakota has risen in recent years. Whether surface mining or shaft mining, the costs are increasing. Surface mining, for instance, requires enormous investments in massive equipment. Factors such as labor, equipment, material costs, depth, grade of ore, and milling technology all influence the cost of mining gold and silver. All of these costs of producing an ounce of gold must be weighed against the value of an ounce of gold on the market. Thus, the most important factor in gold mining is the price of gold on the world market. Higher gold prices can offset these costs and allow successful operation of both shaft and surface mines.

The Homestake Mine closed because operating costs rose while the price of gold on the market dropped below $300 an ounce. While operations ended in 2001, work at the mine will continue in order to secure the 500 miles of tunnels and ensure that the site is environmentally sound.

Environmental concerns are not only an issue for mine closings, but also for operating surface mines. Initiatives to require open cut mines to restore the land to the original contours and increasing severance taxes were turned down in statewide elections. As surface mining continues, mining companies must assure the public that their environmental impact will include restoration, enhancement, and enrichment.

COPPER, LEAD, AND ZINC

Three of the other mutually occurring minerals also can be found in the Black Hills. Historically, some lead has been mined near Deadwood, Galena, and Silver City. Zinc was mined beginning during World War II, with operations ending in 1948. Total zinc production during that time was about one-half million pounds. Copper has never been found in a high enough concentration to merit mining. These three minerals offer little future potential for economic development based on present day knowledge.

URANIUM

Uranium, the principle mineral of atomic energy, has been found in over forty locations in South Dakota. The most economically feasible deposits are in areas of sandstone bedrock or lignite coal. Some uranium has been discovered in shales but not in sufficient concentrations to make them economically feasible to mine.

To date most of the state's uranium production has come from sandstone deposits at the Edgemont area in the Black Hills. Some uranium has also been extracted from lignite beds near Slim Buttes and the Cave Hills. This area has uranium production possibilities that could be further expanded. However, uranium mining in South Dakota is extremely subject to national demands. Presently, there is not sufficient demand to keep this mineral industry operating in the state. In the future, uranium could also be recovered as a by-product of potential lignite coal production.

IRON AND MANGANESE

Iron ore and manganese deposits in South Dakota are closely related. While iron ore is the principal mineral in iron and steel, manganese is an important ferro-alloy of steel. It is also used in storage batteries and the chemical industries.

South Dakota has several very interesting iron ore deposits. Iron ore has been found in the state in varying degrees of concentration. They range in purity from: magnetite (72%) and oxide hematite (70%); to limonite (60%); to carbonite siderite (40%); to manganese-iron carbonates of varying qualities.

There are three major areas of known iron ore deposits in South Dakota. The Black Hills and the surrounding areas contain deposits of hematite, magnetite, and limonite ores. The Hills also have the potential for taconite concentrating production. Northwestern South Dakota in portions of Butte, Corson, Dewey, Harding, and Perkins counties has siderite, hematite, and limonite concentrations occurring with manganese deposits in stream gravels. The third major area lies along the Missouri River south of Pierre and extending to Pickstown. There, another manganese and iron deposit offers some future potential.

In recent years, modern-day prospectors have detected some magnetic anomalies in Yankton, Spink, Union, Day, and Marshall counties. These tests indicate the presence of some iron. However, there has been no interest in further exploring or developing these presences.

The only current iron ore production is in the Nemo area. Production is sold by contract to the South Dakota State Cement Plant in Rapid City.

OTHER METALLIC MINERALS

Because of the formation of the Black Hills, South Dakota, like the Rocky Mountain states to the west, is blessed with a wide variety of other metallic minerals. Some of these minerals have been worked at times. Still others, while present, generally are not recognized even by prospectors, who could slip and hit their heads on one and not realize what mineral it is. Except for beryllium, none of these minerals is presently of any economic significance.

Beryllium is a feldspar coproduct. It is mined in association with feldspar and mica deposits in the Custer area. Production is small in both tonnage and dollar value. Like many of the less important minerals of the Black Hills region, production varies from year to year, and needed amounts are essentially storehoused by contract miners until the market demands.

Tin is present in the form of casserite. It was discovered in the Black Hills in 1876. It has been mined at Tinton and near Hill City. No production has occurred since 1952.

Tungsten, the metal with the highest melting point, also has not been mined since 1952. It is found near Hill City and in the Spokane District. The United States essentially imports all the tungsten it consumes, saving its own reserves for the future.

Molybdenum, a metal alloy used in high temperature steels has been found in both the Black Hills and Harding County. Deposits are small and their content is low in purity. There is no production and essentially no potential for further development.

Thorium and Rare Earths are commonly associated in nature. Thorium is a an element used in the manufacture of gas mantles. Rare Earths are used in arc lights, projection lamps, and glass. Both these minerals have been reported in the Black Hills. However, no significant deposits have been found, but there is potential.

Vanadium has been a byproduct of uranium mining at Edgemont. Small yearly consumption demands by American industry offer little hope for any development of this mineral.

Other minor minerals include antimony, arsenic, bismuth, selenium, sulfur, and tellurium. None of these metals is commercially developed to any extent. Columbium and tantalum, two other mutually occurring minerals, have been utilized at times of need. Tantalum is used in skull plates and sutures. There has not been any tantalum production in South Dakota since World War II.

NON-METALLIC MINERALS

Non-metallic minerals are the second most important category in mineral production in South Dakota. Because of their nature and bulk, they also account for the most volume. In dollar value, sand and gravel, portland cement, and limestone compete annually for the role of major non-metallic mineral. Non-metallic minerals offer a wide variety of uses, ranging from bulk, to ballast, to cement, to building stone, to industrial materials. The demand for, and value of, each mineral is dependent upon how its unique characteristics relate to human needs.

CEMENT

Cement can on occasion rank second to gold in economic importance to the state's mineral economy. The South Dakota State Cement Plant in Rapid City is owned by the state. It is operated for profit by a commission appointed by the governor. Profits are returned to the state's general fund annually. The cement produced at the plant is marketed in South Dakota and seven neighboring states. Yearly production can fluctuate substantially with demands from the residential and highway construction industries.

Portland cement dominates the industry in production and value. Masonry cement is a very distant second in importance. Over one-half of the portland cement is marketed to ready-mix concrete companies. Masonry cement is utilized primarily by the construction industry.

SAND AND GRAVEL

In terms of volume, dimension stone, sand and gravel, and crushed stone are produced in greater amounts than any other minerals in South Dakota. Sand and gravel are also the most economically recoverable mineral resource in the state. Commercially feasible deposits of sand and gravel are found in every county. They currently are being quarried in sixty-one counties, with Brookings, Pennington, and Minnehaha being the most important. Sand and gravel deposits in eastern South Dakota are glacial in origin, while those in the western part of the state are from terraces and outwash deposits. Some silica sand is quarried in the Black Hills.

Generally, sand and gravel will rank second only to gold in production dollar value. Sand and gravel are utilized to render bulk, durability, and strength at low costs. Most of the sand and gravel production is utilized in the construction industry. Highways are the major consumer, utilizing sand and gravel for road base and covering. Other major uses are concrete aggregates, asphaltic aggregates, fill, and snow and ice control. Construction sand and gravel are also utilized for airports, public buildings, railroad ballast, and manufacturing.

BUILDING STONE

Building stone, or dimension stone, is quarried in several areas in South Dakota. In South Dakota the principal dimension stones are granite, quartzite, and limestone. These stones are important because they each have unique qualities such as color, polish, strength, and durability. The most important building stone comes from the Milbank area. Milbank granite is quarried at several sites around the city. It is known worldwide as a monument stone that is prized for its medium-to-dark red colors. The Dakota Granite Company in Milbank operates the largest diamond saw in the world. This saw is fourteen feet in diameter and is utilized to slice and finish blocks of granite.

Building stones also have been quarried at other sites historically. Beautiful Sioux Quartzite was utilized in many older buildings and homes in the eastern part of the state. It was quarried at Dell Rapids, Sioux Falls, East Sioux Falls, and Rowena. Today, Sioux Quartzite is principally utilized as crushed stone. Minnekahta Limestone from the Black Hills was used in several buildings in the Rapid City area.

LIMESTONE

Limestone, the principal dimension stone, often competes with sand and gravel or cement for the ranking of second to gold in the value of production. It is utilized for building stone, concrete, aggregate, ballast, agricultural lime, and filter beds.

The most important limestone deposit in the state is the Minnekahta Limestone formation in the Black Hills. This 40-foot-thick deposit is quarried at Rapid City, Deadwood, Spearfish, Sturgis, Minnekahta, and Hot Springs. The State Cement Plant is the major user of this deposit. This formation alone is large enough to take care of the state's needs for over 12,000 years.

Other major limestone deposits in the Black Hills include the 200-foot-thick Deadwood Formation, the Pahasapa Formation, which is 300 feet to 600 feet thick, and the Greenhorn Formation, which is 40 feet thick. Several other formations suitable for quarrying exist in the Black Hills; near the Badlands and on the Rosebud; from Yankton to Fort Thompson on the Missouri River; and near Mobridge.

CLAYS AND AGGREGATE

Common clay is mined in the Black Hills region for use in the State Cement Plant and the clay products industry in the Rapid City area. Small amounts of bentonite are mined at Belle Fourche. Lightweight shale aggregate is quarried near Rapid City. Clays and aggregates account for less than one percent of the state's mineral production.

PEGMATITE MINERALS

Pegmatite is a unique type of granitic rock. Unlike granite's small crystals, pegmatites are comprised of very large crystals ranging from a few inches to over a foot in diameter. In addition to the crystals, pegmatites contain potash feldspar, mica, beryl, or lithium. Potash feldspar is important in glass, ceramic, and chemical industries. Mica is utilized in gypsum wallboard, roofing, cement, paint, oil well mud, and rubber industries. Rose Quartz, a pegmatite, is mined for decorative and collecting purposes. Pegmatite production is limited to Custer and Pennington counties.

115

GYPSUM

Gypsum is formed from calcium sulfate resulting from the evaporation of ancient sea water. It is mined in the Black Hills and is used as an ingredient at the State Cement Plant at Rapid City.

SALT

Halite, or salt, has been important since people first occupied the land. Salt deposits have been found in South Dakota in Brown, Butte, Harding, and Spink counties. While deposits exist, they are of no commercial importance at this time.

GEM STONES

In recent years, one of the fastest growing segments of South Dakota's mineral industries has been gem stones. Production, demand, and value have been increasing virtually every year. While production value and quantity are relatively small in comparison to other minerals, gem stones are mined for collectors, jewelers, and others.

Gem Andalusite, a metamorphic rock found in the Black Hills, is the only known deposit in the United States. Agates, barite, chalcedony, jasper, staurolite, garnet, and petrified wood are collected as gem stones. Igneous pegmatites sought by collectors are rose quartz, cat's eyes, spodumens, hiddemite, triphone, and amethyst.

MINERAL FUELS

Mineral fuels found in South Dakota include coal, uranium, petroleum, and natural gas. Uranium production was included with metallic minerals. While coal, petroleum, and natural gas are present in the state in large amounts, none of these fuels has been extensively developed. This is both a result of quality and quantity of the deposit and the lack of satisfactory economic reward for potential development.

COAL

Large portions of the northwestern corner of South Dakota are underlain by lignite coal deposits. In fact, these coal deposits underlie portions of seven counties: Butte, Corson, Dewey, Harding, Meade, Perkins, and Ziebach. Historically, small amounts of coal in Dewey and Corson counties have been strip mined.

Lignite is the lowest grade of coal. It is high in moisture content, burns poorly, and emits odors and smoke. Its greatest value is for coal-burning electrical generation plants. Neighboring coal fields in Wyoming and North Dakota are presently utilized for power generation. The state's lignite coal deposits are extensive and have development potential.

There is also a small deposit of better grade bituminous coal in Fall River County. Because of its size there is little potential for development.

PETROLEUM AND NATURAL GAS

The northwestern corner of South Dakota offers excellent mineral potential. This area is actually an extension of the Williston Basin of Montana and North Dakota. Oil and gas potentials in the South Dakota portion of the Basin have not been developed to the extent that they have in the neighboring states. However, the average South Dakotan is not very aware of the extent to which oil production is actively occurring in the northwestern corner of the state. Three other portions of the state have oil and gas potential. Two of the three are in the Black Hills and Bennett County. The Black Hills deposit is an extension of the Denver-Juleburg Basin. The Bennett County potential is part of the Kennedy Basin. The other potential area for oil and gas is in southeastern South Dakota where Iowa's Forest City Basin extends into Union and Clay counties.

Historically, several hundred wells have been drilled in South Dakota. The success rate for these oil and gas wells, however, has not been high in the state. Indeed, the success ratio is about eight times lower than the national average (1:43 vs. 1:5). It is important to note that most wells have not been drilled to the depth of those in the Williston Basin.

Petroleum production comes primarily from the Buffalo Oil Field in Harding County and the Baker Field along the border of Fall River and Custer counties. Natural gas production is minimal, coming primarily from the same two fields.

SUMMARY

The value of any mineral depends on demand. When gold was in great demand and its value was high, gold mining flourished in South Dakota. Now that the value is lower and the costs of extraction and finishing are higher, the oldest continuously operating gold mine in the United States ceased operation in 2001.

South Dakota has many other minerals besides gold. Whether and when extration of those minerals increases depends on extration costs, mineral value, environmental concerns, and demand for the mineral. As the role of gold in South Dakota's mineral economy diminishes, cement, sand and gravel, limestone, and other dimension stone will play increasingly important roles in the state's overall mineral economy.

Chapter Ten

INDUSTRIAL AND COMMERCIAL GEOGRAPHY OF SOUTH DAKOTA

INTRODUCTION

When one thinks of industry or commerce in South Dakota, the first thing that usually comes to mind is agriculture. This is because agriculture is the basis upon which the vast majority of South Dakota's industry and commerce is built. The importance of agriculture is evident everywhere one goes in the state. It begins with the planting of field crops and birth of livestock. It grows to harvest or market time, when crops are taken to the grain elevators and livestock to the stockyards.

Agriculture's importance does not end there. It is evident in mills, meat packing plants, and food processing plants. The importance is also evident commercially in the communities where one finds the implement dealers, the seed companies, vet supplies, and chemical dealers. Indeed the role of agriculture in the economy touches every business and service in the state. Losses in farm income result in closing and bankruptcies of businesses as well.

Agriculture is also the basis upon which South Dakota has built its economy. It has allowed or enabled the state to develop or attract other industries to its communities, industries that utilize the state's other resources or that assemble goods and parts from elsewhere. It is also the agricultural base that allowed some communities to establish "incubator" centers to nurture the growth of new industries.

THE LOCATIONAL FACTORS

With this in mind, what does South Dakota have to offer in terms of attracting and maintaining industry and commerce? Perhaps this can best be answered and understood geographically by examining the major and minor locational factors traditionally utilized in Economic Geography.

The first major factor to be examined is access to a labor supply. This is the most important locational factor in almost every industrial study. In the case of South Dakota, the state has a labor force totalling about 400,000 people. Of that total almost ten percent are employed in the manufacturing segment of the economy. Of the 30,000 plus industrial workers in the state about two-thirds are male and one-third are female.

In recent years, unemployment in South Dakota has consistently been below the five percent mark. This is partially due to the fact that the state has consistently lost population through out-migration to other areas. It is more recently a result of a growing economy in industry, commerce, and service areas.

South Dakota has a well-educated labor supply, with the average worker having had some college education. This is one of the higher levels of average education among the fifty states. In addition to the annual graduation of high school and college students, the state also has a solid vocational program that produces a yearly pool of skilled laborers.

Industrial salaries in South Dakota remain below the national average. This is despite the fact that food product workers significantly exceed the national average for that industry. The state also has one of the lowest work stoppage records in the nation. South Dakota workers have developed an excellent reputation for an honest day's work, loyalty, quality, and good health.

In recent years the state has made some significant progress in increasing the average wage paid to employees. Despite recent progress, most industrial and commercial salaries are still below national averages. This is a problem that will continue to be addressed in the years ahead, although salaries will remain a volatile political issue.

A second major locational factor is access to raw materials. South Dakota's raw materials are related to agriculture, mining, and forestry. The state is noted for its livestock industry and the production of crops. Historically, South Dakota was the major gold producer in the U.S. Today in addition some gold, it also produces silver, bentonite, stone, and some oil and natural gas. The forestry industry centers in the Black Hills and is based primarily on the ponderosa pine tree.

Access to transportation is a positive factor for South Dakota. The state has developed a good transportation system as a result of the needs of agriculture, mining, and tourism. South Dakota is served by two interstate highways, I-29, which runs north-south, and I-90, which runs east-west. The state's road system is comprised of 1,300 miles of cement roadway and 16,000 miles of bituminous road. It is served by 150 Class A point-to-point motor carriers, 2,000 Class B irregular route carriers, and 150 Class C contract carriers.

South Dakota is served by eight railroads: including the Dakota Minnesota & Eastern, Burlington Northern-Santa Fe, and the Dakota Southern. Railroads, along with trucking, provide the major means by which the state's bulky agricultural, mineral, and industrial products are shipped to market. The state also owns almost 1,000 miles of track that it purchased from the Milwaukee Road. The state-owned track has been upgraded to make it suitable for continued agricultural use and industrial expansion.

In 2001, air service to South Dakota extended to eight cities. Sioux Falls' Joe Foss Field and the Rapid City Regional Airport serve as gateway cities to the rest of the nation and world. Regularly scheduled feeder air service links the cities of Aberdeen, Brookings, Huron, Pierre, Watertown, and Yankton with major air terminals. There are also commercial aviation facilities and services and private plane services available at the nine larger airports and many smaller airports and air strips.

Access to markets from South Dakota is excellent, since the state is located near the geographic center of North America. South Dakota is essentially in a one-to-five-day reach of any major point in the country. Indeed many South Dakota products are available on a worldwide basis. The eastern half of the state is in the central time zone, which is attractive to businesses with relations on both coasts and in Europe.

South Dakota is in a very strong position relative to access to utilities. The state has access to large amounts of electrical power through the hydroelectric plants on the Missouri River, from steam-generating plants, and from thermal plants. Approximately 70 percent of the electricity comes from cooperatives and 30 percent from privately owned pro-

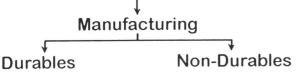

PRIMARY SECTOR
↓
Natural Resources

SECONDARY SECTOR
↓
Manufacturing

Durables   Non-Durables

TERTIARY SECTOR
↓
Retailing
Wholesaling
Transportation
Professions
Others

QUATERNARY SECTOR
↓
Financial Institutions
Higher Education
Research and Development
Specialized Medical Services

Figure 4.
The Sector Model.

ducers. Natural gas availability is limited to the extreme eastern and western parts of the state.

Access to water is an especially significant factor for the state. Currently, most of the water utilized for industry in the state is from ground water supplies. Quality and quantity available can vary greatly from place to place. The reservoirs on the Missouri and other surface waters offer excellent potential for industrial development.

Access to capital for potential development is readily available in South Dakota. The state has taken a very progressive step in assisting industry with capital needs. The Governor's Office of Economic Development has assembled development programs that enhance industrial growth through financing, employee training, marketing and promotion. Additionally, communities can utilize revenue bonds, tax breaks, and other programs to assist development efforts. Most of the larger communities in the state and many of the smaller towns have developed programs to encourage or actively seek industrial development.

The state's excellent education system provides access to management personnel. Many industries like to locate in college communities and utilize students as management trainees. University communities also tend to attract industries that seek some research assistance or a part-time labor supply that is highly educated.

One of South Dakota's greatest industrial assets is access to a tremendous variety of sites. Statewide, there are almost 150 development corporations that can provide industrial sites for virtually any industry. Local industrial groups and the state government are available to assist in site selection. Some developers have speculative buildings ready for occupancy. Industrial sites can range from a small building on Main Street to a major industrial park. The state's larger communities can offer industrial sites that can compete with developments across the United States.

South Dakota also has become an attractive site for manufacturing because of its taxes, or rather, lack of taxes. The state has no corporate income tax, no personal income tax, no personal property tax, and no business inventory tax. It also has among the lowest worker's compensation and unemployment insurance costs in the country. In addition to all these tax incentives, the local real property taxes range from only one percent to four percent, with a five-year tax abatement available to certain developments.

Other locational factors that should be noted about South Dakota are the state's and communities' excellent recreational opportunities and facilities; the very favorable tax structure; the many fine communities, schools, and hospitals; and the four-season climate.

THE SECTOR MODEL

Industrial and commercial development of South Dakota can best be seen by utilizing the sector model to present an overview of economic progress in the state. The sector model examines the state's development in the primary sector, the secondary sector, the tertiary sector, and the quaternary sector (Figure 4).

THE PRIMARY SECTOR

Industrial and commercial development in the primary sector includes those activities directly concerned with the collection and utilization of natural resources. Examples of primary sector economic activities include agriculture, collecting, hunting, mining, and related areas.

Historically, the development of the state utilizing the sector model approach can be said to begin with the collecting and hunting activities of the Paleo-Indian. It continued through the occupance of the Arikaras, Sioux, and European and American fur trappers. Indeed fur trapping is still an actively pursued industry in South Dakota.

The most important primary sector activity today, of course, is agriculture. This activity can again be traced back to the Arikara and Sioux peoples. American homesteaders and European immigrants settled the land, bringing with them agricultural practices and adapting them to the environment and the environment to them. Over time, farming and ranching developed into the most important economic activities in the state, forming the backbone of the state's economy.

In 1874, gold was discovered in the Black Hills. As the prospectors' placers played out, professional mining took over. For 124 years this was best symbolized by the Homestake Mine in Lead. With the closing of the Homestake shaft mine, only the Wharf open-pit gold-mine will be operational. Other primary activities in mining and quarrying include sand and gravel pits in almost every county in the state; limestone in the Black Hills, used for cement and agricultural lime; dimension stone such as the world-famous Milbank granite, marketed on every continent; silver and some rare pegmatite minerals in the Hills; and oil and natural gas production, occurring on a limited scale in select West River areas.

Lumbering is another primary sector activity that has become increasingly important. The Black Hills region has about three times more trees today than when Custer arrived there in 1874. Because of excellent forestry methods, this region today has a growing forestry economy that can operate for years to come while practicing sustained-yield forestry. Unfortunately, in the summer of 2000, the deliberately set Jasper Fire burned over 83,000 acres in the Black Hills.

THE SECONDARY SECTOR

Industrial and commercial development in the secondary sector is concerned with the processing of primary resources into usable goods. Secondary industries utilize not only the primary goods from the local area, but also primary and secondary goods from other regions in producing new products. This sector is generally referred to as manufacturing.

Manufacturing results in the production of a full range of goods. A distinction generally is drawn between durable and non-durable goods:

1. Non-durables can be thought of as subsistence goods such as food and drink.
2. Durables include more lasting products which are purchased less frequently.

In South Dakota, manufacturing employment is almost evenly split between durable and non-durable manufacturing.

The most important single industry in the state is in the non-durables category, namely meat packing. Almost one of every six manufacturing workers in South Dakota is employed in meat packing. John Morrell & Company is the state's largest meat packing plant and largest industrial employer with almost 2,500 workers. It is located in Sioux Falls. Other large packing plants are located in Huron, Rapid City, Mitchell, and Yankton.

Meat packing is the largest industrial employer in South Dakota.

This industry slaughters approximately 3 million hogs, 650,000 cattle, and 400,000 sheep and lambs yearly. Poultry plants in Watertown and Sisseton process turkeys, geese, and ducks.

Other secondary industries directly related to agriculture are numerous. Among the more important industries are large milk, cheese, and butter producing plants at Sioux Falls, Milbank, Big Stone City, Rapid City, and Sisseton. In recent years, frozen potato products, namely French fry, and a "Dakota Style" potato chip industries have developed at Clark. Rapid City and Aberdeen have major grain milling facilities. South Dakota also has major bakeries at Sioux Falls and North Sioux City. In fact, the cookie factory in North Sioux City is one of the largest chocolate cookie manufacturing facilities in the world. Rapid City, Aberdeen, Sioux Falls, and Huron are major beverage and bottling centers, primarily for soft drinks.

The state also produces a variety of textile products. Perhaps the most famous are the hot air balloons manufactured by Raven Industries in Sioux Falls. South Dakota has also become nationally known for quality bedding, which is sewn at Webster and Flandreau. Clothing is manufactured in Sioux Falls, Watertown, Freeman and Parkston.

The primary forest industry of the Black Hills provides materials for both secondary non-durable and durable manufacturing. Logging companies, sawmills and planing mills are concentrated in the Hills at Spearfish, Hill City, Custer, Whitewood, Sturgis, Piedmont, and nearby Belle Fourche. Other durable wood industries include milling, moldings, and doors at Sioux Falls; cabinets at Tea; and structural wood products in Sioux Falls and Rapid City, and wooden play systems in Brookings.

Non-durable wood products produced in South Dakota are related to pulp, paper, and printing. A pulp mill utilizing flax operates in Watertown. Paper bags and cardboard boxes are manufactured in Sioux Falls. However, the largest nondurable wood products industries are related to printing and newspapers. These two industries are found statewide in virtually any larger community or county seat. A total of 2,800 people are employed in printing and 1,700 more in newspaper publishing. The greatest concentration of these people are in Sioux Falls and Rapid City.

The non-durable chemical industry is concentrated in Mitchell where toner products are produced and in Freeman where serums and veterinary vaccines are made. Fabricated rubber products are manufactured in Watertown and Aberdeen, while plastic products are made in Huron, Brookings, and Sioux Falls. The durable paving industry is concentrated in Sioux Falls and Rapid City with concrete companies and in Mitchell with an asphalt specialty.

In recent years, South Dakota has experienced an increase in durable metal products industries. Iron castings are made in Aberdeen and Brookings. Aluminum extrusions are shaped in Yankton. Aluminum storm doors and windows are manufactured in Brookings. Metal shelving is produced in Brookings, and fabricated steel is manufactured in Sioux Falls. The metals industries today employ over 2,500 people in the state.

South Dakota also produces a variety of machinery and related products. Farm machinery is produced in Sioux Falls, Aberdeen, Madison, and Salem. Hoists are made in Watertown and Yankton. Machine tools are manufactured in Aberdeen and Philip. Industrial gears are produced in Aberdeen and metal-working machinery in Watertown. General machinery is manufactured in Elk Point, Alcester, Colton, Madison, and Sioux Falls.

The largest single employer in South Dakota is Gateway Companies with over 6,700 employees in North Sioux City and Sioux Falls. Gateway is one of the largest computer manufactures in the world. Other electrical products and related equipment manufacturing include electronic products in Sioux Falls; satellite receivers in Rapid City; scoreboards and message boards in Brookings; transformers in Colman; heating and cooling equipment in Canton and Watertown; Audio Transformers in Watertown and Huron and semiconductors in Aberdeen, Rapid City, and Watertown.

Transportation products produced in the state are truck bodies and trailers in Watertown, Mitchell, Elk Point, and Sioux Falls; and fire trucks and truck assessories in Brandon. Major national hardware companies have warehouses located in Brookings and Milbank, which serve large areas of the country.

Other industries significant to South Dakota include: computer equipment in Mitchell; medical products in Brookings and Aberdeen; sporting goods in Tabor, Mitchell, and Wanblee; and jewelry in Rapid City, Deadwood, Hill City, Lemmon, and Sturgis.

Industrial development in South Dakota did not just happen, it is primarily the result of individual efforts. Many of these efforts occurred at different intervals and places in the state's historical development. Local inventors, entrepreneurs, and industrialists saw needs and developed manufacturing facilities to address them. Consequently, a community might have a particular industry which seems to be located there without reason. The reason is primarily that the industrialists selected that community in which to live and work.

Modern industrial locational decisions are often made by professional site selectors who work for a company seeking a community in which to locate a manufacturing facility. The site selector, through an elimination process, provides the manufacturer with a professional recommendation as to where he or she believes the new facility would be the most successful.

Competition for new industry is very keen. In a given year in the United States, there are about 1,200 major industrial expansions. There are over 35,000 communities in the country seeking to attract new industry. Not only are Sioux Falls and Aberdeen competing with Blunt and Kadoka but also with Chicago and San Diego. For this reason the most successful communities have a well-organized and professionally staffed industrial development office and program. The results of such programs are evident in recent industrial expansions in Sioux Falls, North Sioux City, Watertown, Aberdeen, Brookings Huron, and Rapid City.

The potential for further industrial development in South Dakota is excellent. The state has a well-educated labor force with a solid national reputation. The state government has established an impressive economic development fund to stimulate growth. State and community leaders are working with industry, education, and financial institutions to assist in further industrial growth.

THE TERTIARY SECTOR

South Dakota also has experienced significant change in the tertiary and quaternary sectors. The tertiary sector is the distributive component of the economy. It includes retailing, wholesaling, transportation, and the professions. Changes in these areas tend to reflect a greater movement and concentration in the larger communities. Retail growth has become especially notable in Sioux Falls and Rapid City with the development of the major malls. Other large communities have witnessed the growth of smaller malls and the revitalization of Main Streets. Two truly unique retail operations that have had major economic impacts on their communities are Wall Drug in Wall and Cabela's in Mitchell. Unfortunately, at the same time, many of the smaller communities have lost businesses and services to the larger cities and towns.

THE QUATERNARY SECTOR

The quaternary sector also reflects the growth of the personal services industry. Here are the services that require high skill or educational levels. It includes financial institutions, higher education, research and development, and specialized medical services. The state has also experienced extensive growth in the areas of Customer Service, Telemarketing, and Telecommunications. South Dakota has become nationally famous for its banking and insurance laws. These laws have stimulated the location of major national and regional credit card and insurance facilities in the state. The largest of these is the Citibank operation in Sioux Falls. Citibank of South Dakota has over 3,000 employees. Sioux Valley Hospital with over 3,500 employees is the state's single largest service employer outside of government or the military.

Higher education continues to be a major emphasis in the state. The public and private institutions are strong and deliver quality educations to their students. Corporate and community research and development efforts are expanding in the state. Among the newest innovation in this area is the Industrial Incubator Center in Brookings. Medical specialists and related facilities are becoming increasingly concentrated in Sioux Falls, Rapid City, Aberdeen, and Yankton. In fact, one out of every eight jobs in Sioux Falls is now related to medical services.

CONCLUSION

All in all, South Dakota has experienced great progress over the last twenty-five years in all four economic development sectors. State government, operating primarily through the Governor's Office of Economic Development, is actively pursuing further industrial and commercial development in all sectors. With the statewide and community efforts that are being made to enhance economic development at all levels, there is good reason to expect continued industrial and commercial expansion in South Dakota's future.

One of the principal goals of all these efforts is to bring greater variety to the industrial and commercial development of the state. South Dakota realizes that it can no longer operate like the mythical farmer with all his eggs in one basket. Just as the American farmer has needed to diversify in order to survive and grow, so too must South Dakota's industrial and commercial development. The diversification of manufacturing and commerce will provide the state with protection from recession, greater opportunities for new ideas and development, and higher wages for employees as there becomes greater demand for laborers in the work place.

Chapter Eleven
TOURISM AND RECREATION

INTRODUCTION

Tourism and recreation are among the fastest growing segments of the economic geography of South Dakota. It is estimated that seven percent of the state's work force is employed in tourism. Tourism and recreation are important to South Dakota because:

1. They provide pleasure and activities for the people of South Dakota.
2. They attract out-of-state visitors who bring additional revenue to the communities and state.

Tourism has been important to South Dakota for some time. In fact, South Dakota is one of the few states that can identify its first tourist. In South Dakota history, it is record-

The Sturgis Motorcycle Rally attracts as many as 500,000 visitors from around the world to this annual summer event. Courtesy Edward P. Hogan.

ed that in 1811, Henry M. Brackenridge, a Pittsburgh lawyer, visited present-day South Dakota and was shown the area by Manuel Lisa, the famous fur trader. South Dakota hosted other early visitors including naturalist John J. Audubon, adventurer Prince Maximilian of Wied, and artists Karl Bodmer and George Catlin.

LEISURE TIME AND WEALTH

In order to understand the increasing importance of tourism and recreation, it is helpful to understand the nature of "leisure." If one were to take a normal, twenty-four-hour weekday, a day's time essentially would be divided into three parts: biological time—to sleep, eat, and perform other natural functions; subsistence time—to work, go to school, or engage in other responsibilities; and free time—or leisure time. It is leisure time that is becoming an increasingly important part of everyone's lives.

Leisure time can consist of many things. It may be engaging in a hobby, reading, watching TV, playing softball, or traveling around the world or just across town to see friends. Everyone seems to have his or her own definition of the nature of leisure time. It is important for people to realize that leisure is not a block of time but rather a use of time.

An understanding of free time helps one to understand its growing importance. For centuries, leisure was only for the wealthy. The poor labored long and hard just to survive. With the Industrial Revolution came a spreading of wealth. Over time, people's attitudes moved away from the Protestant ethic that all work was good. With that change came a demand for leisure among the middle class. Today, some people see leisure as being as valuable as money. This is a tremendous change in attitude and ethic.

In America today, workers normally have a five-day work week, generally eight hours a day or less in length. In some jobs employees are using flex time and working four-day weeks with ten-hour work days. Today, the average worker has fifty-two two-day weekends a year, plus ten to thirty days of paid vacation, and eight to fourteen paid holidays. This means that out of a 365 day year, one works from 217 to 243 days a year and is off 122 to 148 days. In other words, some people are off work forty percent of the year.

With growth of the middle class in America and other countries came a spreading of wealth. As one's standard of living increased people demanded more food, good entertainment, and recreation. With the increase in wealth also came a greater ability to travel. Wealth and technology gave people even greater mobility for work and leisure.

As people's wealth increased, more money became available to spend. When this wealth was combined with paid vacations it resulted in more travel. This is especially true over the last thirty-five years during which the number of leisure-time travelers has skyrocketed.

Income, age, and occupation also play vital roles in travel. Generally the higher one's income, the more he or she travels. Studies also show that most people travel as families and that most travelers are under thirty years of age. The next largest group of travelers are people between forty-five and fifty-four years of age. Unfortunately, the older people get, the more likely health problems will interfere with travel. For this reason, people over sixty-five years of age are the least likely to travel. Blue collar employees travel in a larger percentage than any other group. White collar professionals take far more trips per person and actually dominate travel by occupation. Most travel done by professionals is a result of business or business and pleasure combined.

THE GEOGRAPHY OF TOURISM AND RECREATION

In examining the geography of tourism and recreation in South Dakota, it is important to remember the state's character and relative location. It is the extensive physical and cultural diversity of South Dakota that makes the state "Great Places, Great Faces."

Geographically, it also is important to appreciate the relative location of South Dakota. Relative location is related to tourism and recreation in regard to proximity, time, costs, and accessibility to other areas. It affects the number of visitors to South Dakota in that most tourists travel near home. This is illustrated by a comparison of the tremendous numbers of people who travel the Blue Ridge Parkway in the Eastern United States, versus the number who visit *Mount Rushmore.* Blue Ridge Parkway attracts far more visitors because the number of people living near that location is so much greater.

Time affects location of travel in that people must travel during the block of time available to them. Thus, two- or three-day weekends keep people closer to home, while three-week vacations allow them to travel a greater distance. Costs show similar patterns. Normally trips or vacations to nearby locations are less expensive than long trips.

Geographically, it is known that a concentration of attractions, activities, and events will lure larger numbers of people. This is because the force of locational concentration affords visitors more attractions to choose from. This is evident in the spinoff effect generated in Florida by Disney World, followed by Busch Gardens in Tampa, the Epcot Center near Orlando, Universal Studios, and hundreds of other attractions and service and support functions. It is also evident in South Dakota with *Mount Rushmore,* Custer State

Bear Butte at the northern edge of the Black Hills is a center of Native American spiritual traditions.

Park, Keystone attractions, Flintstone Bedrock City, Deadwood gambling, and many more attractions in the Black Hills area.

Location is also important to the perceptions of tourists. People develop mental images and mental maps of places. These images and maps may or may not be true. What are people's mental images and maps of South Dakota? How accurate are they? By and large, the American people possess a rather meager level of geographical awareness. Some people cannot tell the difference between South Dakota and South Carolina. Remember, too, that South Dakotans may be the only people in the country that call their capital city "Peer" instead of the French pronunciation of "Pierre."

Where people vacation often varies depending upon income, age, education, career, and geographical origin. People are also influenced in their travel decisions by their employer, by state tourist bureaus, and by tour operators and travel agents.

South Dakota receives tourists from every state and virtually every country each year. This amazing fact is documented by registration records at major attractions. Geographically, because of relative location the typical visitor to South Dakota comes from nearby states. This may vary a bit from fall to summer.

Year round, the largest number of out-of-state visitors to South Dakota are from neighboring Minnesota. Other major sources of our visitors are Iowa, Wisconsin, Illinois, Nebraska, Missouri, Michigan, and North Dakota. The only state that is distant, yet sends large numbers of visitors, is California. That large number results from the mobility of California's population. Ohio and Washington are also major providers of tourists to South Dakota.

The out-of-state visitor to South Dakota is here for vacation, recreation, business, or to visit family, friends, or an old home town. Recent data indicate that tourism generates over $1.2 billion in economic activities each year and employs over 30,000 people. It should be noted that almost forty percent of the states do over $2 billion a year each in tourist revenue. It is important to realize that despite tourism's overall importance to the state's economy, South Dakota ranks forty-ninth in tourist expenditures. Despite on-going improvements, South Dakota has outstanding tourism potential and challenges.

While tourism alone is important, it is only one segment of the total economic impact of tourism and recreation on the South Dakota economy. Combined, the impact of tourism and recreation on the Gross State Product exceeds $3.0 billion a year. This total includes not only the impact of out-of-state visitors and tourism, but also gaming, sports, recreational activities, the arts, other cultural attractions, and various support services.

THE ECONOMIC GEOGRAPHY OF TOURISM

As a result of major efforts of the Governor's Office of Economic Development, South Dakota is learning more and more about its out-of-state visitors each year. It is known that almost 6,500,000 tourists visit the state each year. For example, about sixty percent of the tourists to South Dakota have attended college. Almost fifty percent have incomes of over $60,000 a year. Over three-fifths of them are under fifty-five years of age. They travel in parties that average 3.2 people. Two-thirds of the travel parties today have no children in the group.

The major expenditures of visitors are for entertainment and retailing, food and beverages, automobile and traveling, and lodging. In recent years, entertainment and retailing have become increasingly important as tourist activities, replacing food and beverages as the major expenditures. Approximately thirty percent of the tourist dollar is spent on entertainment and retailing. About twenty-seven percent goes to food and beverages and another twenty-five percent to automobile and traveling. The remainder is spent on lodging.

While in South Dakota, the average tourist party spends about $145 a day. Normally, the visitors spend four days in South Dakota. This indicates that the state is developing more tourist attractions that keep visitors here for longer periods of time and thus increase the impact of tourism on the economy.

Where does the tourist's travel dollar go? Over seventy percent goes for the costs of goods and services. About twenty percent pays the salaries and wages of people employed in tourism and recreation. The remainder goes toward tax collections of various government agencies. In South Dakota tourism generates over $19,000,000 a year in gasoline taxes. It provides over five percent of the state's total sales tax collections and also supports local sales tax collections.

The impact of tourism is strong and growing in importance for a state with South Dakota's light population and geographic position. Tourism directly generates over 30,000 jobs. This is about 7.2 percent of all the jobs in South Dakota. Separate from tourism, an additional 8,000 jobs are related to gambling. This means that gaming accounts for about 2.0 percent of all jobs in South Dakota. About three-fourths of the gaming jobs include other business activities and responsibilities.

PUSH-PULL FACTORS

Tourism and recreation, like other migrations, are subject to push-pull effects. A number of social, cultural, economic, and geographic factors motivate one to travel. Thus, tourism is a result of push, deterrents, and pull phenomena.

PUSH FACTORS

Push factors are those that motivate one to travel. Scientists have identified a large number of such factors. However, most believe that self preservation is the principal factor. People today perceive a need to get away, to relax, to follow the sun. At the same time they carry with them a spirit of adventure seeking the excitement of the new and unknown. Travel also brings the traveler esteem and envy from neighbors, friends, and fellow workers.

Push factors include curiosity of visiting other places or cultures; attending or participating in sporting activities and events; pleasure seeking through art, entertainment, and gambling; professional travel to conventions, field research, or school; personal factors such as seeking one's roots or visiting family and friends; and physical and mental health.

DETERRENTS TO TRAVEL

Deterrents to travel can include poor health, family problems, a lack of time, security, and a lack of money. Health is a significant deterrent to travel among the elderly and the ill. It is also somewhat of a deterrent to the handicapped. Family problems can also deter travel. When these problems exist, travel is reduced. A fear of the unknown is another deterrent. Finally, it is difficult to travel today without significant funds or credit. People who cannot afford to travel defer their vacations.

PULL FACTORS

Push and deterrent factors come together in an examination of pull factors influencing the geography of South Dakota's tourism and recreation industry. Pull factors are geographical assets that lure the visitors or keep residents at home. Tourism and recreation areas must be accessible to the public. In the case of South Dakota, much of our state's accessibility is tied to the Interstate Highway System. Both I-90 and I-29 are primary arteries for tourists. They also serve as primary routes for local residents who want to shop, see a game, or attend a concert in Sioux Falls, Rapid City, or other cities along these routes.

Sioux Falls, Rapid City, Aberdeen, and other cities also are accessible by airline service. These three cities, in particular, have been successful in attracting conventions and other visitors by air. The amenities needed and desired by visitors and local residents include restaurants; hotels, motels, and convention facilities; theaters, arenas, shopping centers and districts, and theme parks.

TOURISM, RECREATIONAL ATTRACTIONS, AND ACTIVITIES

South Dakota's physical environment plays a vital role in attracting visitors and retaining resident tourists. The primary tourist attraction in South Dakota is the Black Hills. This unique miniature version of the Rocky Mountains affords the viewer a unique variety of landforms in a relatively small area. In the Black Hills visitors can see the granite peaks, the Red Valley, and spectacular landforms such as Spearfish Canyon, and Bear Butte. The Needles offer a rare geologic formation with rocks standing like pencils from their bases. Wind Cave National Park is the eighth longest known cave in the world containing thirty-four miles of passageways. Jewel Cave National Monument is even larger, being the third largest known cave in the world and extending underground over sixty-nine miles.

Other physical attractions include the Badlands National Park covering almost 250,000 acres of western South Dakota. This unique landscape of colored layers of ash and sand is one of the most photographed areas in the country. Sica Hollow, a state park in northeastern South Dakota, is a land of Indian legends and eerie natural phenomena including "swamp gas." Petrified Wood Park near Lemmon contains fossilized logs of the geologic past. Slim Buttes and Cave Hills in the northwestern corner of the state offer other unique areas of geographic beauty. Indeed there are many people who appreciate the subtle beauty of prairies and river valleys that make up the bulk of the state's geography.

The Great Lakes of South Dakota and other water bodies are also important recreation and tourist areas. Lake Oahe north of Pierre, Lake Sharpe, Lake Francis Case, and Lewis and Clark Lake, their dams and the Missouri River are all major recreation and tourist stops. In fact, Gavins Point is one of the busiest attractions in the state. Other lakes attract cabin owners, travelers, fishermen, boaters, skiers, and sightseers. Among the more popular are Big Stone and Lake Traverse, Lake Poinsett, Roy Lake, Oakwood Lake, Sylvan Lake, and Legion Lake.

Geographically, the diversity of vegetation also is appealing to the sightseer. The eastern prairies and farmlands, steppe vegetation of the west, and forests of the Black Hills are all of interest. Vegetation types also have become increasingly important in cities and towns. Among the most notable are the nationally acclaimed McCrory Gardens in Brookings and the Japanese Gardens in Sioux Falls.

One final portion of the physical environment that must be considered is the climate. The state has four well-defined seasons. As a result, it is able to offer resident and visitor alike a tremendous variety of outdoor activities and challenges. Climate allows for downhill and cross-country skiing. It provides sunny days for bathers and windy days for sailors.

The state's abundant wildlife contributes to recreation and tourism through both observation and participation activities. The observation of various wildlife species is of increasing interest to the public. Observable wildlife includes the famous buffalo herds, prairie dog towns, pheasants along the roadside, fish jumping in the lakes, and Canadian geese migrating north in great waves.

South Dakota is an excellent fishing area. The great lakes along the Missouri River have attracted thousands of fishermen annually with excellent walleye, northern pike, and now salmon. Bass and catfish are also caught. The Black Hills has good trout fishing, while in the glacial lakes of eastern South Dakota, walleye, northern pike, and panfish abound.

Hunting in the state is diversified, yet is almost synonymous with pheasants. The beautiful ringneck pheasant, the state bird, is the most popular upland game in the state. Each fall, thousands of hunters take to the fields in search of this elusive bird. Sharp tailed grouse and prairie chickens are hunted in the west and south respectively. Waterfowl hunting is concentrated around the lakes and sloughs of the east and along the Missouri River.

The Mammoth Site near Hot Springs is one of the state's major archaeological attractions.

Sylvan Lake in Custer State Park typifies the unique scenery of the Black Hills.

Particularly popular are mallard ducks in the east and Canadian geese along the Missouri. Big game hunting consists primarily of deer, antelope, and very limited buffalo hunting.

The cultural environment also plays a vital role in the state's tourism and recreation activities. It is reflected in archaeological sites, historical areas, museums, government, education, religion, cultural traditions, and entertainment and sports.

South Dakota has a number of significant archaeological attractions. They range from dinosaur remains in the Black Hills to the famous mammoth site near Hot Springs, and to Arikara sites along the Missouri River.

Historical sites and buildings are numerous. The most famous, of course, is *Mount Rushmore*, the nation's "Shrine to Democracy." This national memorial is the world's most famous mountain sculpture. It features the faces of presidents Washington, Jefferson, Teddy Roosevelt, and Lincoln. It is recognized all over the world and is the state's most well-known feature. Another famous historical feature is the city of Deadwood, home of the gold rush in South Dakota history. Deadwood was famous also for Wild Bill Hickok, Calamity Jane, and all the other colorful people and events of gold mining history. Deadwood has been experiencing a second gold rush with the incredible growth resulting from the legalization of gambling in that community.

The state contains numerous historic buildings. These include family homes, churches, commercial structures, and governmental buildings. They are widely distributed across the state. Perhaps the most famous are in Sioux Falls, Watertown, Pierre, Yankton, and other larger towns. However, virtually every city and town in the state contains one or more his-

The gaming industry has become a major economic player in Deadwood, on the Indian reservations, and through the state-operated video lottery.

toric structures. Some of these have also been converted into museums or art galleries. Especially interesting are the Pettigrew House and Museum located in Sioux Falls and the Adams Museum in Deadwood. Among the major historical and cultural museums in the state are the Cultural Heritage Center in Pierre, the Agricultural Heritage Museum and South Dakota Art Museum in Brookings, the Shrine to Music Museum and W. H. Over Museum in Vermillion, the Siouxland Heritage Museums, Center for Western Studies, and Civic Fine Arts Center in Sioux Falls, the Friends of the Middle Border Museum and the Oscar Howe Art Center in Mitchell, the Dacotah Prairie Museum in Aberdeen, the Heritage Center at Pine Ridge Indian Reservation, the Akta Lakota Museum in Chamberlain, the Kampeska Heritage Museum in Watertown, the Museum of Geology and the Minnilusa Pioneer and Sioux Indian Museum in Rapid City, and the Dakota Territiorial Museum in Yankton.

South Dakota offers a variety of other cultural attractions. Hutterite colonies in the eastern portion of the state and Indian reservations in the west provide the observer with a view of two unique cultural landscapes. The beautiful state capitol building in Pierre; the tail fins of B-52 bombers visible as one drives past Ellsworth Air Force Base; and the campuses of the state's many fine colleges and universities are further examples of cultural attractions. South Dakota is also a land of churches. A drive through the countryside offers views of scenic church after church.

The state is also a center for cultural traditions. They range from such events as Czech Days at Tabor, to the Schmeckfest at Freeman, to St. Patrick's Day in Sioux Falls. Increasingly important are arts festivals such as the nationally famous Summer Arts Festival in

Mount Rushmore, the "Shrine to Democracy," is the most popular tourist attraction in South Dakota.

Brookings and Northern Plains Tribal Arts Festival in Sioux Falls. These festivals feature local and regional artists, handicrafts, music and dance, and foods.

Entertainment also is a major portion of tourism and recreation in South Dakota. Perhaps the most popular entertainment is shopping. For many people entertainment means dining out at one of the many restaurants in the state. Night life and night clubs are clustered in larger cities as are theaters and cinemas. The State Video Lottery is also a popular pastime in restaurants and bars.

The addition of legalized gaming in Deadwood and selected Indian Reservations has been extremely well received by tourists and South Dakotans alike. It is having an extremely significant impact on those areas' economies and development. In fact, the amount of money bet in Deadwood alone in a year exceeds the dollars expended by out-of-state tourists.

Other major entertainment activities include down-hill ski slopes at Terry Peak in the Black Hills and at Great Bear outside Sioux Falls, Flintstone Bedrock City amusement park in Custer, and Story Book Island in Rapid City. As nice as these and similar developments are, they are dwarfed in importance by the Corn Palace in Mitchell and the world famous Wall Drug in Wall. These unique entertainment features are two of the most important and famous attractions in South Dakota. The "World's only Corn Palace" features Byzantine towers and exterior murals of corn and grain. It attracts hundreds of thousands of visitors yearly. Wall Drug near the Badlands became world famous from its "Free Ice

The Corn Palace in Mitchell is a major tourist attraction. The exterior murals and decorations change yearly.

Water" and "See Wall Drug" signs that have found their way all over the world. Today it is the world's largest drugstore and a very popular tourist spot.

Sports are another major part of our state's recreation and tourism industries. Statewide, the most popular sporting events are at the high school level. The annual basketball championships are major rituals in South Dakota. The many colleges and universities also afford major sporting events to the residents and visitors. This is especially true during homecomings such as Hobo Day and Viking Days. Amateur sports include baseball, softball, soccer, hockey, and swimming.

The state occasionally attracts professional events such as golf tournaments, exhibition football, the Globetrotters, and boxing. Sioux Falls is the home of minor league basketball and baseball teams, an arena football team, and a US Hockey League team. Most of the larger cities and towns have well-developed city recreation programs. These programs may include golf, swimming pools, ball fields, hockey, tennis courts, horseshoes, and numerous other sport and recreational activities.

The people of South Dakota love outdoor recreation, especially in the summer months, and take full advantage of the many opportunities that occur. This is most evident on the lakes and rivers of the state. The state has the largest number of boats per capita in the nation. Almost everyone fishes, swims, or water skis. Outdoor recreation is no longer limited to good weather. Recent years have seen tremendous growth in outdoor winter recreation. Fish houses dot the frozen lakes, and snowmobile tracks parallel most roads in open country.

"Free Ice Water" signs advertising this unique tourist oasis can be found around the world. Wall Drug symbolizes the people of South Dakota's belief in entrepreneurship.

Studies of out-of-state visitors and in-state residents regarding tourist and recreational activities present a rather clear picture of what people prefer. By far the most popular leisure activity is driving for pleasure. Studies of visitors indicate that the highlight of their trip to South Dakota is generally seeing the Black Hills, especially *Mount Rushmore*. Other favorite tourist attractions are the Badlands; good roads; the lakes; the Needles; wildlife; the Black Hills Passion Play at Spearfish; the caves; the Corn Palace; Deadwood; *Crazy Horse Memorial* at Custer; and Wall Drug.

Major recreation activities of South Dakotans in addition to driving are fishing, attending sporting events, and swimming. Other favorites include picnicking, horseback riding, hunting, hiking, boating, camping, tennis, bicycling, and all types of skiing.

CONCLUSION

The geographic wealth of South Dakota is reflected once again in the state's tourism and recreational activities. The physical and cultural geography of the state have produced an abundance of tourism and recreational activities and areas. The state is well prepared to benefit from the increasing amounts of leisure time that are believed to lie ahead. South Dakota's location is such that with increased investment and creativity, it will play a much more vital role in the geography of America's tourism and recreation.

Chapter Twelve
TRANSPORTATION AND UTILITIES

The people of South Dakota benefit from well-developed and extensive transportation and utility infrastructures. It is said that South Dakotans are among the world's most mobile people. At the same time, they have access to an outstanding utility system. Both of these infrastructures offer people outstanding potential for future development.

The state's transportation system developed over time. There is evidence of early Indian or fur-trading trails crossing portions of present-day South Dakota. A map by William De L'Isle indicated that in 1701 a trail extended from the Mississippi River westward to the Falls of the Big Sioux River. Later, as Anglo-American occupance began, new trails were developed. They were planned and constructed to enable emigrants to reach the new lands in the Dakotas and other areas or for miners to reach the various gold fields in the West.

The roads that were constructed following settlement primarily paralleled railroad tracks and rivers or connected towns. Later roads were based on the congressional townships of the United States Land Survey. With that survey as the basis, the state was divided

The South Dakota Department of Transportation has utilized long-range planning to develop an extensive transportation infrastructure. South Dakotans are among the world's most mobile people.

by meridians and base lines into townships and ranges. The division lines in turn were developed into the township road system that criss-crosses the state.

The arrival of the Dakota Southern Railroad in 1873 was to provide the state with the principal means of passenger and product movement of several generations. Over 4,500 miles of rail were laid in the state. Unfortunately, the end of passenger service and railroad abandonment have dramatically reduced that figure in recent years. In fact, the automobile is credited with causing the first abandonment of 350 miles of track in South Dakota as early as 1928.

Evidence of rail line abandonment is present across the state. One need not look far across the landscape to see the graded areas that once served as rail bed. Other evidence includes grain elevators stranded like isolated islands with a sea of grass where iron rails once ran. Abandoned rail beds also serve as snowmobile trails, hiking paths, and farm roads.

With the invention of the horseless carriage at the turn of the twentieth century, South Dakota entered the automobile age. Indeed, in some communities, local inventors and mechanics labored hard, but unsuccessfully, to develop an early automobile industry in the state. With the automobile and truck came the need for highways. Highways in turn enabled farmers and ranchers to bring more of their products to markets. They also opened the state to more tourists.

In the early 1900s, South Dakota residents were able to work on road construction in lieu of paying taxes. The system changed and in 1916 the state's constitution was amended to allow the state to construct roads. There were no gravel roads in South Dakota until 1921, and no concrete roads until 1923. The state's first concrete road extended from Dell Rapids to Sioux Falls.

Over the years, the road system was upgraded adding more and more hard-surfaced roads. The road system was further enhanced by the development of the Interstate Highway System. The Interstate System was approved by Congress in 1956 primarily for defense purposes. However, it was only a matter of time until farmers, truckers, shoppers, tourists and pleasure drivers discovered these excellent roads.

The decline of the railroad closely corresponded with the arrival and growth of commercial airlines. It was further enhanced by the construction of some excellent landing fields and airbases during World War II when several South Dakota cities were utilized as Army Air Corps training stations. By 1970, over seventy-five approved airports had been built in the state. Commercial airlines, regional carriers, and charter services are available at several airports. Private aircraft utilize the other facilities.

South Dakota has been a leader in efforts to achieve sufficient power supplies. Efforts have ranged from individual attempts to design the first successful "perpetual motion machine," to Progressive Era calls for damming the Missouri River for power generation, to Pathfinder, one of the United States' first nuclear power plants. Historically, it has also utilized some natural gas wells in isolated areas to heat individual buildings or to fuel the perpetual flame in Capitol Lake.

Geographically, an understanding of the state's present transportation and utility systems provides a basis for understanding today's economic activities and for planning tomorrow's growth and development. It also enables one to recognize the overall importance of each element in the total infrastructure.

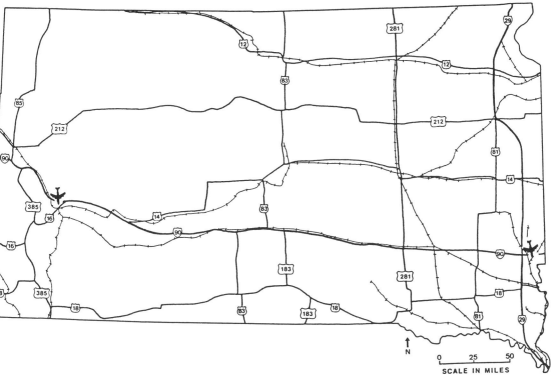

Map 30. **Major Transportation Systems of South Dakota.**

TRANSPORTATION

HIGHWAY AND ROAD SYSTEM

The South Dakota state highway system is comprised of 7,910 miles of interstate, arterial, and state secondary roads. The interstate highway system in the state is comprised of 678 miles of dual-lane, controlled-access roads (Map 30). Interstate 29 extends from Kansas City, Missouri, northward to the Canadian border. In South Dakota, I-29 enters the state at Sioux City, Iowa, and extends northward to the border with North Dakota. Interstate 90 is a true transcontinental highway, extending from Boston, Massachusetts, to Seattle, Washington. In South Dakota I-90 enters the state east of Sioux Falls and extends westward to the Wyoming border.

Some 2,256 miles of the remaining state highway system roads are comprised of high-volume arterial highway which includes east-west Highways 12, 212, 14, 16, 18, and 50, and north-south Highways 81, 281, 83, and 385. The state highways also include 279 miles of low-volume arterial road, 3,288 miles of minor arterial road, and 1,409 miles of state secondary road. In addition to the state highway system, the people are served by over 20,000 miles of county roads and over 50,000 miles of secondary rural road, plus municipal streets and alleys. This means that the state has about one mile of road for every nine people.

The road system is vital to both the state's everyday financial operation and future economic development. There is great concern about the thousands of bridges that exist in the state. Numerous state and local studies indicate that South Dakota is at a point where substantial amounts of tax monies are going to have to be devoted to bridge replacement. This is a need that will have to be met in the near future.

The state is also actively upgrading existing major state highways. Plans are also being discussed that propose construction of a major, four-lane artery from northeastern Colorado to the Black Hills area; a divided highway from Mitchell through Huron and Aberdeen to Jamestown, North Dakota; and a tourist loop from Chamberlain to Pierre and back to I-90.

Over 16,000 trucks are registered in the state. Some 8,000 of them are registered for interstate service. In addition to Class A carriers, the state is also served by irregular route carriers and common carriers. The state is essentially one day's shipment to Denver, Chicago, or St. Louis. Coastal locations such as New York City, Miami, Houston, or Los Angeles are four to five days shipping time distant.

RAILROADS

The people of South Dakota consider the railroads to be essential to their economic well being. This was demonstrated with the enactment of a one-year sales tax that enabled the state to purchase 764 miles of abandoned rail lines. That brought state ownership to almost 1,000 miles of the some 2,000 miles of track in South Dakota. The railroads serving South Dakota are the Dakota, Minnesota and Eastern; the Burlington Northern-Santa Fe; the Daktoa Southern; the D&I Railroad; CP Rail; Ellis and Eastern; the Red River Valley; and the Sisseton Milbank. These railroads operate on corporate track, state-owned track, and privately owned track (Map 30).

Principal resources shipped by rail are agricultural, mineral, or forest products. In recent years, there has been an increase in the use of unit trains, whereby the entire train's freight capacity is devoted to carrying one product to market.

The Dakota, Minnesota and Eastern has its national headquarters in Brookings. The D M & E was purchased from the Chicago Northwestern by a group of employees and experienced managers. It has upgraded operations along its route in both South Dakota and Minnesota and is positioned to be the dominant railroad in the region.

Unfortunately, South Dakota does not have any passenger service available in the state. It is not served by the Amtrack system. The only passenger rail service in the state is a short tourist train that runs in the Black Hills. There are plans to develop a steam-powered rail line from Rapid City Regional Airport to the Dunbar resort in Deadwood. Over the years, several communities have discussed developing similar tourist trains in hopes of attracting more business to their local economies. To date excessive costs of such development have prevented implementation of these ideas.

AIRLINES

Airline service to South Dakota is increasingly concentrated in Sioux Falls, Aberdeen, and Rapid City. Several major airlines serve these cities. In recent years, actual airline companies serving an area have changed rapidly as a result of corporate takeovers, mergers, and bankruptcies. However, through it all, these three major gateways have maintained and expanded their services and destinations.

In addition to these two major regional airports, regularly scheduled airline services are currently available in Aberdeen, Brookings, Huron, Pierre, Watertown, and Yankton. South Dakota cities are connected with Minneapolis, Chicago, St. Louis, and Denver by

Denver by subsidized regional carriers. The state and local governments are continually working to retain intrastate airline systems to provide air travel among South Dakota's larger communities.

PIPELINES

Pipelines are presently utilized for transportation of petroleum, natural gas, and water. In recent years, South Dakota has also been at the developmental forefront of further uses of pipelines for transportation. The state was selected to be the site of the ETSI Pipeline, which would have transported Wyoming coal to the Missouri River. The pipeline would have run across western South Dakota. In addition to transporting Wyoming coal through South Dakota, it would have also provided water to many small communities in the western portion of the state. From the Missouri River, the coal would have been shipped by rail to the Tennessee Valley Authority for electrical power generation.

The ETSI Pipeline was stopped as a result of lawsuits by neighboring states backed financially by railroads that would have competed with it. South Dakota in turn sued one of the railroads and won a substantial judgment. That decision was appealed by the railroad and reversed.

If the state or ETSI wins in the end, one can expect an expanded role for pipelines in the transportation of minerals other than oil and gas. Because of its water resources, the state can be expected to continue to be interested and involved in potential pipeline developments.

UTILITIES

ELECTRICITY

South Dakota is noted for low energy costs. A major reason for this is the existence of the four hydroelectric dams on the Missouri River. Electrical power also is provided by lignite coal plants in neighboring states, a natural gas plant in Huron, and even some local diesel-powered plants.

The four dams on the Missouri River are operated by the United States Bureau of Reclamation. Bureau of Reclamation power is sold to cities and towns, cooperatives, and private power companies. Private investor-owned utility companies are members of the Mid-Continent Area Power Producers (MAPP), which is a ten-state cooperative electrical needs planning organization. There are twenty-six rural electric systems throughout the state that receive their energy from two large wholesale cooperatives, East River Electric Power Cooperative and Rushmore Electric Power Cooperative. The remainder of the electric power is supplied to consumers through municipal and tribal power companies.

South Dakota is blessed with an abundance of low-cost, clean electrical energy. Indeed electrical rates in several South Dakota communities are among the lowest in the country. The state's electricity consumption is less than sixty percent of its production. This, combined with excellent planning by power suppliers, bodes well for future electrical needs.

NATURAL GAS

Natural gas service in South Dakota is limited to the eastern and western parts of the state. In the eastern part of the state, Northern Natural Gas Company is the principal supplier to four distribution companies: Northwestern Public Service Company, Western

Power and Gas Company, Iowa Public Service Company, and Central Gas Company. Western South Dakota is served by Montana-Dakota Utilities Company, with service extending from the Montana border to Ellsworth Air Force Base.

OTHER UTILITIES AND TECHNOLOGIES

Water and sewer are also utility services to the people of the state. They are generally operated by municipalities and rural water cooperatives. Irrigation Districts provide water for agricultural use to participating members. Telephone service is supplied to virtually everyone who wants it by investor-owned, private, and municipal companies. State government also operates its own telephone system.

The Rural Development Telecommunications Network was established and is operated by South Dakota to provide two-way video and audio communication between seventeen sites situated in larger communities across the state. The RDT Network also includes an uplink/downlink satellite component that will allow one-way video/ two-way audio communication from the seventeen studios to virtually every high school in the state.

AN OVERVIEW

South Dakota is in a strong position to meet not only the transportation and utility demands of its residents but to supply these services to an expanding population and economy. The state, municipalities, cooperatives, private and investor owned services have developed excellent transportation and utility infrastructures. They also have developed the long-range plans essential to bringing the roads and power services on line as needed.

Chapter Thirteen

POPULATION AND SETTLEMENT GEOGRAPHY

INTRODUCTION

Examination of South Dakota's population and settlement, both past and present, provides a vital understanding of the people who occupy the landscape. Population geography studies basic characteristics of the state's population, distribution of people, including those factors that influence population growth or decline, patterns of settlement, and trends that affect the present and future.

In 2000, the state's population totalled 754,844. This number was the largest population in the state's history. This population number is but a small fraction of the nation's more than one-quarter of a billion people. South Dakota's population ranked forty-fifth among the fifty United States in population in both 1980 and 1990. Despite its recent growth, in 2000 the state dropped to forty-sixth place in rankings. The light population of South Dakota also can be reflected by density, the number of people per square mile. Most of South Dakota remains very uncrowded. The state's population density is just over nine persons per square mile, compared to the nation's density of over seventy per square mile.

Yet as one studies South Dakota's population and its pattern of settlement, he or she cannot help but notice that population density and patterns differ greatly from place to place. Some of the state's larger communities, such as Sioux Falls and Rapid City, are thriving, while many of the smaller towns struggle for survival as their populations dwindle. Crowded city streets and shopping centers teeming with customers stand in marked contrast to country roads that extend to the horizon without a single vehicle in sight.

Many rural communities with boarded store fronts tell us of the state's changing patterns of population, economy, and settlement. Growing suburban developments echo the sounds of the carpenter's hammer and saw in contrast to the silence of lonely deteriorating abandoned farmsteads. Crowded day-care centers and elementary school classrooms and a growing number of nursing homes to care for our elderly give clues to the state's age structure. These are but a few examples of the many contrasts that characterize the population and settlement of South Dakota.

POPULATION GEOGRAPHY

People are perhaps the single most revealing element in the geographic study of places and regions: their numbers, or population; their pattern of distribution, or settlement; changes in number and the underlying reasons for population growth or decline in an area; and the movement or migration of people from place to place. Each of these demographic characteristics can tell us a great deal about environmental conditions and land use practices, economic conditions, and the way people feel about places.

SETTLEMENT

To a predominantly farming people, good soil, ample rainfall, an adequate growing season, and available land are extremely important environmental factors. When farming conditions are good, the population may experience rapid growth, but during periods of prolonged drought when the soil turns to dust and crops wither, the population may dwindle. During times of economic hardship, whether caused by drought or some other factor such as very low prices for crops and livestock, many families leave their farms or ranches. Some leave the state, thereby reducing the state's population. Still others move within the state, often to a town or city in search of wage-paying jobs and contribute to a change in local populations and the state's pattern of settlement.

Population change results from only two factors: natural change or migration. Natural changes are a growth or decline in population resulting from an imbalance between the number of births and deaths. Migration is the gain or loss in population that occurs when people move into or away from a place. Birth and death rates have not changed significantly in South Dakota during recent decades. Therefore, most of the changes in population and settlement have occurred as a result of migration, people moving to, from, or within the state.

Where people live, or their pattern of settlement, is most generally related to economic factors. People tend to settle in those places where they believe they can improve their economic well-being. Often, people will favor one location over others because they are better able to utilize the natural environment and its resources at a particular time and stage of technological development. Without the needed tools and skills to develop and use natural resources, they are of no value.

Many pre-European Native Americans, for example, roamed the plains in small hunting bands. The vast herds of bison were their chief resource. They lacked the tools and skills to farm the rich prairie soils. As nomadic hunters, their populations were low in number and their settlements were widely scattered. These hunting peoples had few villages. Their camps were often established along the shore of a lake or stream, from which water could be obtained and wood was available for fuel, the making of tools and weapons, and other purposes.

This is not to say that the Native American population did not thrive within the environment of South Dakota. Indeed, evidence indicates that from 1800 to 1825 the Dakota Sioux experienced a 400 percent growth in their population. They comprised over one-sixth of the Indian population of the Great Plains. Growth was the result of their dominance of the region. In addition to having surpassed the Arikara as the dominant tribe, the Sioux also increased agricultural production and controlled the buffalo ranges, the fur and horse trade, and the arms trade. They had no major enemies during this time and their population blossomed.

The earliest Anglo-American settlers attracted to what is now South Dakota clung very closely to the Missouri River and its major tributaries. Fort Pierre, Bon Homme, Yankton, and Elk Point were located on the Missouri River. Sioux Falls, the state's first Anglo-American settled community, grew at a site on the Big Sioux River. These settlements depended on the streams for a reliable water supply, transportation, and in some instances, such as Sioux Falls, for water power to drive early mills that provided flour and lumber.

During the mid-1800s, windmills needed to bring water from deep within the earth, and steel-tipped moldboard plows capable of breaking and turning the thick prairie sod, had not yet reached Dakota. During the latter part of the 19th century, however, these technological developments did make it possible for people to begin moving away from the rivers and to begin turning the vast prairie grassland into some of the world's richest farmland.

With the discovery of gold in the Black Hills during the mid-1870s, thousands of people migrated to the area of what is now southwestern South Dakota in the hope of making a lucky strike and fast wealth. For a short time, this was the area of highest population and population density in the state.

Today, however, more than fifty percent of South Dakota's population lives within fifty miles of the state's eastern border in a narrow corridor that includes the cities of Yankton, Vermillion, Madison, Brandon, Sioux Falls, Brookings, Watertown, Milbank, and Sisseton. Here conditions are very good for farming. A dense quilt-like pattern of farms, many small farming communities, and larger urban centers dot the landscape. In addition to farming, many processing and service industries such as John Morrell and Company and Citibank in Sioux Falls provide employment for a large and growing population. Indeed, throughout the region, in addition to industry and services, employment is also generated by government, finance and insurance, medical centers, the media, the elementary and secondary schools, and the state's colleges, universities, and technical schools. In response to the needs of a large population, transportation linkages are well developed in eastern South Dakota and provide easy access to cities, towns, and farms.

Moving from east to west across South Dakota, rainfall amount diminishes and conditions become increasingly drier. Farms are much larger and much of the land is devoted to livestock grazing or is unused for economic purposes. As one moves westward, it becomes obvious that people are fewer in number and the population density becomes increasingly sparse. Only Rapid City and the Black Hills area—with the military, tourist-related services, mining and lumbering industries, and other diverse economic functions—stand apart from the otherwise very sparsely populated western half of the state.

With the exception of the Black Hills region, the economy of South Dakota has long been dominated by agriculture. When farming and ranching have prospered, the state's population has grown. When the agricultural economy has been poor, population growth has slowed or even declined. Only during the 1980s did the population continue to grow at a healthy pace despite a troubled agricultural economy. This suggests that South Dakota's economy is beginning to diversify. Today the state's people are not as dependent upon farming and ranching as they have been in decades past. New industries and businesses have meant more jobs for South Dakotans. In turn, fewer people have had to leave the state in search of work opportunities, so the population continues to grow.

Most new industries and businesses are located in the larger urban centers. For this reason, most of the state's larger cities have grown in size during recent decades. At the same time, many of the smaller communities, particularly those which depend on the agricultural economy, have lost population.

Many factors have influenced the population decline in small towns and rural areas. Improved transportation has made it much easier for rural people to travel to and shop in larger communities that offer a greater variety of goods and services. On the farm, the use of large mechanized agricultural equipment has replaced much of the need for human hand labor. The average size of farms has increased greatly and continues to do so. Larger farm size in turn reduces the number of rural farm families and the need for local, small stores and services. The average size of farm families also has declined through the years further reducing the rural population.

Rural-to-urban migration has been a major characteristic of South Dakota's population throughout the twentieth century. After 1970, the trend toward an increasingly urban population has stabilized somewhat. Since 1990, one-half of the state's population is classified as being urban, that is, living in communities with 2,500 or more people. The other one-half of the population is classed as being rural. The rural population is comprised of two groups: the rural non-farm and rural farm. Almost eighty percent of the rural population are non-farm, living in open country or in towns with fewer than 2,500 people. The remaining rural population live on farms and engage in agriculture. Despite the continued decline in the farm population, a large, rural, non-farm population has enabled South Dakota to remain one of the nation's most rural states.

POPULATION

The geographic study of population characteristics of a place—be it a community, county, state, or region—requires geographers and other social scientists to turn to census data for the needed information. The United States takes a census every ten years ending in "zero" (1970, 1980, 1990, 2000, etc.). In addition to a "head count" of the population, the census provides geographers and other social scientists with a great deal of other valuable information about the state and its people.

Using historical census data, for example, one can clearly see that South Dakota's population has had its ups and downs. During some decades the population has grown and during others it has declined (Fig. 5). In 1870, only 11,776 people were counted in what later was to become South Dakota. With the coming of the railroads, the discovery of gold in the Black Hills and the rush that followed and a period of good farming conditions, the population grew to nearly 350,000 by the census of 1890. The population continued to grow until 1930 when it reached 692,849 people. This number was not exceeded again until the growth period of the 1980s. The population announced in the 2000 Census was the greatest in the history of South Dakota.

Figure 5.
South Dakota Population, 1870 to 2000.
Source: U.S. Census.

Year	Number	Year	Number
1870	11,776	1940	642,961
1880	98,262	1950	652,740
1890	348,600	1960	680,524
1900	401,570	1970	665,524
1910	583,888	1980	690,768
1920	634,547	1990	696,004
1930	692,849	2000	754,844

During the 1930s the state's population experienced its first decline. The Great Depression and dust bowl conditions of the "Dirty Thirties" forced thousands of people from the land. With very few jobs in the state's cities at the time, many families were forced to out-migrate from South Dakota to seek their fortunes elsewhere. Indeed, the state's population declined by almost 50,000 people from 1930 to 1940.

With the outbreak of World War II, South Dakota experienced another heavy loss of population. This was due to military service needs, and the vast job opportunities in the urbanized industrial areas of the nation. By 1945, the population of South Dakota had declined to 589,290 people, a figure that represents a 13.9 percent decline in just five years.

With the end of World War II, a return of adequate rainfall, and improved economic conditions during the late 1940s, the state's population once again began to grow in a trend that continued through the 1950s. During the 1960s, however, the population once again declined, from approximately 680,000 people to 665,000 people. More than 90,000 people left South Dakota during that decade. This occurred even though the natural birth rate kept the net loss between 1960 and 1970 to about 25,000 people. Once again, it was drought that affected the agricultural economy. Since 1970 the state's population has grown slowly but steadily to its 2000 total of 754,844 people. The key to future population growth rests in the growth of diversified industries and businesses. If jobs increase in number, so too will the state's population.

From the census data it is also apparent that South Dakota's settlement pattern is changing. It was previously mentioned that during the twentieth century rural population has declined and urban population has grown. It is also important to remember that not all parts of the state have shared equally in the state's recent population growth. In fact, two of every three South Dakota counties has actually lost population since 1970. Most counties that have gained population are those in which a city is located such as Minnehaha and Lincoln (both Sioux Falls) and Pennington (Rapid City).

THE DENSITY

The density of population in South Dakota ranks among the nation's lowest with just over nine persons per square mile. It must be remembered, however, that population density figures can be quite misleading because people are not spread evenly about the land. Minnehaha County, which includes Sioux Falls, is the most densely populated, with more than 135 persons per square mile. Harding County, on the other hand, located in the state's far northwestern corner, has fewer than one person per square mile. Two patterns become evident from examining population density. First, density is greatest in the more humid and urbanized eastern part of the state. Second, the most densely populated counties are those in which larger communities also are located.

THE AGE AND SEX COMPOSITIONS

The age and sex compositions of the state's population convey a visual image of the people (Figure 6). This image is displayed in a population pyramid. In 2000, over one-half of the state's population were female and the remaining proportion male. This results in a sex ratio with almost ninety-seven males for every one-hundred females. This indicates that the state's population is becoming somewhat older. At birth, more male babies are

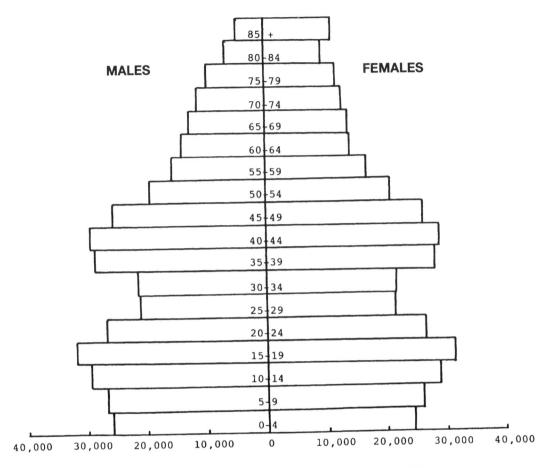

MALES

FEMALES

85 +	
80-84	
75-79	
70-74	
65-69	
60-64	
55-59	
50-54	
45-49	
40-44	
35-39	
30-34	
25-29	
20-24	
15-19	
10-14	
5-9	
0-4	

40,000 30,000 20,000 10,000 0 10,000 20,000 30,000 40,000

Figure 6. **Age and Sex Composition of South Dakota, 1999.**
State Data Center

born. By age eighteen years, the sex ratio is about even. The older one gets, the more females than males exist. This is due to a variety of factors including a longer life expectancy for women and higher age specific and accidental death rates for males.

The population pyramid also conveys the age composition of South Dakota's population. It does so in five-year intervals. An ideal population pyramid is bell shaped with a broad base, tapering upward to its summit. In South Dakota's case, the 1999 population pyramid indicates some significant insights. Instead of a broad base, it reflects a narrowing base. This is a result of a declining birth rate. This parallels national trends to a large extent. The birth rate in the United States has generally declined since 1961 with some exceptions. The larger populations at the thirty-five-year to fifty-four-year age groups reflect the state's growth during the 1945-to-1965 period, both from births over deaths and from declines in out-migration.

The pyramid also reflects a growing elderly population as well as one that is becoming increasingly female dominated. This in turn has some very significant implications. Among them are a growing age-dependency population, a larger number of elderly people who generally have limited incomes, and a larger group of people who require medical services, nursing homes, specialized care and so forth.

The heart of a population pyramid is the working age population or those people between twenty-five years and sixty-four years of age. In South Dakota this group is increasing steadily in number but not significantly in percentage of the total population. Essentially, this is indicating that the state is able to keep more people here as it provides more job opportunities for the residents. It does not indicate an end to out-migration, only a slowing of it.

The median age, which now exceeds thirty years, is the highest in the state's population history. An increasing median age reflects a declining or low birth rate, the out-migration of youth, and an increasing elderly population. South Dakota's median age is expected to continue slowly to increase until such time as the birth rate changes or extremely significant economic opportunities occur.

NATURAL INCREASE

Natural increase is the increase of births over deaths. From 1990 to 1999, some 98,048 births occurred in South Dakota. During that same period, 62,765 deaths took place. If no in-migration or out-migration was occurring, the population would have increased by 35,283 people. During that period, the state's population actually inceased by 37,129 people. This is an extremely significant figure.

MIGRATION

From 1980 to 1990, over 50,000 people out-migrated from South Dakota, continuing a trend that existed since the 1930s. Because of out-migration, the state has lost vast numbers of vital people who would have had the opportunity to bring their talents to the growth and development of the state. While out-migration slowed but continued into the early 1990s, it appeared that the loss of population would never end.

Out-migration is age specific. That means it impacts certain age groups more than others. In the case of South Dakota, the greatest impact of out-migration is on younger populations. It is also somewhat sex oriented at least initially. Normally, the first group to out-migrate is young women who recently completed high school or college. Within six months or so of graduation, the young men also begin to leave in large numbers.

Historically, the major reasons for leaving South Dakota are low wages, job opportunities, climate, the social and cultural environments, and the appeal of other areas. Interestingly, a study of out-migrants by one of the authors of this book indicated that two-thirds of those leaving said they would stay in their hometown if they could find an adequately paying job.

Since the mid 1990s, the good news for South Dakota is the fact that for the first time in decades, population growth exceeded natural increase. Not only has out-migration declined dramatically, but positive in-migration also occurred. Part of the increase in in-migration is a result of net international migration of almost 5,000 people during the 1990s. The immigrants came primarily from Africa, Eastern Europe, and the former Soviet Union.

MARRIAGE AND FAMILIES

Among the many traditional values held by South Dakotans is marriage and family life. About sixty percent of the state's adult population is married. There are more than 260,000 households, each having an average of approximately 2.67 persons. The relatively small family size can be explained by two factors. First, a very high percentage of the state's married couples are beyond the child-bearing age. Second, a growing number of young couples delay starting families in order to improve their financial condition, since both the husband and wife serve in the labor force.

THE LABOR FORCE

Some sixty-six percent of all South Dakotans over sixteen years of age are in the labor force. More than half of all women over sixteen years of age are employed, as are about seventy-five percent of the men. Unemployment in South Dakota is generally low. This is because the combination of growth in industry and business and the loss of people to out-migration result in low unemployment. It is important to realize that over half of the workers in the state are economically distressed. Even more serious situations can and do occur on the Indian reservations where unemployment and poverty totally dominate the economic communities.

INCOME

One of the most serious problems facing the state is that of increasing the standard of living. One major way of achieving that goal is to increase wages and total incomes. Median family income in South Dakota in always well below the U.S. average. This reflects both the low salaries of the state and its agricultural nature. A total of 16 percent of the population is at or below the poverty level.

ETHNIC COMPOSITION

Nearly 93 of every 100 South Dakotans are white. Of the non-white population, almost 50,000 of the state's residents are Native American. Fewer than 6,000 people are of other racial groups. The Native American population is the fastest growing segment of the state's population. The Native Americans are increasingly confining themselves to a few reservations and the largest urban communities. Indian population will also continue to migrate to other parts of the nation. However, many Native Americans tend to move off and on the reservations quite frequently.

HOUSEHOLDS

In 1990, South Dakota had over 259,000 households. This figure includes over 180,000 family households. Some 152,500 of the family households are headed by married couples. Another 20,700 are headed by a female householder with no husband present. The remaining 7,000 are other head households. South Dakota, like most states, is experiencing an increase in single-parent households.

CITIES AND TOWNS

Most people in South Dakota today live in cities and towns, despite the fact that it is still one of the nation's most rural states. Trends indicate that the urban and non-farm populations will continue to grow. Urban communities are incorporated communities of 2,500 people or more. Some 50 percent of the state's population is urban. All persons living in communities of less than 2,500 people, or in open country and not engaged in agriculture are classed as rural non-farm. They comprise 39 percent of the state's population. The remaining 11 percent of the people are classified as the farm population. The farm population in South Dakota declined by almost one-third from 1950 to 1990. They are all persons living on farms and principally engaged in agriculture.

Geographically, one of the most exciting ways to examine a community is through the morphological approach, viewing the community as a person. Like people, each community is a unique entity despite some common characteristics and responsibilities. A city or town, like a person, has a skeleton. In the case of the community, it is comprised of the streets, alleys, sidewalks, railroad track, and streams upon which a town is built. The body of homes, stores, schools, hospitals, industries, and other structures are all attached to the skeleton. Like a person, unless all the parts are in the right places, the community has difficulty functioning properly. Both people and a city have a face.

The face of the community is extremely important. To you, your community's face is the mental image that comes to mind when you visualize your hometown. Also like people,

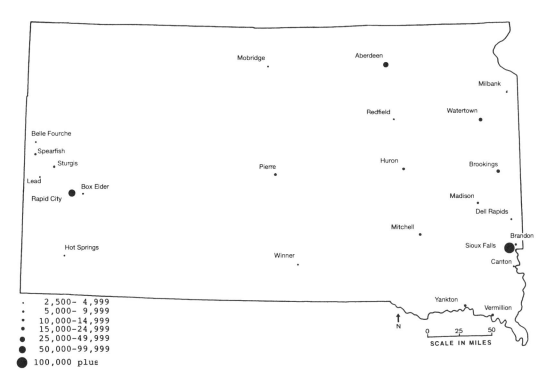

Map 31. **Major Cities and Towns of South Dakota.**

153

some are attractive and some are not. The face is essential to community growth, for in order to survive, it must be appealing enough to attract younger populations to come and live with it. This is why so many larger cities have used urban renewal as a form of plastic surgery to attract new populations.

Both people and cities have jobs, responsibilities, leisure, and rest. These are called functions. The job functions of cities and towns are industry, commerce, mining, government, and transportation. The personal and cultural responsibilities are education, communication, religion, and health. The various recreational activities and services available in the community provide the leisure function. Finally, rest is provided by the residential function of the community.

Communities, like people, also have reputations. These can be good, indifferent, or bad. Reputations can and will change over time. There is gossip about communities as there is gossip about people. Numerous other human emotions come into play here including love, hate, envy, jealousy, and lust. Think about it. What kind of a person is your community? Is it a dear friend? Do you enjoy hanging around with it? Your answer to these and other questions tells you a great deal about yourself and your community.

Communities also serve trade areas. Some are very small with very limited areas from which to draw economically. Others such as Sioux Falls, Rapid City, and Aberdeen, serve large areas and even cater to people living in other states. Trade areas range from minimum convenience communities with a cafe, grocery and gas, to primary wholesale-retail centers with all the major retail, service, and wholesale functions.

South Dakota has 309 cities and towns ranging in size from Hillsview with 3 people in 2000 to Sioux Falls with almost 125,000 people. Despite the large number of communities, it is important to realize that 285 of those towns are rural non-farm settlements of less than 2,500 people. Another 22 cities have between 2,500 and 50,000 people. Two communities are metropolitan cities of over 50,000 people (Map 31).

In 2000, the state's ten largest cities, in their rank order, were:

Sioux Falls	(123,975)
Rapid City	(59,607)
Aberdeen	(24,658)
Watertown	(20,237)
Brookings	(18,504)
Mitchell	(14,558)
Pierre	(13,876)
Yankton	(13,528)
Huron	(11,893)
Vermillion	(9,765)

US Census Bureau, 2000

TRENDS

The future of South Dakota's population depends primarily on economic factors and migration trends. Population change occurs in two ways: through births and deaths and by in-migration or out-migration. Earlier it was mentioned that seven decades of out-migration were marked by a sharp decline in the state's population during the 1930s and again during the 1960s. It was also stated that even though births outnumber deaths by nearly a two-to-one margin, the state's population grows quite slowly. The reason for this slow growth is because one of South Dakota's chief exports is its people, particularly its young people, through out-migration. As this trend is reversed, and when births outnumber deaths by a two-to-one ratio, South Dakota could experience very rapid population growth.

Most South Dakotans love their state and take great pride in the many fine things that it has to offer. They love the state's way of life, friendly, helpful people, uncrowded space and many excellent recreational opportunities. South Dakota's excellent schools, low cost of living, and the relative lack of crime and pollution are just some of the factors that often are mentioned by residents in praise of the state.

Still, many South Dakotans continue to leave the state or plan to do so at some future date. In studying migration patterns, geographers and others consider what are called "push-and-pull" factors. Push factors include all reasons for leaving (out-migration); pull factors are those which influence where people move or why they remain.

For most South Dakotans, push factors are economic, social, familial, or environmental: they are unable to find high paying jobs or employment suited to their training; as a dominantly rural state, many people, particularly the young adults, feel that the state lacks the "action" and "excitement" that are offered by larger cities elsewhere; their families, friends, and teachers are encouraging them to leave; and the weather, rolling plains landscape, vast "empty spaces," and lack of forests are judged to be negative factors by some residents.

Pull factors, those which attract out-migrants to other locations, include better jobs and higher wages; a preferred social or cultural environment, often in a larger city than South Dakota offers; or a more pleasant physical environment such as mountains, ocean, or a warmer climate.

The single most important cause of migration, be it push or pull, is economic motivation: people move first in search of higher salaries and secondly seeking better jobs. The third major reason for leaving is in search of a better climate in which to live. Another major factor influencing migration is quality of life. Not all people, of course, judge quality of living in the same way. Many younger people, for example, might be attracted by the excitement and opportunities they believe to exist in a large city. At the same time, many older urban residents, tired of the city's hectic pace, crowded conditions, and other factors may look to a place like South Dakota as being ideal for living, raising a family, and working.

Looking ahead, demographers and other population scientists project continued new growth for the state's population. Some predict that it may reach 775,000 by the year 2010, whereas others are far less optimistic. Rural and small town population, it is believed, will continue to decline as a percentage of the state's total population. The larger cities will continue to be the major centers of economic growth and development as well as population growth.

Diversification of the state's economy and an increase in higher paying jobs, including many not related to agriculture, will gradually reduce the loss of population to out-migration. As cities grow, so too will services and amenities that will make South Dakota an even more attractive and enjoyable place to live and call home. South Dakota will likely never be among the most populous states. Obviously, most South Dakotans have no desire to see it become heavily populated. Indeed, most would be simply delighted if it reached a level of economic opportunity where their children and grandchildren could afford to call South Dakota home.

Chapter Fourteen
REGIONS OF SOUTH DAKOTA

INTRODUCTION

People have a tendency to establish divisions to identify places. These divisions may be physical, political, social, cultural, economic, or based upon some other type of classification. We then make generalizations about these places based upon the criteria we are using. For example, the Americas become Anglo-America and Latin America, as a result of such cultural factors as language and customs. Anglo-America in turn becomes Canada and the United States. The United States further can be divided into 50 states, 435 congressional districts, hundreds of area codes, and thousands of zip codes.

The nation also can be divided into physiographic regions such as the Atlantic Coastal Plain, the Great Plains, or the Rocky Mountains. Culturally, it can be divided into New England, the South, the Middle West, the American West, and so on. Economically, it can become production and trade areas, Federal Reserve Districts, and so forth. In other words, there are literally hundreds of regions to which one place might belong. This means that a map is like a mosaic. It is comprised of numerous distinct pieces that fit together to become a whole.

So far in this work, the various regions that exist in South Dakota have been discussed in relation to the topics that were being examined. Physiographic regions such as the Coteau de Prairies and the Black Hills have been studied. Climatic zones, soil regions and vegetation belts have been examined. Familiar regional terms such as East River, West River, reservation area, and trade area have been discussed. These places all fit together to complete the mosaic picture of South Dakota. They provide the color, texture, relief, and surface that results in the visual identification of South Dakota.

Geographically, a region is defined as a homogeneous area determined by arbitrarily selected criteria. Those criteria traditionally utilized by geographers in conducting a regional geography include location, terrain, climate, natural vegetation, soils, water, human occupance, and human development. The latter generally includes agriculture, industry, tourism and recreation, transportation, power and utilities, population, cities and towns, and the future of the region. In other words, a traditional regional geographic study links the data of the natural sciences with the social sciences.

The concept of region is essential to geographic understanding. A region encompasses the totality of people and place occupying that space. Each region has a central core area that reflects the geographic characteristics that give it its unique individuality and personality. The central core of the region is a recognizable geographic space defined by selective criteria. The overlap areas between the cores should not be thought of as clearly identifiable lines or boundaries but rather as transitional zones, where regions meld.

It also should be noted that over time, regions can grow, retreat, change direction, or even disappear. Realize too that sequent occupance over time plays a vital role in regional understanding. The regions of South Dakota to the Teton Sioux in 1825 are quite different than those to the South Dakotan in 2000. The human/land relationship in a given environment can then change quite dramatically with different peoples at different times.

Realizing then that a region will give one a geographic understanding of a part of South Dakota, let us examine what the state looks like regionally. There are numerous criteria that could be used to delimit the regions of the state. Because this is a geographic study, it will use only the major factors that have been investigated in this book. Remember, a region can be defined by one or more selective criteria. Utilizing traditional criteria, the regions of South Dakota are delimited using terrain, climate, soils, natural vegetation, human occupance, and human development.

As the regions of South Dakota are developed, remember what has already been learned by reviewing a series of maps to help establish regions. Map 3 represents the state's three major physiographic regions: the Central Lowlands, Missouri Plateau, and Black Hills.

Map 5 depicts the four climatic zones that exist in the state: the two Humid Continental zones of the east, the Dry Continental of the west, and the Unclassified mountain zone in the Hills. Now let us overlay these two maps in order to develop an understanding of a geographic region (Map 32). Notice how the Humid Continental zones and the Central Lowlands overlap. Notice too the similarities in areal extent of the Dry Continental zone and the Missouri Plateau and of the Black Hills and Unclassified Climate. What has just been achieved here is to establish three regions utilizing only two criteria, in this case terrain and climate.

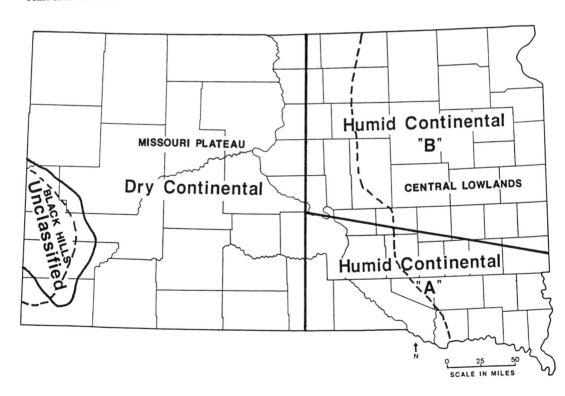

Map 32. Physiographic and Climatic Regions Overlay of South Dakota.

158

While this would be sufficient for some geographic studies, the use of additional criteria helps give better definition to the state's regions. So let us look at some more maps. Map 8 depicts three major soil zones: the Chernozem Zone, Chestnut Zone, and Gray Wooded Zone.

Map 6 delimits vegetation types with short to tall prairie grasses covering the east, steppe vegetation in the west, and coniferous forest in the mountains. Note the very similar boundaries of the vegetation and soil regions. Now mentally overlay these maps to the climate and terrain. Now the intellectual concept of regions become much clearer and better defined.

In developing geographic regions, we can also add people to the picture. This can be achieved by looking at the human occupance and the human development of South Dakota. A map depicting occupance by the Santee and Yankton Sioux of the east and Teton or Western Sioux provides a basis for understanding sequent occupance by Native Americans (Map 11).

A similar map could show occupance by settlers as non-Indians occupied the state. The homesteaders of the east, the miners of the Black Hills, and finally ranchers and farmers who settled the central and west after the turn of the century. From such maps regions of occupance will emerge. Finally occupance could also be added to the map showing physical regions.

Human development further helps define the regions. Maps of South Dakota's agriculture can demonstrate the difference between major farm areas and ranching lands. A map

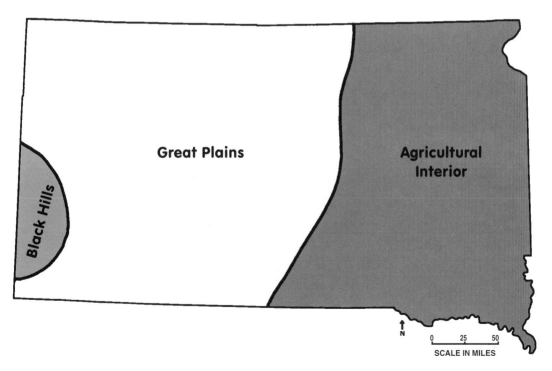

Map 33. **The Three Geographic Regions of South Dakota.**

159

Sioux Falls, in the Agricultural Interior, is the largest city in the state and is consistently rated among the top places to live in the United States.

of manufacturing densities can delimit the regions further. Overlaying such maps showing regions of human development causes new regional patterns to emerge.

In summary, the geographic regions of South Dakota can be determined by the physical environment, the cultural environment, or the combined physical and human occupance criteria. With each new layer of information one notices how a clearer regional pattern emerges. Actually, the regions of South Dakota are fairly simple to delimit, but the more variables that are considered, the more accurate are the regions.

Now let us turn attention to naming the regions of South Dakota. This can be achieved in several ways. Local people, themselves, can name regions as has been done with such perceptual regions as the Sioux Empire or Great Northwest. Or, they can defer to nationally or internationally recognized regions utilized within the discipline of geography. In this instance, we will do the latter. Geographically, we identify three major regions of South Dakota: the Agricultural Interior of the east, the Great Plains of the west, and the Black Hills in the far southwestern part of the state (Map 33). Each of these three regions also extends beyond the borders of South Dakota. The Agricultural Interior extends as far east as the Appalachian Mountains. The Great Plains extends from the Canadian prairies to the Rio Grande River of Texas. The Black Hills extend from Glendive, Montana, into Nebraska.

With the regional borders delimited, it is now possible to describe the regional geography of South Dakota. This can be achieved by simply examining the geographic criteria used to determine the regions as they apply to each region.

THE AGRICULTURAL INTERIOR

The Agricultural Interior of South Dakota is the state's easternmost region. At the same time, it is the northwestern most portion of the country's Agricultural Interior. Physiographically, the Agricultural Interior of South Dakota is a portion of the Central Lowlands. Terrain in this region is a result of recent glaciation during the Wisconsin Stage. The effect of ice flowing and retreating over the landscape is a gently rolling hill plain appearance covered with potholes and lakes and drained by the Big Sioux, Vermillion, James, and Lower Missouri rivers.

Climate of the region is Humid Continental with a longer summer in the south and longer winter in the north. Average annual precipitation ranges from eighteen to twenty-four inches. Rich chernozem soil blankets the land. This lush soil is a result of the combination of parent materials, deep rooted tall prairie grasses, and moderate rainfall. It is one of the most fertile areas in the world. Natural prairie grasses are gone for the most part, but the environment that once was so beneficial to the grasses is today host to excellent crop production. Larger animals such as bison and antelope no longer roam, but jackrabbits, cottontail, and gophers abound. Precipitation is generally good in this region, although flooding and drought can and do occur.

This region once served as home to early people known as Mound Builders. It was later occupied by Sioux people known as the Santee Sioux and the Yankton Sioux. The region was the first portion of South Dakota opened to settlement. Thousands of people came into this region as a result of the Homestead Act of 1862. The region boomed in the late 1800s, then suffered a tremendous decline during the Dust Bowl and Depression of the 1930s.

161

Today the Agricultural Interior of South Dakota is one of the finer agricultural areas of the nation. It is noted for production of livestock, being important in the raising and marketing of cattle, hogs, and sheep. Its major crops are corn, soybeans, hay, oats, and rye.

The region is also the major industrial center of the state with large industries in Sioux Falls, Brookings, Aberdeen, Huron, Watertown, Yankton, and Mitchell. It is noted for meat packing, dairy products, grain milling, and machinery, as well as medical products, fabricated metal products, and electrical products. The most important mineral products are sand, gravel, and stone. The region has an ever-growing tourist industry centered in Sioux Falls and Mitchell.

Population tends to be concentrated close to the South Dakota-Minnesota border. Sioux Falls, with almost 125,000 people in the urban area, is the state's largest city. It is a center for financial activities, communication and media, medical services, and transportation in the region. Sioux Falls contains the largest airport in the state. Aberdeen is the second largest city in the region with a population of about 25,000 people. Aberdeen is the major trade center of northern South Dakota. Brookings is the home of South Dakota State University, and Vermillion is home to the University of South Dakota, the two largest institutions of higher education in the state.

Future trends for the Agricultural Interior of South Dakota appear to be very bright. Over the last thirty years, this region has been able successfully to address a serious problem of out-migration. The recent rapid industrial expansion of the region combined with a substantial growth in financial institutions and commercial shopping facilities have helped reduce out-migration. The region is moving forward in the twenty-first century with facilities such as the EROS Data Center and businesses and industries such as Gateway, Citibank, Morrell, Raven, Sioux Valley Hospital, 3M, and Larson Manufacturing.

THE GREAT PLAINS

The Great Plains Region of South Dakota is comprised essentially of the western two-thirds of the state with the exception of the Black Hills region. The Great Plains Region is traditionally associated with the 100th meridian of west longitude. Actually, in South Dakota the Great Plains is physiographically comprised of the western portion of the glaciated east and the Missouri Plateau. Land here rises in a series of steps and hills as one moves from east to west. Two major forces, water and wind, have shaped this region's landscape. Perhaps this is symbolized best in the Big Badlands area, where water and wind have created uniquely beautiful landscapes of castellated peaks and deep dark valleys of weak shales.

Climatically, the region is part of the Dry Continental zone. Here most of the region will receive thirteen to eighteen inches of precipitation. Summer days can get very hot, often exceeding 100°F. Winters are cold, and blizzards can occur. Wind is ever present, and rainfall often occurs as thunderstorms.

Soils of this region are of the chestnut classification. Chestnut soils typically develop in zones with the temperatures, precipitation, and vegetation found here. Natural vegetation here is steppe. Steppe vegetation is short to mid grasses that are patchy or scattered in distribution. Animal life is dominated by speed animals such as antelope and coyote.

Several rivers flowing from the west eastward to the Missouri River drain the region. Major western streams include the Cheyenne and White rivers. The Missouri River enters

**The Pierre Hills reflect the unique beauty of the physical environment of the Great Plains.
Courtesy Edward P. Hogan.**

the region at the border with North Dakota and flows southward, dropping in elevation about one foot per mile until it reaches Gavins Point. The Missouri River has been dammed in four places, resulting in Oahe Reservoir, Lake Francis Case, Lake Sharpe, and Lewis and Clark Lake. These lakes all occupy space behind large hydroelectric power-generating dams.

Human occupance of the Great Plains region has varied greatly over time. In more recent times, it was occupied by the pre-Arikaras about 1250 and the Arikaras in the 1500s. The Arikaras developed a strong culture and society within the region and dominated agriculture and trade for many years. In the 1700s Sioux crossed the Missouri River. They were to replace the dominance of the Arikaras.

The Sioux occupied this land as nomadic peoples living off buffalo herds and agricultural products. Their occupancy of the land was challenged with the arrival of white men in increasing numbers. This challenge resulted in a series of battles and wars that ended in 1890 with Wounded Knee. After that time, Indian lands were opened to settlement and the Indians were confined to reservation areas. Today the greatest concentrations of Sioux people in the region are still in areas of reservation and Rapid City.

Human development of this region has not been as intense as in the Agricultural Interior. This region is a more fragile ecological environment than its eastern neighbor. The Great Plains is a land of ranching and farming. Cattle dominate the area's livestock industry, although hogs and sheep are raised. This is a land of winter wheat and sorghum in the south and central portions and spring wheat in the north.

Industrial development is not extensive here yet, although Rapid City contains some excellent industries including Magnetic Peripherals and the South Dakota cement plant. Other communities such as Pierre are actively seeking industries. Tourism is an important part of the human development of the Great Plains. This region contains Pierre, the state's capital, and the extremely popular Badlands National Park. It is also home of the world famous Wall Drug at Wall. The region also plays an important part in the nation's military defense. Ellsworth Air Force Base east of Rapid City is a home of the new B-1 bomber.

Population centers in the Great Plains include Rapid City, the state's second largest community. The Rapid City area is approaching 60,000 people. It is a financial center, a trade area that extends into Wyoming and Nebraska, and an educational and cultural center as well. Pierre is the second largest city in the region with over 13,000 people.

Future growth of the Great Plains Region is not as predictable as that of the Agricultural Interior. Growth is expected to continue strongly in Rapid City and Pierre. Cities such as Mobridge, Platte, Philip, and Kadoka no doubt will experience some growth. Most of the region will continue to be dominated by ranching and reservation lands. These areas will not change as rapidly as the urban places.

BLACK HILLS

The Black Hills comprise the third region in South Dakota. They are located in the extreme southwestern part of the state. Physiographically, the Black Hills are a miniature version of the Rocky Mountains. They are comprised of the central crystalline core, the limestone plateau, the Red Valley, and the outer hogbacks. Harney Peak at 7,242 feet is the highest point in the Hills.

Climate of the region is an unclassified highland climate. This means that the climate changes significantly with increased elevation. The highest snowfall in the state is in the Hills. Soils here are gray-wooded soils. They developed from parent materials and were strongly influenced by the forests that grow in them.

Natural vegetation is coniferous forests with Black Hills Spruce and Western Yellow Pine covering most of the area. Valleys are covered with grasses. Animal life is more typical of mountain environs. This region once contained grizzly bear, black bear, and white tailed deer. Today it contains deer, buffalo, prairie dogs, and numerous small animals.

Human occupance of this region has changed dramatically over time. Once the land of ancient peoples, who hunted mammoth here, it has experienced many sequential changes. Historically, the Sioux and other Native American peoples revere the Black Hills as holy ground.

American miners saw it as the mother lode. Beginning with the discovery of gold in 1874, thousands of miners came to the Hills in search of wealth. Over time the placers played out and hard rock mining developed. Now it is declining too. The Black Hills also have developed as the tourist center of South Dakota with *Mount Rushmore*, the "Shrine to Democracy," dominating the region's numerous attractions. Other major attractions include Crazy Horse Memorial, Custer State Park, Spearfish Canyon, historic Deadwood, and legalized gambling.

Population in the Black Hills is concentrated in several small cities and in the valleys and canyons. Major cities include Spearfish, Deadwood, Lead, Custer, and Hot Springs. Spearfish now has a population of over 8,606 people. The rest contain 4,000 people or fewer, ranging from Hot Springs with 4,129 to Deadwood with 1,380. Major industries are related to mining and forestry. Minerals include gold, silver, bentonite, uranium, vanadium, sand, gravel, and stone.

Indeed the future of the Black Hills is closely tied to minerals, forests, and tourism. The area contains potential for development in oil, natural gas, and iron ore. It is also witnessing increased interest in expanding the gold mining operations. Tourism will continue to be vital to the region's economy. Scenery must be preserved and enhanced. The Black Hills will continue to develop. However, its growth will not follow the pattern of the Agricultural Interior of the Great Plains regions. Its growth will be unique to its mineral-tourist-mountain economy.

AN OBSERVATION

Through use of the geographical concept of region and the methodology of regional geography, one can see that unique differences exist between the three regions of South Dakota. It can be seen too that each region develops its own unique characteristics and personalities. Indeed each had developed its own ways to work and play. The region is an exceptionally powerful tool of the geographer. It is one that everyone can use to understand his or her communities, state, nation, and world.

Chapter Fifteen

THE FUTURE OF SOUTH DAKOTA

INTRODUCTION

We are about to conclude this exploration of South Dakota. We have criss-crossed the map of the state, examining the physical and cultural environments. Geographically, South Dakota has been studied in detail utilizing both the systematic (or topical) approach and the regional method.

As a result of these studies and using what is known about past, present, and future trends, it is now possible geographically to understand and anticipate what lies ahead for South Dakota. These are not predictions from a crystal ball but rather observable geographical patterns that are emerging in the state.

The physical environment is comprised of the lithosphere, atmosphere, biosphere, and hydrosphere. Each of these areas is deeply interrelated with the other. As a result, characteristics and trends may relate to more than one area.

Obviously, barring major geologic or climatic change, the major terrain features of the state will not undergo dramatic modification. This does not mean that changes will not occur. Indeed, the terrain is modified more than most people realize. Every time we dig a basement, grade a parking lot, or till a field, we bring about change.

Most anticipated changes in the lithosphere are closely related to erosion and runoff. Wherever humankind builds, farms, or develops, some changes occur. Erosion and runoff problems can result from bad practices in any of these areas. Attempts will continue to be made to reduce the erosion of the soils and conserve this great resource. Mother Nature, however, has as her primary goal the reduction of the earth's surface to sea level. As a result, land is constantly being washed away to some degree.

In South Dakota, this forewarns problems with the silting in of the major reservoirs on the Missouri River. In the immediate future, major attention will be required to save our four river lakes. In fact, on a much smaller scale, silting will be an increasingly important problem in most of the state's lakes and sloughs.

How often have you heard, "Weather, we always talk about it but never do anything about it"? Well, future trends indicate that humankind will attempt to do something about it. Scholars are conducting studies now on cyclic trends such as drought, winter storms, and floods. As more and more information is learned, people will better understand these atmospheric trends. Indeed, technology soon may enable one to predict drought or heavy snowfall seasons. Scientists will also increase efforts to achieve some success in weather modification. This could range from increasing rainfall in a portion of Harding County to dissipating a tornado-spawning storm before it reaches Mitchell.

Changes in the biosphere are potentially numerous. One very simple trend is related to shelterbelts. These farm features are now in a state of decline. Future trends point in two opposite directions. One trend is toward elimination of shelter belts. The other is toward redesigning shelter belts to provide additional income to the farmer by utilizing the land for both protection and commercial tree crops.

Continued emphasis on enhancing plant, fish, and wildlife is anticipated. The state is expected to continue to place special emphasis on waterfowl populations. Efforts to protect and enhance other fish and wildlife species can be expected. This is because they have both a natural and commercial value.

The biosphere may well witness the arrival of new plant species through gene splicing. Plants are being developed in laboratories which will enable the enrichment of the physical environment, provide for better utilization of lands by livestock, or yield more desirable qualities for our personal landscapes. It is only a matter of time and money before they begin to impact the state's agricultural community and economy.

Water will be South Dakota's greatest resource in the future, provided the state withstands attempts by neighboring states and the federal government to take control of it. Indeed, potential governmental programs could attempt to take or restrict the state's use of its own waters.

Currently, most of our cities and towns draw their water supplies from ground water. The last ten to twenty years also have shown dramatic increases in the demand for artesian waters for agricultural use. This is true even in traditional ranching country. When you see the center pivot irrigation fields in the Great Plains, have you ever wondered what the people who established the large ranches there 100 years ago would say if you had told them that their grandchildren would be farming corn on the same lands? As irrigation increases, however, artesian formations can experience a loss in pressure and a decline in water availability. South Dakota is going to have to face this serious problem in the not-too-distant future.

Continued efforts to develop a coal slurry pipeline similar to that once proposed by ETSI can be expected. Pipeline companies believe that they can move minerals such as coal cheaper than can the railroads. South Dakota, because of its geography, could be at the center of the pipeline-railroad controversy in the years ahead.

Based on present trends, one can anticipate an increase in irrigation in both East River and West River portions of the state. The U.S. government likely will attempt to become further involved in controlling irrigation. Government also will attempt to expand water regulations to smaller communities. Virtually any size town may well be expected to put in water treatment facilities similar to those in larger cities for waste-water control.

The cultural environment reflects the human occupance and human development of the state. Trends here are primarily related to agriculture, industry and commerce, tourism and recreation, and population.

Agriculture, as you recall, especially the livestock industry, is the most important segment of the state's economy. Future trends indicate that the raising of livestock will continue to be the most important element in the future. Indeed, it may even become more important. Trends indicate that the raising of livestock will become more industrialized.

We likely will see the development of large feedlots in the eastern part of the state. Large-scale commercial feeders will attempt to develop massive facilities for both cattle and hogs. Family farm operators can be expected to oppose such operations since a single facility could have a tremendous impact on the marketing of livestock or the price of feed. Family farm operators will continue to be pressured to leave the land, only to be replaced by corporate farms and ranches.

Crop production will experience changes as well. The continued dominance of corn, wheat, and hay is expected. Other crops will grow in importance, however, especially soybeans in the southeast and east central and sunflowers in the northeast. Additionally, farmers are expected to move to more specialized products for additional income and crop diversity. Among these are mushrooms, artichokes, asparagus, flowers, and various types of trees. Genetic plant research will likely bring about new hybrids and even totally new crops in the future.

As a result of the state's 1987 program to enhance economic development, some significant changes in industry and commercial development can be anticipated. Efforts also will be made to exploit further the mineral resources of the state. Despite the closure of Homestake Mine, it is expected that mining companies will continue their efforts to establish strip mines in the Black Hills in order to recover gold, silver, and other metals. Trends indicate that the general public will continue to resist such developments. Some potential for oil and gas development exists, depending upon national energy needs.

In terms of major industries, meat packing is the most important industry in South Dakota. Present trends indicate that it will continue to be the most important single industry in the future. If large-scale feed lots or production plants are added to the state, more large-scale slaughtering operations will be developed. One result of such developments would be significant increases in the need for water and waste-water treatment facilities in the communities where these plants are built.

In light of the state's various economic development efforts and the fact that it has one of the best-educated labor forces in the nation, a solid basis for industrial expansion exists. As a result, South Dakota may anticipate the expansion of existing industries, the development of more home-grown industries, and the attraction of industries from elsewhere. Major emphasis likely will be placed on attracting clean, high-technology, higher-paying industries.

It must be remembered that because of the small number of manufacturing workers in the state, almost any increase in industrial jobs will have a significant effect. Many industries will continue to seek farm wives as laborers. Others will seek farmers looking for a second income. Still others will be seeking college graduates with specific academic and technological skills or vocational-technical students with special training. The work force should become even more diversified.

The commercial development of South Dakota will continue to concentrate in the larger urban centers. This will make it even more difficult for small-town businesses and smaller towns to survive. Much of the expansion will be controlled by out-of-state companies and national chains that essentially will take the profits out of South Dakota. Resentment to this likely will lead to a corporate or business income tax in the near future.

Financial regulations and banking laws are favorable to continued development of the financial sector of the business world. In addition to regional and national credit card centers, the state can expect further development in areas of insurance, banking, pension funds, and investing. Downtown Sioux Falls will emerge as a substantial financial center similar to those in Hartford, Connecticut; Omaha, Nebraska; or Des Moines, Iowa, but on a smaller scale.

Transportation will continue to be vital to the state's well being. The maintenance of the Interstate highways and the upgrading of state highways must continue to receive great attention. Numerous bridges will need to be replaced. The remaining railroad track will be upgraded or rebuilt in areas where growth is occurring. Airline service will become increasingly concentrated in Sioux Falls and Rapid City. Smaller towns with existing air service will experience increased difficulty in maintaining such services. Indeed, even Rapid City might have problems with larger airlines.

Tourism, recreation, and gaming will continue to be vital to the economy. This is true despite the fact that these activities rank low in total dollars spent by tourists, in comparison to other states. This industry realizes that major efforts must be made to enhance tourism and recreation. The first area to be addressed is the need to expand tourism opportunities along both I-90 and I-29. In addition to recent developments such as the tribal casinos, the major resorts at Chamberlain and the proposed Dunbar in Deadwood, and the enhanced Falls Park in Sioux Falls, other major developments must occur. East River especially must strive to attract new developments. The most popular tourist areas in the nation are manmade. Thus, theme parks and other cultural attractions have much to offer. Developments also will take place along I-29, but it is not expected to become as significant to tourism as is the more heavily traveled I-90.

Further developments are likely to occur in West River as well. Especially important will be progress on the *Crazy Horse Memorial* near Custer, legalized gaming beyond Deadwood and the Indian Reservations, and other proposals under consideration for the Black Hills region.

Major strides are expected to be taken in the area of recreation as well. In the future people will have more leisure time. There will be more efforts to bring professional and semi-professional sports to South Dakota. Cities will be expected to provide comprehensive, year-round recreation programs for all ages. More camping, fishing, and hunting areas and parks will be needed and no doubt provided.

The future population of the state is expected to exceed 775,000 by the year 2010. It is important to realize that currently over fifty percent of the people live within fifty miles of the state's eastern border. Future trends indicate that this percentage may increase even more. The number of people in rural areas and small towns is expected to continue to decline, although at a slower rate than during recent decades. The out-migration of our youth also will continue to occur but again at a decreasing rate. The number of elderly people in South Dakota will increase, reaching the point that one out of every seven people here will be over sixty-five years of age. This will place some major financial demands on the state.

The American Indian population is expected to continue to grow rapidly. Trends indicate that the Indian population will become increasingly urban. The largest numbers will be in Sioux Falls and Rapid City. White and other non-white populations also will become increasingly urban, gravitating again to the larger cities.

Sioux Falls will move toward the 150,000 population mark. Rapid City will exceed 65,000, and Aberdeen will move toward 30,000. Medium-sized cities such as Watertown, Brookings, Mitchell, and Pierre also will experience slow but steady growth. Problems will occur in the smaller communities where survival will depend upon innovative leadership, citizen involvement, and attracting a major function or service that enables continued existence.

The South Dakota of the future may be significantly different from the land we call home today. Things can change very rapidly. Change can be planned or forced. Progress can result from innovation and invention. Ideals can be enriched or destroyed. It is all up to us as citizens. South Dakotans must be actively involved in the state and community if valued resources and traditions are to be preserved. Residents of South Dakota must actively work to enable the state to achieve the dreams they have for it. The people of South Dakota must direct the state around the obstacles that lie ahead and over the pathways that lead to a better future.

The South Dakota of the future must be what we the people make it. For it to be otherwise means that we as citizens have yielded our rights and responsibilities to others. People are the future of South Dakota. The state's citizens are those who will nurture the land, the communities, and this way of life for future generations. South Dakotans have a proven history of responsible stewardship to this land we live on and love.

This *Geography of South Dakota* has been designed to provide the reader with a basis for understanding the past and present of South Dakota, and an introduction to what may lie ahead. This learning adventure is intended to enable one to understand this unique geographic place that we know as South Dakota. It is also designed to enable the reader to serve as a critic for the environment by understanding the state's location relative to other places and the interaction that occurs here between humans and the physical and cultural environments. As a result of geographically investigating South Dakota, we can better appreciate the interaction between and among peoples and places. We can also understand the concept of geographic region as it applies to South Dakota. As geographically informed people, we are now able to understand and utilize the geography of South Dakota in our roles and responsibilities as citizens in this wonderful state we call home. We must be prepared to serve as good stewards of our environment to enhance our understanding and guide our future.

BIBLIOGRAPHY

Aase, J. H., *The Mineral Industry of South Dakota, 1980*. Vermillion: Department of Water and Natural Resources, 1982.

Agricultural Experiment Station, *The Hutterites and Their Agriculture, 100 Years in South Dakota*. Bulletin No. 669, SDSU, Brookings, SD, 1974.

Agriculture Extension Service, *South Dakota Weeds*. Brookings, SD: State Weed Control Commission, March 1967.

Alex, Lynn Marie, Prehistoric and Early Historic Farming and Settlement Patterns. *South Dakota History*, 13:4-21, 1983.

Allen, John Logan, *Passage Through the Garden*, Urbana: University of Illinois Press, 1975.

Ambrose, Stephen E, *Undaunted Courage*, New York: Touchstone, 1996.

Anderson, Lawrence C., *South Dakota Hutterite Colonies*. Map. Mankato, MN: Mankato State Univ., Dept. of Geography, 1988.

Andreas, Alfred Theodore, Andreas' *Historical Atlas of Dakota*. Chicago: Donelley, 1884.

Antonides, R.J., *Some Guidelines for Organizing Economic Development Efforts in South Dakota Along Trade Area Lines*, Extension Circular 651. Cooperative Extension Service: SDSU and US Department of Agriculture, 1966.

Arikara Indians of South Dakota. Archeological Research Project, Work Projects Administration. Vermillion, SD: University of South Dakota Museum, 1941.

Army Corps of Engineers. *Flood Plain Information, Rapid Creek, Rapid City, South Dakota*. Omaha District, June 1973.

Army Corps of Engineers. *Flood Report - Cheyenne River Basin, South Dakota Black Hills Area*. 1973.

Atwood, Wallace, *The Physiographic Provinces of North America*. Boston, MA: Ginn & Company, 1940.

Baer, Linda, *Is the Exodus Over?* Brookings, SD: Agricultural Experiment Station, South Dakota State University, Update Series C229, No. 12, August 1985.

Bailey, Reeve M. and Allum, Marvin O., *Fishes of South Dakota*. Ann Arbor, MI: Museum of Zoology, Univ. of Michigan, 1962.

Baskett, Jr., Tom and Sanders, Jerry, *An Introduction to Custer State Park and the Southern Black Hills*. Billings, Montana: RAWCO, 1977.

Beadle, W.H.H., *Dakota: Its Geography, History and Resources*. D.D. Merrill, 1888.

Bischoff, August G. translated by Anton H. Richter. A 1909 Report on Russian-German Settlements in Southern Dakota. *South Dakota History* 11:185-198. 1981.

Bohi, Charles W. and H. Roger Grant, Country Railroad Stations of the Milwaukee Road and the Chicago & Northwestern in South Dakota. *South Dakota History* 9:1-23. 1978.

Borchert, John, *America's Northern Heartland: An Economic and Historical Geography of the Upper Midwest*. Minneapolis: University of Minnesota Press. 1987.

Borchert, John, *Minnesota's Changing Geography*. Minneapolis: University of Minnesota Press, 1959.

Borchert, John and D.P. Yaeger. *Atlas of Minnesota Resources and Settlement*. Minneapolis: Univ. of Minnesota Press, 1968.

Borchert, John, *The Urbanization of the Upper Midwest: 1930-1960*. Report No. 2, Minneapolis: Upper Midwest Economics Study, 1963.

Borchert, John and Russell B. Adams, *Trade Centers and Grade Areas of the Upper Midwest*. Urban Report No. 3, Minneapolis: Upper Midwest Economic Study, 1963.

Borchert, John, Thomas L. Anding and Morris Gildemeister, *Urban Dispersal in the Upper Midwest*. Urban Report No. 7. Minneapolis: Upper Midwest Economic Study, 1964.

Bragstad, R.E., *Sioux Falls in Retrospect*. Sioux Falls, SD, 1967.

Bray, Martha Coleman, *Joseph Nicollet and His Map*. Second edition. Philadelphia: American Philosophical Society, 1994.

Briggs, Harold E., The Development of Agriculture in Territorial Dakota, The Culver-Stockton Quarterly 7:1-38. In the *Collected Papers of Harold E. Briggs*. 1931.

Briggs, Harold E., "The Settlement and Economic Development of the Territory of Dakota." *South Dakota Historical Review*, 1, April 1936, pp. 151-166.

Brown, Jesse and Willard, A.M., *The Black Hills Trails*. Rapid City, SD: The Rapid City Journal Company, 1924.

Beutler, Martin, "Impact of South Dakota Agriculture 1991-1995", *Economic Commentator*, No. 379, South Dakota State University, August 1997.

Bureau of Intergovernmental Relations. Office of Energy Policy. *South Dakota Energy: Production, Consumption, and Policy*. September 1982.

Carruth, Hayden, "South Dakota: State without End." *The Nation*, 116, 24 January 1923, pp. 87-90.

Case, LeLand, *Lee's Official Guidebook to the Black Hills and the Badlands*. 2nd ed. Sturgis, SD: The Black Hills and Badlands Association, 1953.

Casey, Robert J., *The Black Hills and Their Incredible Characters*. New York: The Bobbs-Merrill Co. Inc., 1949.

Cash, Joseph H., *Working the Homestake*. Ames: Iowa State University Press, 1973.

Chittenden, Hirman M., *History of Early Steamboat Navigation on the Missouri River*. New York: Fransis Pl Harper, 1903.

Chittick, Douglas, *Growth and Decline of South Dakota Trade Centers, 1901-1951*. Brookings, SD Agricultural Experiment Station, Bulletin No. 448, 1955.

Chittick, Douglas, "The Future of Small Towns in South Dakota." *South Dakota Farm and Home Research* 12 (1961): 16-20.

Churchill, C.L., Brashier, Clyde K., and Limmer, Dan. Evaluation of a Recreational Lake Rehabilitation Project. Brookings: SDSU, 1975.

Churchill, Edward P. and Over, William H., *Fishes of South Dakota*, Pierre, SD: South Dakota Dept. of Game and Fish, 1938 ed.

Clark, Champ, *The Badlands*. New York: Time-Life Books, 1974.

Comprehensive City Plan, City of Sioux Falls, South Dakota. Prepared by Harland Bartholomew & Associates, City Planners, St. Louis, MO, November 1950.

Condra, George Evert, *Geography of Nebraska*. Lincoln, NE: The University Publishing Company, 1906.

Connolly, Joseph P. and Rothrock, E. P., *Mineral Resources of South Dakota*. Pierre: State Department of Agriculture, November 1942.

Consulting Services Corporation, *South Dakota Non-Resident Travel and Recreation Survey*. Pierre: Industrial Development Expansion Agency, June 1967.

Coursey, O.W., *Pioneering in Dakota*. Mitchell, S.D.: Educator Supply Co., 1937.

Cram, Geo F., *Indexed Railroad and Township Map, Dakota*. 66 Lake Street, Chicago: By the author, 1879.

Crawford, Ronald R., "The Minnesota River Lowland: An Area Study." Thesis, Department of Geography, South Dakota State University, Brookings, SD, 1977.

Crop Production in South Dakota, South Dakota Department of Transportation, Division of Railroads, Pierre, SD, August 1979.

DeVoto, B., *The Journals of Lewis and Clark*. Boston: Houghton-Miffin, 1947.

Division of Resource Management, *South Dakota Water Plans, Vol. I & II*. Pierre: SD Department of Natural Resources Development, 1973.

Driver, Harold E., *Indians of North America*. 2nd ed. Chicago: The University of Chicago Press, 1969.

East Dakota Conservancy Sub-District, Lake Herman Report. Brookings, SD. 1969.

Eiselen, Elizabeth, A Geographic Traverse Across South Dakota: A Study of the Subhumid Border. Ph.D. diss., Geography, Univ. of Chicago at Illinois. 1943.

Elias, Thomas S., *The Complete trees of North America-A Field Guide and Natural History*. New York: Van Nostrand Reinhold Company, 1980.

Federal Writer's Project in South Dakota, *Custer State Park in the Black Hills of South Dakota*. Rapid City, SD: Works Project Administration and the Custer State Park Board, 1938.

Federal Writers' Project, *South Dakota: A Guide to the State*. New York: Hastings House, 1952.

Fenneman, Nevin M., *Physiography of Western United States*. New York: McGraw-Hill Book Company, 1931.

Field, Donald R. and Robert M. Dimit, *Population Change in South Dakota Small Towns and Cities, 1949-1960*. Brookings: SD Agricultural Experiment Station, Bulletin No. 571, 1970.

Fieldler, Mildred,. *Railroads of the Black Hills*. Seattle: Superior Publishing Company, 1964.

Fite, Gilbert Courtland, *Peter Norbeck: Prairie Statesman*. Columbia, Missouri: The University of Missouri Studies, University of Missouri, 1948.

Flint, Richard Foster, *Pleistocene Geology of Eastern South Dakota*. US Department of the Interior. US Geological Survey, Professional paper 262. Washington, D.C.: US Government Printing Office, 1955.

Fouberg, Erin Kimberly Hogan, *Tribal Territory, Sovereignty, and Governance: A Study of the Cheyenne River and Lake Traverse Indian Reservations*. New York, Garland Publishing, 2000.

Froiland, Sven, G., *Natural History of the Black Hills and Badlands*. Sioux Falls, SD: The Center for Western Studies, 1990.

Fuguitt, Glan, "County Seat Status as a Factor in Small Town Growth and Decline." *Social Force* 44 91965): 245-251.

Gab, Orville E., "The Coteau des Prairies: An Area Study." Thesis, Department of Geography, South Dakota State University, Brookings, SD, 1979.

Gaines, John F., *A Geographic Study of the Nebraska Loess Plain in Nebraska*. Lincoln, NE, 1951.

Goss, Sydney G., "Factors Associated with Population Changes in Rural South Dakota Communities." Thesis, Department of Sociology, South Dakota State University, 1974.

Goss, Sydney G., R.T. Wagner, and R.M. Dimit. "Population Change in South Dakota Small Towns: 1960-1970." SD Agricultural Experiment Station, Bulletin No. 636. 1975.

Governor's Office of Economic Development, *South Dakota: In Comparison*. Pierre: Governor's Office of Economic Development, 1988.

Griesenbrock, Jan, "The Impact of Flooding in Brookings County, South Dakota: 1936-1985." 1986.

Hamburg, James F., "The Influence of Railroads Upon the Processes and Patterns of Settlement in South Dakota." Ph.D. diss., Geography, Chapel Hill, Univ. of North Carolina, 1969.

Hamburg, James F., "Railroads and the Settlement of South Dakota During the Great Dakota Boom, 1878-1887." South Dakota History. 5(1975): 165-178.

Hamburg, James F., "Paper Towns in South Dakota." *Journal of the West* 16: 40-42.

Hammer, Kenneth M., "Come to God's Country: Promotional Efforts in South Dakota Territory, 1861-1889." *South Dakota History* 10 (1980).

Hannus, L. Adrien, "The Lange/Ferguson Site: An Event of Clovis Mammoth Butchery with the Associated Bone Tool Technology: The Mammoth and Its Track." Ph.D. dissertation, University of Utah, 1983.

Harms, L.L., "Quantification of Pollutants in Surface Runoff from Agricultural Lands in Brookings County, SD." Ph.D. dissertation, SDSU, 1973.

Harrower, Henry Draper, *The New States: A Sketch of the History and Development of the States of the North Dakota, South Dakota, Montana, and Washington*. New York: Ivision, Blackman & Company, 1889.

Hart, John F., *The Look of the Land*. Foundations of Cultural Geography Series. Englewood Cliffs, N.J.: Prentice-Hall. 1975.

Hart, J.F., "The Middle West." *Annals, Assoc. of American Geographers*, 2 (June 1972): 258-282.

Hart, John F., The Spread of the Frontier and the Growth of Population. *Geoscience and Man* 5:78-81. 1974.

Hart, John F. and Neil E. Salisbury. "Population Change in Middle Western Villages: A Statistical Approach." *Annals of the Association of American Geographers* 55(1965): 140-160.

Hart, John F., N.E. Salisbury and E.G. Smith. "The Dying Village and Some Notions about Urban Growth." *Economic Geography* 44(1968): 343-349.

Hauk, Joy Keve., *Badlands: Its Life and Landscape*. Interior, SD: Badlands Natural History Assoc., 1971.

Haupt, Herman., *Suggestions to Encourage Settlement and Secure Rapid Development of the Wheat Lands of Minnesota and Dakota: Tributary to the Northern Pacific Railroad.* Minneapolis Tribune: Book and Job Printing Establishment. 1881.

Health Education and Welfare., *Environmental Impact Statement - Urban Renewal Project, Rapid City, South Dakota.* Housing and Urban Development, 1974.

Hill, Loren, G., "A Trade Area Study of Kadoka, South Dakota." Thesis, Department of Geography, South Dakota State University, 1979.

Hillestad, Linda, "The Changing Impact of Natural Disasters in Brookings County, South Dakota." Thesis, Department of Geography, South Dakota State University, 1982.

History of Southeastern Dakota. Sioux City, IA: Western Publishing Company, 1881.

History of the Sinai Community. Arlington, S.D.: *The Arlington Sun*, 1979.

Hoag, Donald G., *Trees and Shrubs for the Northern Plains.* Fargo, N.D.: North Dakota Institute for Regional Studies, 1965.

Hodge, William T., *Climates of the States.* Vol. 2. Detroit: Gale Research Company, 1978.

Hogan, Edward Patrick, Opheim, L.A., and Zieske, S.H., *Atlas of South Dakota.* Dubuque: Kendall/Hunt Publishing Co., 1970.

Hogan, Edward Patrick, "Every Eighth South Dakotan." Sioux Falls: SD Association of Health Care Facilities, 1973.

Hogan, Edward Patrick, *Geography of South Dakota.* SDSU, Brookings, SD, 1976 (mimeographed).

Hogan, Edward Patrick, *The Reasons for Out-Migration of South Dakota Youth.* Ph.D. dissertation, Saint Louis University, St. Louis, MO. 1969.

Hogan, Edward Patrick, *South Dakota, An Illustrated Geography.* Huron: East Eagle Publishing, 1991.

Hogan, Edward Patrick and Roybal, Joe, *South Dakota House Types.* Brookings, SD: Department of Geography, SDSU, 1979.

Holden, David J., *Dakota Visions.* Sioux Falls, SD: Center for Western Studies, 1982.

Hoover, Herbert T., and Zimmerman, Karen P. *The Sioux and Other Native American Cultures of the Dakotas, An Annotated Bibliography.* Westport, CT: Greenwood Press, 1993.

Hoover, Herbert T., and Zimmerman, Karen P. *South Dakota History, An Annotated Bibliography.* Westport, CT: Greenwood Press, 1993.

Horizons-Sioux Falls in the 1970s. Prepared by Sioux Falls Industrial and Development Foundation and Northern States Power Company, 1970.

Hotchkiss, Caroline W., The Great Plains in Their Relation To Human Occupation and Development: A Series of Lessons for Seventh or Eighth Grade. *The Journal of Geography* 9:225-229. 1911.

Howland, Lee A., "The James River Lowland: A Regional Study." Thesis, Department of Geography, South Dakota State University, Brookings, SD, 1989.

Hudson, John C., "A Location Theory for Rural Settlement," *Annals of the Association of American Geographers* 59(1969): 365-381.

Hudson, John C., "The Plains Country Towns." *In The Great Plains: Environment and Culture*, pp. 99-117. Edited by Brin W. Blouet & Frederick C. Lubke. Lincoln: Univ. of Nebraska Press, 1979.

Hudson, John C., "Migration to an American Frontier," *Annals of the Association of American Geographers*, 66:242-265, 1976.

Hudson, John C., "North American Origins of Middlewestern Frontier Populations, *Annals of the Association of American Geographers*, 78:395-413, 1988.

Hudson, John C., *Plains Country Towns*, Minneapolis: University of Minnesota Press, 1985.

Hudson, John C., "Towns of the Western Railroad, *Great Plains Quarterly*, 2:41-54, 1982.

Hudson, John C., "Two Dakota Homestead Frontiers." *Annals of the Association of American Geographers* 63(1973): 442-446.

Huemoeller, A. William, Kenneth J. Nicol, Earl O. Heady and Brent W. Spaulding, *Land Use: On Going Development in the North Central Region.* Ames, IA: Center for Agricultural and Rural Development, Iowa State University, 1976.

Hunt, Charles B., *Physiography of the United States.* San Francisco: W.H. Freeman and Co., 1969.

Huseboe, Arthur R., *An Illustrated History of the Arts in South Dakota.* Sioux Falls, SD: Center for Western Studies, 1989.

Huss, Dorothy, Kuni, Robert S., Lampe, William and Moxon, Margaret, *Huron Revisited.* Huron: East Eagle Company, 1988.

Jennewein, J.L., and Boorman, J., eds., *Dakota Panorama*. Sioux Falls: Dakota Territorial Centennial Commission, 1961.

Johansen, John P., *Recent Population Trends: In Relation to Resource Development in South Dakota*. Rural Sociology Department, Bulletin B44, SDSC, 1954.

Johnson, A.W., "The Physical Geography of Minnesota." *Journal of Geography*, 14 (Feb. 1916): 161-165.

Johnson, James R. and Nichols, James T., *Plants of South Dakota Grasslands: a Photographic Study*. SDSU Agricultural Experiment Station Bulletin No. 566. Brookings, SD: Agricultural Experiment Station, 1970.

Johnson, James R., and Nichols, James T., *Plants of South Dakota: A Photogenic Study*. Brookings, SD: Agricultural Experiment Station, South Dakota State University, Bulletin 566, 1982 rev.

Kapler, Todd, Overview of the Fur Trade in the Upper Missouri Region, section 8, page 1-22. Excerpt from a National Register Nomination of Historic Place on Fort Pierre prepared by the State Historical Preservation Center, Vermillion, SD, 1989.

Karolevitz, Robert F., *Challenge the South Dakota Story*. Sioux Falls, SD: Brevet Press, Inc., 1975.

Kerr, F.F., and Tipton, Merlin J., *Eastern South Dakota Ground Water Supplies*. Brookings, SD: Cooperative Extension Service, South Dakota State University, Fact Sheet 201, 1975.

King, Phillip B., *The Evolution of North America*. Princeton, NJ: Princeton University Press, 1959.

Kingsbury, George W., *History of Dakota Territory*. 2 vols. Chicago: S.J. Clarke Publishing Company, 1915.

Kirk, Ruth, *Badlands*. Badlands National Monument, SD: Badlands Natural History Association, 1976.

Kohn, Clyde F., The Geography of Rural Settlements and Population. In *Status of Research in American Geography, 1952*, by the Division of Geology and Geography, National Research Council. Washington, D.C.: National Academy of Science, 1952.

Kohn, Clyde F., Settlement Geography. In *American Geography: Inventory & Prospect*, edited by Preston E. James & Clarence F. Jones, 125-141. Syracuse University Press. 1954.

Kovats, Julius A., Black Hills Gold Mining, 1876-1935: Toward A Time-Space Model. Ph.D. diss., Geography, The University of Oklahoma. 1978.

Kraenzel, Carl Frederick, *Great Plains in Transition*, Norman: University of Oklahoma Press, 1955.

Land Utilization and Marketability Study, Downtown Center Renewal Project. Larry Smith & Co., Chicago, IL, May 1969.

Landis, Paul H., *Growth and Decline of South Dakota Trade Centers, 1901-1933*. South Dakota Agricultural Experiment Station, Bulletin No. 279, 1933.

Lang, Mahlon George, *The Role of Agriculture in South Dakota's Economy: An Approach to Analysis*. Brookings, SD: South Dakota State University, Master of Science Thesis, 1972.

Lass, William E., *A History of Steamboating on the Upper Missouri River*. Lincoln: Univ. of Nebraska Press, 1962.

Lawrence, Antoine, *Birth of the Rosebud Country*. Winner, SD: Sodak Printers, 1975.

Lawson, Merlin P. and Maurice E. Baker, *The Great Plains: Perspectives and Prospects*. Lincoln: Univ. of Nebraska Press, 1981.

Little, Elbert L., *The Audubon Society Field Guide to North American Trees: Eastern Edition*. New York: Alfred A. Knopf, 1980; Toronto: Random House of Canada, 1980.

Lobeck, A. K., *Geomorphology*. New York: McGraw-Hill Book Company, 1939.

Long, John H., ed. *Historical Atlas and Chronology of County Boundaries*. 5 vols. Boston: G.K. Hall & Co., 1984. Vol. 5: *Minnesota, North Dakota, South Dakota*, comp. Mark P. Donovan (North And South Dakota) and Jeffrey D. Sibert (Minnesota).

Lowie, Robert H., *Indians of the Plains*. Lincoln: University of Nebraska Press. 1982.

Lyons, T.D., "Dakota Blizzard." *The Commonweal*, 33, 27 December 1940, pp. 251-253.

Madson, John, "The Prairie Blizzard." *Audubon*, 72, March 1970, pp. 54-56, 65.

Mather, Cotton E., "The American Great Plains." *Annals of the Association of American Geographers* 6(1972): 258-282.

McCoy, Allis P., *Dakota Homestead*. Chicago: Adam Press, 1974.

McGregor, D.J., *Mineral and Water Resources of South Dakota*, Bulletin #16. Vermillion: SD State Geological Survey, 1964.

McGuiness, C.L., *Water in South Dakota*, Report #2. Vermillion: SD State Geological Survey and State Water Resources, 1962.

Meleen, Elmer E., and Over, William H. pt I. *A Preliminary Report of the Mitchell Indian Village Site and Burial Mounds*. pt. II *Notes on the "Moundbuilders" of South Dakota*. Vermillion, SD: University of South Dakota Museum, 1938.

Miller, Robert H., *Mineral Resources of South Dakota*. Pierre: South Dakota Industrial Development Agency, February 1959.

Mineral and Water Resources of South Dakota. South Dakota State Geological Survey. Washington, D.C.: United States Government Printing Office, 1964.

Mineral and Water Resources of South Dakota. SD State Geological Survey. Washington, D.C.: US Government Printing Office, 1975.

Minshull, Roger. *Regional Geography: Theory and Practice*. Chicago: Aldine Publishing Company, 1967.

Missouri River Basin Commission, *James River Basin Sub-regional Analysis: Agricultural Technical Paper*, Missouri River Basin Commission, 1980.

The Mitchell Centennial History Committee. *Mitchell Re-Discovered: A Centennial History, 1981*. Mitchell, South Dakota: McLeod's Printing and Office Supply, 1981.

The Mitchell Prehistoric Indian Village: An Overview. Mitchell Prehistoric Indian Village Preservation Society, Mitchell, SD, n.d.

Montana-Dakota Utilities Co., Northwestern Public Service Co., and Ottertail Power Co., "This is Big Stone Plant." (Mimeographed).

Montgomery, V.E. and Garry, R., *Out-of-State Travelers in South Dakota: June, July, August, 1972*. Vermillion: Business Research Bureau, May 1973.

Montgomery, V.E., and Garry, Steven J., *Out-of-State Travelers in South Dakota: June, July, August, 1975*. Vermillion, SD: Business Research Bureau, 1976.

Montgomery, V.E., and Volk, A.A., "The Economy of the Black Hills of South Dakota." Vermillion, SD: Business Research Bureau, School of Business, Univ. of South Dakota, Bulletin Number 52, October 1957.

National Oceanic and Atmospheric Administration. "State of South Dakota Tornado Statistics by Counties 1953-1974." National Weather Service computer printout.

National Park Service. *The Archaeology of the Plains: An Assessment*. Dept. of Anthropology, Univ. of Utah, 1955.

Nelson N., *The Retail, Wholesale, and Service Businesses in South Dakota*. Vermillion, SD: Business Research Bureau USD, Bulletin 130, 1981.

Nelson, N., *Out-Of-State Travelers in South Dakota, Summer 1985*. Pierre: Department of State Development, 1985.

Nelson, Paula M., *After the West was Won: Homesteaders and Town Builders in Western South Dakota, 1900-1907*. Iowa City: University of Iowa Press, 1986.

Nelson, Wendy, "Sylvan Lake Restoration," *South Dakota Conservation Digest* 51 (1984): pp. 20-4.

Nichol, Ralph E., "Steamboat Navigation on the Missouri River," *South Dakota Historical Collections* Vol. XXVI, 1952.

O'Harra Cleophas Cisney, *O'Harra's Handbook of the Black Hills*. Rapid City: The Black Hills Handbook Company, 1913.

O'Harra, Cleophas Cisney. *The Geology, Mineralogy and Scenic Features of Custer State Park, South Dakota*. Rapid City, SD: South Dakota School of Mines Bulletin Number 14, Depts. of Geology and Mineralogy, South Dakota School of Mines and Technology, January 1926.

Olson, Gary D., The Historical Background of Land Settlement in Eastern South Dakota. In *Big Sioux Pioneers*, edited by Arthur R. Huseboe, 17-28. Sioux Falls, SD: Nordland Heritage Foundation, 1980.

Over, William H., *Amphibians and Reptiles of South Dakota*. rev. 2nd ed. Vermillion, SD: University of South Dakota, 1943.

Over, William H., *Flora of South Dakota*. Vermillion, SD: The University of South Dakota, 1932.

Over, William H. and Churchill, Edward, P., *Mammals of South Dakota*. Vermillion, SD: Univ. of South Dakota Museum and Department of Zoology, 1941.

Over, William H. and Thomas, Craig S., *Birds of South Dakota*. Vermillion, SD: University of South Dakota Museum, 1946.

Page, J.W., The Geographical Factors Controlling the Sites of Towns. *Journal of Geography* 11:92-96. 1912.

Parker, Donald Dean, ed., *Early Residents of Brookings County South Dakota*. n.p.: Brookings County Historical Society, 1960.

Parker, D.D., *History of Our County and State*. Brookings: South Dakota State College, 1959.

Parker, Dr. Donald Dean. *Pioneering in the Upper Big Sioux Valley*. Brookings, S.D.: Donald Dean Parker, 1967.

Parker, Watson. *Gold in the Black Hills*. Lincoln, NE: University of Nebraska Press, 1966.

Patterson, Donald Dean, "An Appraisal of The Use of Soil Survey Information As The Basis For Valuing Land For Tax Purposes In Spink County, South Dakota." M.S. thesis, South Dakota State College of Agriculture and Mechanic Arts, 1964.

Pearl, Richard M., *1001 Questions About the Mineral Kingdom*. New York: Dodd, Mead and Co., 1959.

Peterson, E. Frank, *Historical Atlas of South Dakota*. Vermillion, SD. 1904.

Peterson, William H. and Vandall, Arthur B., *Blizzard and Cold Weather Tips*. Brookings, SD: Cooperative Extension Service, South Dakota State University, Fact Sheet 352, 1967.

Plan for the Classification, Preservation and Restoration of Lakes in Northeastern South Dakota. By James Hayden and Jerry Siegel, Chairmen. State Lakes Preservation Committee, South Dakota, July, 1977.

Power, Hon. F.D., "Historical Sketch of Davison County." In *Twentieth Century Atlas of Davison County, South Dakota*, pp. 45-56. Compiled by Frank E. Peterson. Vermillion, SD: by the compiler, 1901.

Projections of South Dakota Population 1980-2000. Pierre, SD: Planning Information Assistance Section, SD State Planning Bureau, 1980.

Recollections of Dakota Territory. Ft. Pierre, S.D.: William Rhoads, 1931.

Reese, M. Lisle, *South Dakota A Guide to the State*. New York: Hastings House, 1952.

Remote Sensing Institute. *Remote Sensing for Evaluating Flood Damage - Rapid City, South Dakota Flood of June 9, 1972*. Brookings, SD: SDSU Remote Sensing Institute, 1972.

Ridgley, Ronald H., Railroads and the Development of the Dakota's: 1872-1914. Ph.D. diss., Modern History, Indiana University. 1967.

Ridler, Jim, Lake Herman Model Implementation Program. Soil Conservation Society of America. South Dakota Chapter, Newsletter. April 1979.

Riegel, Robert Edgar, *The Story of the Western Railroads: From 1852 Through the Reign of the Giants*. Lincoln: University of Nebraska, reprint. 1926.

Riley, Marvin P., *The Hutterites and Their Agriculture: 100 Years in South Dakota*. Brookings, SD: Agricultural Experiment Station, South Dakota State University, Bulletin 669, 1974.

Riley, Marvin P. and Butler, Eugene T., *South Dakota Population, Housing, and Farm Census Facts*. Agricultural Experiment Station, SDSU, Brookings, SD, Bulletin No. 611, May 1973.

Riley, Marvin P. and Satterlee, James L., *South Dakota Population, Housing, and Farm Census Facts*. Brookings, SD: Agricultural Experiment Station, SDSU, Update Series C229, No. 10, November 1983.

Riley, Marvin P., Satterlee, James J., and Goreham, Gary A., *Population Change of Counties and Incorporated Places in South Dakota: 1950 to 1980*. Brookings, SD: Agricultural Experiment Station, South Dakota State University, Update Series C229, No. 13, March 1984.

Riley, M.P. and R.T. Wagner, *Reference Table: Population Change of Counties in Incorporate Places in South Dakota 1950-1970*. SD Agricultural Experiment Station, Bulletin No. 586, 1971.

Robinson, Doane, *Encyclopedia of South Dakota*. Pierre, S.D.: Doane Robinson, 1925.

Robinson, Doane, *Encyclopedia of South Dakota*. Sioux Falls, SD: Will A. Beach Printing Co., 1925.

Robinson, Doane, *History of South Dakota*. n.p.: B.F. Bowen and Company, 1904.

Robinson, Doane, *History of South Dakota*. Chicago: The American Historical Society, Inc., 1930.

Roger, R.H. & Elliot, F.F., *Types of Farming in South Dakota*, Bulletin 238. (Brookings, SD:) Farm Economic Department, Agricultural Experiment Station, South Dakota State College of Agriculture and Mechanic Arts, 1929.

Rothrock, E.P., *The Surface of a Portion of the James Basin in South Dakota*, Vermillion, SD, Bulletin No. 54, June 1946.

Rumpca, Anslem H., "The Lake Dakota Plain." Thesis, Department of Geography, South Dakota State University, Brookings, SD, 1978.

Russell, Richard J., *Climatic Years*, The Geographical Review, Vol. 24, 1934.

Russell, J.S. and Rhoades, H.F., "Water Table as a Factor in Soil Formation." *Soil Science*, Vol. 82 (1956): 323-24.

Saveland, Robert N., *Geography of Missouri*. Kansas City: Burton Publishing Company, 1954.

Salonen, Debra R., "Taking Hold: A Study of Land Acquisition, Land Ownership and Community Development in Northeast Brookings (1870-1916)." Thesis, Department of Geography, South Dakota State University, 1977.

Sandro, G.O., "A History of Brookings County Prior to 1900." M.A. Thesis, University of South Dakota, July 1936.

Satterlee, James L., Arwood, Don, and Joffer, Pat, *A Graphic Summary of South Dakota*. Brookings, SD: Agricultural Experiment Station, Census Data CEnter, South Dakota State University, 1993.

Satterlee, James J. and Arwood, Don, *Demographic History of South Dakota Counties*. Brookings, SD: Agricultural Experiment Station, South Dakota State University, Census Data Center Newsletter, Centennial ed., vol. 3, No. 8, November 1988.

Satterlee, James L. and Arwood, Don, *South Dakota Municipalities: 1986 Population Estimates*. Brookings, SD: Agricultural Experiment Station, SDSU Update Series C229, No. 24, September 1988.

Satterlee, James J. and Arwood, Don, *Demographic History of South Dakota: Migration*. Brookings, SD: Agricultural Experiment Station, South Dakota State University, Census Data Center Newsletter, Centennial ed., vol. 3, No. 7, October 1988.

Satterlee, James L. and Goreham, Gary A., *Changes in South Dakota Farms, 1935-1982*. Brookings, SD: Agricultural Experiment Station, SDSU, Update Series C229, No. 21, August 1985.

Satterlee, James L. and Malan, Vernon D., *History and Acculturation of the Dakota Indians*. Brookings, SD: Agricultural Experiment Station, SDSU, Bulletin 613, 1973.

Sauer, Carol O., "Historical Geography and the Western Frontier." In *The TransMississippi West*, pp. 267-89. Edited by J.F. Willard and C.B. Goodykoontz. Boulder: University of Colorado Press, 1930.

Schell, H.S., *Dakota Territory During the Eighteen Sixties*, Report #30. Vermillion: Univ. of South Dakota, August 1954.

Schell, Herbert S., *History of South Dakota*. Lincoln, NE: The University of Nebraska Press, 1961.

Schell, Herbert S., *South Dakota: Its Beginnings and Growth*. New York: American Book Company, 1942.

Schell, Herbert S., *South Dakota, A Student's Guide to Localized History*. New York: Teachers College Press, Columbia University, 1971.

Schell, Herbert S., *South Dakota Manufacturing to 1900*, Bulletin Number 40. Vermillion, SD: Business Research Bureau, School of Business Administration, Univ. of South Dakota, 1955.

Scherschligt, O. and Kruger, D., *South Dakota Outdoor Recreation Plan*. Pierre: SD Department of Game, Fish and Parks, 1967.

Siegel, Jerry L. and Susan Rollag, 1983. Wall Lake shoreline erosion analysis, East Dakota Conservancy Subdistrict and Interagency Water Quality Management Council.

Smith, Elbert W., *Pioneering in Dakota*. LaConner, WA: Puget Sound Mail, 1929.

Smith, H.T.U., "Dune Morphology and Chronology in Central and Western Nebraska." *Journal of Geology*, Vol. 73 (1965): 557-78.

Smith, James Richard, *Geography of the Northern Plains and Other Essays*. Sioux Falls, SD: Augustana College Press, 1990.

Smith, M.C. and Henkes, W.C., *The Mineral Industry of South Dakota in 1968*. Mineral Report 16. Vermillion: SD Geological Survey, March 1970.

Sneve, Virginia Driving Hawk, ed. *South Dakota Geographic Names*. Sioux Falls, SD: Brevet Press, Inc., 1973.

South Dakota: A State to Behold. South Dakota Extension Homemakers Council, 1975.

South Dakota Agriculture Census Handbook, Agricultural Experiment Station, SDSU, Brookings, SD, Update Series C229, No. 16, 1984.

South Dakota Agriculture 1987-1988. SD Department of Agriculture. South Dakota Agricultural Statistics Service, 1988.

South Dakota Agriculture 2000. SD Department of Agriculture. South Dakota Agricultural Statistics Service, 2000.

South Dakota Business Directory 1988-1989. Omaha, NE: American Directory Publishing Company, 1988.

South Dakota Civil Defense. *After Action Report on the Black Hills Flood Disaster*. 1973.

South Dakota Department of Economic and Tourism Development, Industrial Division, *South Dakota Manufacturers and Processors Directory, 1979*. Sioux Falls, SD: Board of Industrial Development, 1979.

South Dakota Department of Game, Fish, and Parks, Division of Parks and Recreation. *The 1975 South Dakota Comprehensive Recreation Plan*. Pierre, SD: Division of Parks and Recreation, Department of Game, Fish, and Parks, 1975.

South Dakota Department of Natural Resources, Division of Resource Management. *South Dakota Water Plan* Vol. II-B, Section 6, "Resource Inventory of the Bad River Basin." Pierre, SD: Division of Resource Management, Dept. of Natural Resources, 1975.

South Dakota Department of Natural Resources, Division of Resource Management. *South Dakota Water Plan* Vol. II-B, Section 5, "Resource Inventory of the White River Basin." Pierre, SD: Division of Resource Management, Dept. of Natural Resources, 1975.

South Dakota Department of Natural Resources. Division of Resource Management of South Dakota. *South Dakota Water Plan* Vol. II-B, Section 16. Pierre, SD: Dept. of Natural Resources, 1975.

South Dakota Department of Natural Resources. Division of Resources Management. *South Dakota Water Plan*. Vol. II-B, Section 4: *Resource Inventory of the Minnesota Tributaries River Basin*. Pierre, SD: Dept. of Natural Resources, 1976.

South Dakota Department of Natural Resources. Division of Resources Management. South Dakota Water Plan. Vol. II-B, Section 4: *Resource Inventory of the Red River Tributaries*. Pierre, SD: Dept. of Natural Resources, 1975.

South Dakota Department of Tourism. 1999 Intercept Study Final Report. Pierre, SD. January 2000.

South Dakota Department of Transportation. *Construction Programs*. Pierre, SD: Dept. of Transportation, 1978.

South Dakota Department of Transportation. Division of Planning. Office of Planning and Programming. *South Dakota Railroads in Summary*. February 1989.

South Dakota Department of Transportation, Division of Railroads, *Railplan South Dakota*. Vol. 1, Pierre, SD: Dept. of Transportation, 1978.

South Dakota Directory of Manufacturers and Processors 1987-1988. Dept. of State Development. Pierre, SD, 1988.

South Dakota Fifty Years of Progress 1889-1939. Sioux Falls, SD: S.D. Golden Anniversary Book Co., 1939.

South Dakota Geological Survey. *The Mineral Industry of South Dakota in 1968*. Washington, D.C.: U.S. Government Printing Office, 1969.

South Dakota Historical Collections. Vol. X. Pierre, SD: Hipple Printing Co., 1926.

South Dakota Historical Markers. Sioux Falls, S.D.: Brevet Press, 1974.

South Dakota Office of Tourism. "South Dakota Governor's Conference on Tourism-STRATEGY '86. December 1986.

South Dakota Mining Association. "Industry Status Report." Sioux Falls: South Dakota Mining Association, January, 1990.

South Dakota Rural Electrification Association. *SDREA 1975-1976 Directory of Rural Electric and Telephone Cooperatives*. Pierre, SD, 1975.

South Dakota State Geological Survey. *The Biology of South Central South Dakota*. by S.S. Visher, Bulletin No. 5, 1912.

South Dakota State Geological Survey. *The Geography of South Dakota*. by S.S. Visher. Bulletin No. 8, 1918.

South Dakota State Geological Survey. *A Geology of South Dakota*. Part I: *The Surface*, by E.P. Rothrock. Bulletin No. 13, 1943.

South Dakota State Geological Survey. *A Geology of South Dakota*. Part III: *Mineral Resources*, by E.P. Rothrock. Bulletin No. 15, 1944.

South Dakota State Geological Survey. *Amphibians and Reptiles of South Dakota*, by William H. Over. Bulletin No. 12, 1923.

South Dakota State Geological Survey. *Hydrology of the Dakota Formation in South Dakota, Report of Investigations*, by Robert H. Schoon. Bulletin No. 104, 1971.

South Dakota State Geological Survey. *The Badlands Formations of the Black Hills Region*, by Cleophas C. O'Harra. Bulletin No. 9, 1910.

South Dakota State Geological Survey. *The Geography, Geology, and Biology of Mellette, Washabaugh, Bennett and Todd Counties, South-Central South Dakota*. Bulletin No. 5, 1912.

South Dakota State Geological Survey. *Geology of Southern Jackson County and Vicinity*, by Charles L. Baker. Bulletin No. 73, 1953.

South Dakota State Geological Survey. *Mineral and Water Resources of South Dakota*. Bulletin No. 16, 1964.

South Dakota State Highway Map. Rand McNally and Co., 1989.

South Dakota State Planning Bureau. *South Dakota Planning Bureau. South Dakota Facts: An Abstract of Statistics and Graphics Concerning the People and Resources of South Dakota*. Pierre, SD: State Planning Bureau, 1975.

South Dakota State Planning Bureau, *South Dakota Facts: An Abstract of Statistics and Graphics Concerning The People and Resources of South Dakota*. Pierre, SD: State Planning Bureau, 1976.

South Dakota State Planning Bureau, Planning Information Assistance Section. *South Dakota Population Projections: 1980, 1985, 1990*. Pierre, SD: Planning Information Section, State Planning Bureau, 1978.

South Dakota State University. Agricultural Experiment Station. *Deciduous Trees for South Dakota Landscapes*, by Dale E. Herman. Bulletin 578. 1971A.

South Dakota State University. Agricultural Experiment Station. *Climate of South Dakota*. Bulletin 582. 1971B.

South Dakota Task Force on Tourism, "South Dakota-A Travel Marketing Plan for South Dakota." December, 1986.

The South Dakota Tourism Study. Prepared for SD Dept. of Tourism, by Grant & Associates, Inc.; Hunt & Hunt; US Travel Data Center; RL Associates. November 1987.

South Dakota Water Plan: Resource Inventory of the Vermillion River Basin, by Thomas Lowe. SD Dept. of Natural Resources Development. Division of Resources Management. vol. II-B., Sec 13, 1977.

South Dakota Water Plan: Resource Inventory of the Big Sioux River Basin. SD Dept. of Natural Resources Development. Div. of Resources Management. vol, II-B, sec. 11, 1972.

South Dakota Water Plan: Resource Inventory of the James River Basin. SD Dept. of Natural Resources Development. Division of Resources Management. vol. II-B, sec. 10, 1978.

Speck, Robert A., "The Coteau du Missouri." Thesis, Department of Geography, South Dakota State University, Brookings, SD, 1988.

Spencer, Robert F. and Jennings, Jesse D., *The Native Americans*. New York: Harper and Row Publishers, Inc., 1965.

Spicer, Edward H., *A Short History of the Indians of the United States*. New York: Van Nostrand Reinhold Company, 1969.

Spindler, Will Henry, *Rim of the Sandhills*. Mitchell, SD: Educator Supply Company, 1941.

Spuhler, Walter, Lytle, William F., and Moe, Dennis, *Climate of South Dakota*. Brookings, SD: Agricultural Experiment Station, SDSU, Bulletin 582, 1971.

Steele, N. E., *The Geography of South Dakota*. New York: Ginn and Company, 1937.

Stephens, H.A., *Woody Plants of the North Central Plains*. Lawrence, KS: Univ. Press of Kansas, 1973.

Stewart, James R., *A Study of Selected Demographic Factors Associated with Population Change in Incorporated Rural Communities of South Dakota*. Masters Thesis, SDSU, 1976.

Sundy, Donn P., "The Background, Growth and Principal Institutions of Mitchell, South Dakota." M.S. thesis. Univ. of South Dakota, 1976.

The Territory of Dakota. Aberdeen, S.D.: Frank H. Hagerty, 1889.

Thornbury, William D., *Principles of Geomorphology*. New York: John Wiley & Sons, 1954.

Thornthwaite, Warren C., Climate and Settlement in the Great Plains. In *Climate and Man: Yearbook of Agriculture*, Washington, D.C.: U.S. Printing Office, USDA. 1941.

Thwaites, Reuben G., ed. *Original Journals of the Lewis and Clark Expedition*, 1804-1806, Vol. 6, written by Lewis Meriwether. Arno Press: New York. 1969.

Towne, Arthur E., *Old Prairie Days*. Ostego, MI: Ostego Union Press, 1941.

Turner, Frederick Jackson, "The Significance of the Frontier in American History." In *Frontier and Section: Selected Essays of Frederick Jackson Turner*, pp. 32-57. Edited by William E. Leuchtenburg & Bernard Wishy. Englewood Cliff: Prentice-Hall, 1961.

US Department of Agriculture. Soil Conservation Service. *Estimated Land Use Conversions in South Dakota*. Huron, SD: Soil Conservation Service, 1988.

US Department of Agriculture. *Soils and Men, The Yearbook of Agriculture*. Washington, D.C.: Department of Agriculture, 1938.

US Department of Agriculture. *Climate and Man, The Yearbook of Agriculture*. Washington, D.C.: Department of Agriculture, 1941.

US Department of Agriculture. *Grass, The Yearbook of Agriculture*. Washington, D.C.: Department of Agriculture, 1948.

US Department of Agriculture. *Soil Survey Brookings County*, Series 1955, No. 3 (1959).

US Department of Commerce, Bureau of the Census. *1978 Census of Agriculture*. Vol. 1, Part 41, *South Dakota*. Washington, D.C.: U.S. Government Printing office, 1980.

US Department of Commerce. Bureau of the Census. *1980 Census of Population*, Chapter A, *Number of Inhabitants*, pt. 43, *South Dakota*. Washington, D.C.: US Government Printing Office, 1982.

US Department of Commerce. Bureau of the Census. *1982 Census of Agriculture. South Dakota State and County Data*. Washington, D.C.: US Government Printing Office, 1984.

US Department of Commerce. *Climatological Data Annual Summary South Dakota, 1976*. Asheville, N.C. National Oceanic and Atmospheric Administration, 1976.

US Department of Commerce. *Climatological Data South Dakota*. Washington: US Government printing Office, 1900-1980.

US Department of Commerce. National Oceanic and Atmospheric Administration. National Weather Service. *Annual Summary with Comparative Data*. Washington, D.C.: US Government Printing Office, 1979.

US Department of Commerce. National Oceanic and Atmospheric Administration. National Weather Service. *Annual Summary with Comparative Data*. Washington, D.C.: US Government Printing Office, 1980.

US Department of Commerce. National Oceanic and Atmospheric Administration. National Weather Service. *Annual Summary with Comparative Data*. Washington, D.C.: US Government Printing Office, 1981.

US Department of Commerce. National Oceanic and Atmospheric Administration. National Weather Service. *Annual Summary with Comparative Data*. Washington, D.C.: US Government Printing Office, 1982.

US Department of Commerce. National Oceanic and Atmospheric Administration. National Weather Service. *Annual Summary with Comparative Data*. Washington, D.C.: US Government Printing Office, 1983.

US Department of Interior, Bureau of Mines, *Minerals Yearbook: South Dakota*. Washington D.C. Bureau of Mines, 1988.

US Department of Interior, Geological Survey. *Geological Atlas of the United States: Mitchell Folio, South Dakota*. Library Edition: Mitchell Folio, no. 99. Washington, D.C.: U.S. Geological Survey, 1903.

US Department of the Interior, National Park Service, *Early Indian Farmers and Village Communities*. Washington, DC: National Survey of Historic Sites and Buildings, 1963.

US Department of the Interior and US Department of Agriculture. *Black Hills Area Resource Study*. (In cooperation with the states of South Dakota and Wyoming), July 1966.

U.S. Geological Survey. *Mineral and Water Resources of South Dakota*. Washington, D.C.: U.S. Government Printing Office, 1975.

US Geological Survey/National Oceanic and Atmospheric Administration. *The Black Hills-Rapid City Flood of June 9-10, 1972: A Description of the Storm and Flood*. Washington, D.C.: U.S. Government Printing Office, 1975.

Vexler, Robert, *Chronology and Documentary Handbook of the State of South Dakota*. Dobbs Ferry, New York: Oceana Publications, Inc., 1979.

Visher, Stephen Sargent, *The Biology of South Central South Dakota*. Vermillion, SD: South Dakota State Geological Survey, Bulletin No. 5, 1912.

Visher, Stephen Sargent. *Climatic Atlas of the United States*. Cambridge, MA: Harvard University Press, 1954.

Visher, Stephen Sargent. *The Geography of South Dakota*. South Dakota State Geological Survey, Bulletin 8. Pierre, SD: State Publishing Co., 1918.

Wagner, Robert T., Butler, Eugene T., and McComish, Karen A., *Population Projection Models for South Dakota 1980, 1985, and 1990*. Bulletin 631. Brookings, SD: SDSU, 1975.

Weaver, J.E. and Albertson, F.W., *Grasslands of the Great Plains*. Lincoln, NE: Johnsen Publishing Company, 1956.

Weaver, J.E., *North American Prairie*. Lincoln, NE: Johnsen Publishing Company, 1954.

Webb, W.E., Air Towns and Their Inhabitants. *Harper's Magazine* 51:828-835. 1875.

Webb, W.E., *The Great Plains*. Boston: Ginn and Co. 1931.

Wedel, Waldo R., The Great Plains. In *Prehistoric Man in the New World*, edited by Jesse D. Jennings and Edward Norbeck, pp. 193-220. Chicago: The University of Chicago Press. 1964.

Weimer, Robert E., "The Sandhills of South Dakota: A Regional Study." Thesis, Department of Geography, South Dakota State University, Brookings, SD, 1985.

Welch, Thomas P., "The James River Highlands: An Area Study." Thesis, Department of Geography, South Dakota State University, Brookings, SD 1982.

Westin, Frederick C. and Buntley, George J., *A Generalized Soils Map of the East River Area of South Dakota*, Brookings, SD: Cooperative Extension Service, SDSU, Soil Survey Series 5, Fact Sheet 134A, 1962.

Westin, Fred C.; Puhr, Leo F.; and Buntley, George J., *Soils of South Dakota*. SDSU Agricultural Experiment Station Soil Survey Series No. 3. Brookings, SD: Agricultural Experiment Station, 1967.

Westin, Frederick C. and Malo, Douglas D., *Soils of South Dakota*. Brookings, SD: Agricultural Experiment Station, SDSU, Bulletin 656, 1978.

Westin, F.C., *Soil Survey, Brookings County South Dakota*. Washington: U.S. Government Printing Office, 1959.

Whittlesey, Derwent, Sequent Occupance. *Annals of the Association of American Geographers* 19:162-165. 1929.

Williams, Albert, *The Black Hills-Mid-Continent Resort*. Southern Methodist University Press, 1952.

Wiseman, Mavine Schrader, *Dakota Dateline, 1881-1981: The Story of Mount Vernon, South Dakota*. Stickney, SD: Argus Printers for Mount Vernon Centennial Celebration, 1981.

Wishart, David J., Settling the Great Plains, 1850-1930: Prospects and Problems. In *North America: The Historical Geography of a Changing Continent*, edited by Robert D. Mitchell & Paul A. Groves. Totowa, N.J.: Rowman & Littlefield. 1987.

Woolworth, A.R., *Sioux Indians III, Ethnohistorical Report on the Yankton Sioux*. New York: Garland Publishing, Inc., 1974.

Work Projects Administration. *South Dakota Place-Names, Part II Lake Names*. University of South Dakota, Vermillion, SD, 1940.

Wulff, Mrs. Walter, *Big Stone County History*. Ortonville, MN: LA. Kaercher, 1959.

Year, Peggy Ellen, *Ghost Towns in South Dakota: A Geographic Perspective*. Masters Thesis, SDSU, 1981.

ACKNOWLEDGMENTS

This is the third edition of this book, and the improvements were made possible because of the help of many people. We want to thank our families, Joan, wife and mother, who read and reread this text and continually encouraged its completion; Rob, husband and son-in-law, who provided constant support and encouragement, and our children, siblings, in-laws, and grandchildren, Bridget, Edward, Tim, Molly, Patrick, Amy, Kate, Olivia, Fiona, Sophie, Maggie, and Claire, who are always inspirations. Thanks also for the support and encouragement of Rodney, Glenna, Dan and Nancy Fouberg. We are also grateful to our predecessors, the late Edward and Dorothy Hogan of Saint Louis, Missouri, who fostered a love for learning and geography and to Mary Ford and the late William Ford for furthering our love for travel.

A special thank you to our mentors who have guided us along the way, especially Professor John W. Conoyer, Dr. Clement S. Mihanovich, Ms. Judy Kroll, Dean Charles Pirtle, Professor Harm de Blij, Dr. J. Clark Archer, and Dr. Marshall Bowen.

The developing and completing of the first edition of this book required a great deal of nurturing, encouragement, and support. Actually, this process began some forty years ago with the opportunity to study at Saint Louis University under Professor John W. Conoyer, one of the finest geographers of his time and an outstanding teacher.

At South Dakota State University in 1967, Dr. Hilton M. Briggs, Dr. Harold S. Bailey, Dr. Frank Schultz, and Dr. William R. Kenney encouraged the development of a Geography of South Dakota class. A 1990 sabbatical and research funds provided encouragement and some support for this book. Thanks go to the South Dakota Board of Regents, former President Robert T. Wagner, Vice President Carol J. Peterson, and deans Dr. Larry Stine, Dr. Allen Barnes, Dr. Herbert Cheever, and Dr. Rex Myers for their support over the years. We are especially grateful to President Peggy Gorden Elliott for her support of this edition.

The evolution of this book required the assistance of a large number of people. Two of those who helped and encouraged the original effort are no longer with us: Mr. William "Gip" Nolan, an early mentor, and Governor George S. Mickelson, a dear friend, both of whom displayed their love of South Dakota through their own examples and experiences.

We want to acknowledge our dear friends Dale and Pat Larson, who continue to provide the encouragement needed to complete this work. Their support enabled the completion of an earlier book, *South Dakota: An Illustrated Geography*, which evolved from this work. Thanks also to our friends Ron and Barb Nelson for their encouragement over the years.

We also want to recognize our colleagues. At South Dakota State University they are the late Dr. Lee A. Opheim, a teacher, co-worker, and friend for forty years; and Dr. Roger Sandness and Professor Maynard Samuelson, who provided friendship and a supportive team effort for almost thirty years. Thanks also to Dr. Donald Berg, Dr. Janet Gritzner, Dr. Darrell Napton, and Joan Bruinsma of the SDSU Department of Geography. Appreciation also goes to Florence Schade, Helen Horten, Joella Anderson, and Isabelle Apland of SDSU for the opportunity to work with them in such an enjoyable professional environment. Special gratitude goes to Professor Orville Gab who produced the outstanding cartography for

185

this work, and Dr. Charles Gritzner, co-author of *Infinite Variety*, an award-winning educational TV series for South Dakota Instructional Television.

We appreciate the support of the South Dakota Governor's Office for Economic Development for the permission to utilize their outstanding photography collection in this work, and that of Mr. Ken Schaack, a former employee of that office and friend who encouraged this effort.

We are grateful for help and suggestions provided by Dr. Herbert T. Hoover and Dr. Thomas Gasque of the University of South Dakota, Professor Emeritus Joseph Bonnemann and Dr. Donald Berg of South Dakota State University, and Carol Bonnemann. We thank them for thier careful reading of the first edition and positive suggestions.

We also want to recognize Susan Coombes, who provided excellent support and suggestions during the completion of the text. Thanks to Patrick Jochim, of the SDSU Instructional Technologies Center, for his creative graphics. We are especially grateful to the Mary Chilton DAR Foundation and to the Elmen Family Foundation for providing partial funding for the publication of this work.

Finally, thanks to Dr. Arthur Huseboe, Dr. Harry Thompson, and Mr. Dean Schueler of the Center for Western Studies for their faith in and encouragement of the publication of this book. Last, but certainly not least, thanks to our students for their interest, attention, and desire to learn.

Ed Hogan and Erin Fouberg

Index